UP-TO-DATE SCHOOL ESSAYS, LETTERS, APPLICATIONS, PARAGRAPHS AND STORIES

Goodwill's

UP-TO-DATE
SCHOOL ESSAYS
LETTERS, APPLICATIONS
PARAGRAPHS AND STORIES

FOR HIGH AND HIGHER SECONDARY STUDENTS

S.S. BHAKRI
ANAND SAGAR

GOODWILL PUBLISHING HOUSE
B-3, RATTAN JYOTI, 18, RAJENDRA PLACE
NEW DELHI-110008 (INDIA)

Published by :
Rajneesh Chowdhry
for
Goodwill Publishing House
B-3, Rattan Jyoti
18, Rajendra Place
New Delhi-110008
Tel. : 5750801, 5755519
Fax : 91-11-5763428

© Publisher

1st Edition 1973
24th Edition 1984
50th Edition 1993
55th Edition 1995
60th Fully Revised Edition 1999
61st Fully Revised Edition 2000
62nd Edition 2001
63rd Edition 2002
64th Edition 2003

Price : Rs. 40/-

Typeset at
Radha Laserkraft
R-814, New Rajinder Nagar
New Delhi-110060 • Tel. : 5730031

Printed at
Star Offset Printers, New Delhi

Contents

ESSAYS

PART III : SCHOOL'S SURROUNDINGS AND EXAMINATIONS

LETTERS & APPLICATIONS

PART I : LETTERS TO FRIENDS

x

PART II : PERSONAL LETTERS (FAMILY)

PART III : LETTERS CONCERNING SCHOOLS

PARAGRAPHS

STORIES

Essays

PART I

Persons We Come Across

1. THE POSTMAN

A postman is an important public servant. He works in every nook and corner of the country, whether it is a city a town or a village. The postman has to go from door to door and deliver letters, parcels, money orders and gifts.

The postman is familiar to one and all. He wears a *Khaki* uniform. On his head, there used to be a turban, and a Khaki bag in one hand and a bundle of letters to be delivered in the other hand. However, the modern postman is sans the traditional turban. From his looks he appears to be a simple, humble and courteous person. He is welcomed everywhere whether it is a rich man's residence or a poor man's hut.

The postman's job is really very difficult. Whether it is a rainy season, summer season or winter, he has to go from house to house and from locality to locality for delivering letters. Even during the night, he goes to deliver the telegrams. As the postmen have to cover many villages and cities, they have to cross the most difficult terrains. The postman has to pass through deserts and forests and other hostile places.

Some of the postmen are said to have lost their lives due to snake bites or have been killed by tigers and other dangerous animals in the Jungles.

Despite his difficult responsibilities, he gets a very meagre salary. His pay and allowances are small and holidays are limited. When other people enjoy their holidays, he is busy delivering letters to the people and is overburdened during festivals; sometimes, people offer him money and gifts out of courtesy and sympathy.

A postman's life is hard indeed. One has to acquire special qualities for becoming a postman. A person of good health and polite manners along could discharge the duties of a postman. He always wears a smile on his face. But despite all these agonies, he has a dark and bleak future. There are no chances of promotion in his profession. He spends his whole life in poverty and public service. His profile demands that we should hold him in high esteem and respect him for the burden that he carries on his shoulders.

2. THE POLICEMAN

In every country, laws are necessary. Laws help in the maintenance of peace. So, the laws ought to be observed by every citizen. But there are some elements in every society that do not pay any heed to the laws of the land.

The policeman is entrusted with the task of arresting and controlling such people as break laws. He makes people obey these laws. One, who does not obey, is punished by the police. It is because of policemen that our lives and property are safe. Hence, a policeman is an important person in the life of a nation. He acts as a saviour of the society.

4

A policeman is usually a man of sound health. He wears a *Khaki* uniform and carries a cane in his hand. He ties a belt round his waist and wears only shirt and pants. The policemen of every state of India could be distinguished due to their different official symbols.

A policeman is assigned jobs at the police station or check-posts. Sometimes, he is posted at that point of the town or city where there is fear of any disturbance and arson. During public demonstrations and strikes, he plays a decisive role. When the crowds become violent, he also uses his *Lathi* (stick) for controlling the mob. If the situation deteriorates, he could also resort to firing but with the permission of his superiors.

A policeman's job is really tough because he has to be on duty round the clock, though the police force also works in shifts. He is considered to be the custodian of law and order. He maintains peace and harmony. He becomes tough with those who violate discipline and create disorder and confusion. He remains on duty during the winter nights and chilly mornings. His duties are manifold. He also settles disputes and brings two warring parties to the point of reconciliation. He also protects the sanctity of religious processions and keeps the miscreants and hooligans away. In fact, he is an enemy of all those persons who indulge themselves in riots or thefts. He is the protector of the poor and the weak.

As he gets a poor salary, his standard of living is low. He has to support his family with that little income. Although he works hard, yet his pay is meagre. He must be paid well and respected because he is the real guardian of the civil society of the nation.

3. THE STREET BEGGAR

Beggars are very common in India. They are found in almost every village, town and city of India. The main areas of their operations are the places of pilgrimage and worship. They squat on the banks of the rivers, in front of temples and other places of hectic activity. They roam from street to street, from one locality to another and beg for alms, food and money. They accept whatever is given to them; sometimes they pursue the people so consistently that people get fed up of them.

Some people give alms to beggars in order to ward them off and not due to pity. Some beggars are so young and healthy that they do not deserve charity at all. The deserving cases are very few; those who are crippled, lame, deaf, dumb, blind or handicapped, are incapacitated and cannot earn their living. Some are in such a pathetic state as would evoke pity and compassion. Such crippled beggars are well-versed in the art of singing religious songs. Some beggars have really very melodious voice. Their sweet voice attracts the passers-by. Such beggars are found in trains and buses and they enthral the travellers through their religious and devotional songs.

Sometimes, one comes across a deaf and dumb beggar, lifting a blind or lame beggar on his back and begging for alms. It is also usual to see a leper placed in a manually driven cart and carried from place to place. These beggars know human psyche and beg according to the inner feelings of the people.

But most of the beggars thrive due to the generosity of women. These beggars never miss religious gatherings and other festivals. Some wear only a loin-cloth. Some beggars besmear themselves with ash while others have long hair and pairs of tongs. Some meditate under a tree. But many are cheats and charlatans. These beggars deceive the innocent women and at times even rob them off their money and jewellery.

The number of beggars in India is rising. These beggars live on the earnings of others. It is really a curse that even the healthy citizens of India resort to begging. They indulge in various vices like drinking and gambling. Their bodies are diseased. They carry infection with them and roam from place to place. Therefore, they are responsible, to a large extent, for spreading disease and immoral values in the society.

Begging should be banned in India by law. A legislation must be enacted to put an end to this profession. However, deserving cases should be helped and should be given gainful employment. Street begging is really a bane for India. Now a days, people are not swayed by any religious feeling. Hence, beggars are not treated in the manner in which, they hope to be treated.

4. AN INDIAN JUGGLER

India is land of variety and so are her people. Jugglers are a very common sight in India. They provide us with amusement and fun. They are generally found in small towns and villages as well as at fairs. In a big city like Delhi, we come across very few jugglers because there is not much open space where a juggler could give his performance. Besides, here every one is in a hurry. The police do not allow them to show their feats that could attract big crowds. People have so many other attractions and means of entertainment that they show no interest in the hackneyed tricks of the jugglers. The educated people, in particular cannot afford to waste their precious time by watching the performances of jugglers.

A juggler, however, is popular among women, children and old men. They are amazed at his wonderful tricks and gimmicks. They consider him to be a magician.

A juggler is very shabbily dressed. He has a long and loose coat, a big turban, a *Dhoti* and a pair of old socks. Quite often, he has big ear-rings and some rings in his fingers. He has a funny appearance. He carries with him a drum and a flute. He employs a small boy who carries his stock-in-trade in a bag or basket and the bag contains the articles that a juggler needs for the show.

First of all the juggler selects a suitable place for the performance. He spreads a piece of cloth on the ground and begins to play on the flute. The boy with him begins to beat the drum. The juggler is adept at playing on the flute. He can produce different tunes so as to attract a sufficiently large crowd before beginning his tricks. He is clever, witty and quick in movements. He smiles with confidence during his show. He surprises the spectators by his well-timed jokes and witty remarks.

A juggler has many items to show. He generally begins with the card tricks. He can correctly tell the card that has been pulled out of the pack by a spectator. He also shows other feats. Then, he shows ball tricks that are very interesting and surprising. He takes a number of balls and throws them up in the air in quick succession. The balls keep revolving in a circle without any one of them falling on the ground. The success feat depends upon the ingenuity and regular practice.

Sometimes, the juggler asks a man to give him his ring He covers it with a piece of cloth and waves his magic wand over it. When he removes the cloth, the people are amazed to find that the ring has disappeared. The owner is anxious to get the ring back. When the juggler sees that the patience of the owner of the ring is exhausted, he asks some other person in the crowd to search his pocket. Much to the bewilderment of all, the ring is found in the pocket of the owner himself and the same is handed back to the owner.

He also shows a mango branch sprouting into a young tree. His basket trick is also very interesting. He puts a big basket over the boy's body. He runs his dagger through it many times. The people hear the painful cry of the boy. They also see the sword covered with blood. They think that the boy might be dead. But when he removes the basket, they see nobody under it. The boy comes from somewhere in the crowd and is quite safe and sound. Then people shout with joy and praise the trick by claps. Some people give a Rupee or two to the boy.

With the help of his wand, the juggler can multiply the number of his currency notes and coins and becomes rich for a short time. But again, he is the same poor man loitering from place to place in search of bread.

The juggler's skill requires dexterity and practice. He earns a living by his clever feats. Our eyes cannot follow his movements, as he is active and smart. But despite his talent, he is poor.

After the performance, he goes round with his bowl asking the spectators to put something in it. The spectators drop some coins in that bowl. After a lot of toil, he earns his living and remains in tattered others. A juggler is generally semi-fed but he is without any worries. ●

5. AN INDIAN FARMER

India is an agricultural country. Our prosperity depends upon our agricultural production. For achieving this purpose, the Indian farmer's contribution is very vital. India, as a matter of fact, is a land of farmers. Nearly 75 percent of our population lives in villages.

An Indian farmer is respected by everyone. It is he who produces grains and vegetables for the citizens of the country. Throughout the year, the Indian farmer remains busy in tilling the fields, sowing seeds and reaping the crops. His, indeed, is a very busy life.

He gets up early in the morning. Then, he takes his yoke, bulls and plough-share and goes to his fields. In the fields, he ploughs the land for hours together. Then, he takes his breakfast. The breakfast is brought by the members of his family in the fields. His breakfast is very simple. It consists mainly of *Chapatis, Pickle and Lassi*. After taking his breakfast, he again gets busy with his work.

He works very hard. But after his hard labour, he gets a very reasonable amount of reward. He sells his production of foodgrains in the market at a low and nominal price.

He lives a very simple life. His clothes have a rural flair.. He lives in a mud-house, though many farmers of Punjab, Haryana and UP have built *Pucca* houses as well. His property comprises a few bulls, a plough-share and a few acres of land. He lives from hand to mouth.

A farmer is the very soul of a nation. Our late Prime Minister, Shri Lal Bahadur Shastri, gave a slogan, "Jai Kisan." He realised that an Indian farmer feeds the nation. Upon him, depends the agricultural production. They must be provided with all the latest implements of farming. Better seeds, fertilisers, manures, implements for agriculture and chemicals could enable him to grow more. ●

6. A STREET HAWKER

A street hawker is a common sight in all the Indian towns and villages. A street hawker goes from one street to another and from one locality to another for selling his articles or food-stuffs.

A street hawker usually comes with a basket full of articles, placed on his head. He hawks his articles. Every street hawker brings articles and eatables of different kinds. Usually, in the morning, street hawkers come with vegetables and fruits in their baskets. They sell the fruits and vegetables and earn their livelihood in this manner.

Those people, who live in villages and towns, hear the calls of the street hawker early in the morning. He brings fresh fruits and vegetables with him. Upon hearing his voice, housewives flock around him. They buy fruits and vegetables from him. Street hawkers have to face very odd customers sometimes who go on arguing (bargaining) about the prices of various commodities. Sometimes, they have to bow to the wishes of the customers by reducing their rates.

Then, there are other street hawkers who come on bicycles, loaded with clothes, utensils and other articles of daily need and consumption.

All these are, no doubt, tough jobs. A street hawker has to labour a lot in order to earn his living. His profits are very meagre. He is generally a poor man. His clothes are also dirty. But with this small income, he makes his both ends meet. Normally, a street hawker has a cart of three wheels or four wheels. Poor street hawkers have to carry their goods on their heads. The street hawkers sell fruits, vegetables, bread, eggs, salted grams, *Chana Bhatura, Pao Bhaji,* plastic items and toys.

Some of the street hawkers carry very inexpensive things. By selling their complete stock, they earn a very small amount of money. This shows the poor condition of these street hawkers. If a hawker is a little innocent, he is teased by the street urchins. These clever urchins sometimes steal his articles while the poor fellow has to bear the loss.

On the whole, a street hawker's condition is pitiable because he wanders from morning till evening from place to place in order to earn his daily living. In India, the hawkers are quite large in number because, by investing a little amount of money, they can start a business. And India is a country of the poor people. But there is no harm in earning one' living with hard labour. Every individual should earn his own living instead of becoming a burden on others. It is dignity of labour that should be respected.

7. A GOOD CITIZEN

A good citizen has to imbibe many qualities. The fact that he has some duties and responsibilities to bear, is true. But at the same time, he also enjoys some rights and privileges as a citizen of a free State. While he has every right to participate in the judicial, legal, political, religious and social affairs of the nation, he has also some responsibilities. He must not injure the sentiments of others and must protect the weak from the strong. Being loyal to the nation and the society, under all the circumstances, is his first and foremost duty.

A good citizen must be ready to sacrifice his life for the sake of his motherland. He is also required to be a good citizen and a nationalist. He should have firm and deep faith in his motherland. He has to obey the law of the land. But he has also to keep in his heart, the welfare of the country, the welfare of his state, the benefit of society and the long term interests of the nation.

A good citizen must respect the cultural heritage of his country. He should respect the heroes, the prophets, the sages and saints of his country. He must respect the race to which, he belongs. He must always keep in mind the future of his country. He must raise the standard of living of his country by working honestly.

During the times of aggression or foreign attacks, he must be ready to shed his blood for the sake of his motherland. Therefore, defence of the country is the supreme duty of a good citizen.

A good citizen must live in peace and harmony with his neighbours and fellow citizens. He must love the institutions of his country. A good citizen must always respect the laws of the State and should have no patience with those who are criminals and anti-social elements.

He must be vigilant against the enemies of the country. He must not do something that may help the anti-nationalists or the enemies of the country. He must cling to high ideals. He must be aware of what is happening in his country.

Unity of the nation should be his topmost priority. He should work for the unity of the country. A goodwill for all, the protection of the weak, help of the victims and a sympathetic attitude towards his fellow citizens are the qualities that are needed in a good citizen.

A good citizen should have a spirit of co-operation, friendliness, humanity, dedication and devotion towards his family and society. He must respect other faiths. He must not do something that brings disgrace to his society or to his country. "Greatest good of the greatest number of people" should be his principle. All these good qualities, if possessed, make us good citizens. ●

8. AN IDEAL TEACHER

In Mr SC Mehta, I have found an ideal teacher, Mr Mehta is a young man of 35, with sound health and sound mind. He is really a man of intellect and intelligence. He is a storehouse of knowledge and wisdom. Sometimes, I wonder how he has acquired so much of knowledge.

While in the class, he is a strict disciplinarian. He teaches sincerely and enthusiastically. He explains till every student is satisfied. His method of teaching is very good. His sound arguments, easy explanations and well-knit thoughts make the students listen to him most attentively. He keeps the class lively and in good humour. He does not allow any kind of boredom or idleness to descend upon the class. His witty remarks are really pleasing and delightful.

Further, he is also a good sportsman and an acknowledged athlete. That is why, he is very much interested in games and sports. He always instructs the students "to play while play and study while study." He himself is a good debater and keeps the audience spellbound by his powerful oratory. He has mastery over various subjects. But his study of English literature is so deep and vast that he is held in high esteem by the students and the staff alike.

He is an industrious teacher and takes pains while teaching. He is the master of style and Ruskin has said "Style is the man." His lucid language, sound knowledge and a good understanding of the subject make him one of the most admirable teachers of our institution. He is very kind and sympathetic towards the poor and intelligent students. Students love him and like him because of his sterling character and other qualities of head and heart. His speeches on Independence Day and Republic Day are really inspiring and thought-provoking. His wit and wisdom is a subject of discussion.

On the whole, in Mr S C Mehta, I have found not only an ideal teacher, but also a great philosopher, friend and guide.

PART II

About Myself

9. HOW I FELT BORED DURING THE SUMMER VACATION

A fortnight before the summer vacation were to commence, we stopped taking interest in studies. We made various ambitious plans for touring places. But man proposes and God disposes. On the very first day of the vacation, my mother developed sericus pain and she had to be operated upon. My tour to Srinagar was cancelled. This decision did not make me unhappy because the pressing problem of mother's illness led to a loss of interest for the tour.

My mother was hospitalised the very next day. Worry was writ large on father's face and tears rolled down my mother's cheeks. Unfortunately, a serious trouble developed after the operation. I took the responsibility of preparing breakfast, lunch and dinner. After giving it to my brothers and sisters, I went to the hospital.

In the hospital, the screaming, wailing and praying patients made me unhappy. Mother's condition used to upset me. When I came, my youngest sister, who was three years of

16

age, would cry and could long to go to mother. She would refuse to take milk or food. I could not arrange bath for the youngers for two days. Our clothes were dirty and the kitchen was in a bad shape. The rooms were also untidy.

Cooking was a big problem for me. The dishes were often spoiled. Many times, I burnt my hands. Now, I realised the value of hard work my mother used to put in. I could not eat the food that I cooked.

I could not talk out my heart to any one. My brothers and sisters were too young to give me any comfort. My friends had gone out of station. Sometimes, I used to dream of their happiness and compare it with mine. My life had become a dull routine; going to the hospital and preparing lunch, dinner and breakfast. It bored me a lot. I suspended the reading of detective stories. I did not visit cinema halls. The days passed and the summer vacation came to an end. I was bored so much that I never wished for any more summer vacation. ●

10. MY UNCLE GOT A LOTTERY

My uncle was a poor clerk. His six children were ill-fed and ill-dressed. It was a difficult for him to meet the household expenses. He was often frustrated. But frustration did not alter his good nature. He was polite, helpful and accommodating. He used to get loan from my father who would never take it back. He was worried about the future and marriages of his children. He would condemn the dowry system. He used to calculate the expenses on the marriages and would be satisfied to think that he would get a few thousand Rupees as Provident Fund.

But one day, fortune smiled on him. He became the proud possessor of a prize-winning lottery ticket. The whole family was overjoyed. My father thanked God for helping his brother. After a few days, he started entertaining fears whether he would get the money or not. However, the price money of Rupees five lakhs was paid to him.

My uncle was soon a changed man. His children started talking of shifting to a new house. He himself gave priority to the purchase of a house. He would ask the price of every house and expressed contempt for living in a locality where the poor lived. He would boast of being intelligent, hard-working and honest. His visits to our house became less frequent because he started feeling that my father should visit his house. He started thinking about resigning from his job because it lowered his status in the society. He thought of setting up a business. He consulted a large number of people regarding the pros and cons of different types of businesses. He planned to make a huge investment. He would go to different factories to know about the nature of business, the values of investments put in and the profits being generated by the entrepreneurs.

Whenever any one gave any suggestion, he would be suspicious. He branded people as rogues who wanted to grab his money. He criticised his relatives for giving very small dowries to their daughters. He often said on oath that he would neither give nor accept a small dowry. He hated the person who reminded him of his old days. He wanted to break off with his old friends, old days of life and the old social circles. ●

11. FIVE THINGS I LOVE THE MOST

This world is full of many wonderful and lovely things. Man has been trying to mobilise the resources of his intellect for making various types of inventions and discoveries and endeavouring to make the things more lovely and worth enjoying. This process of beautifying the worldly things is a continuous process. There is no end to it. As there are many beautiful and lovely phenomenon in this world, it becomes very difficult to pick and choose one out of them. Somehow, with the greatest care, I have selected five phenomenon that I would like to adopt in my future life.

First of all, I have a great love for nature. I am fed up with these artificial and momentary pleasures that is derived from the city life. I am thinking of settling in some village where I should be able to enjoy nature. I wish to make friendship with nature because nature can be a true friend and real guide of a man. It never deceives a person who loves her. Wordsworth, the great lover of nature, has also acknowledged this fact in his poems. I am very much anxious to go and enjoy steep hills, greenery of the open valleys, cool breeze and other natural sites. There, I would find people who are quite different in nature from the city dwellers. The motto of their lives is — "Simple Living and High Thinking." Thus I would have the privilege of coming in contact with simple and straight-forward people.

Secondly, I am very much interested in adopting 'teaching' as my profession. I am deeply pained to learn that illiteracy is widespread in India. For the successful functioning of a democracy, it is essential that we should reduce the levels of illiteracy. I have a great love for this profession. I want every young man and woman to get education. There is a dire need for spreading education to every nook and corner of the country. I hope that by opting for this profession, I would be serving the country in the best possible manner.

Thirdly, I have a keen desire to read fiction. Munshi Prem Chand, Bhagwati Charan Verma and Pawan Verma are my favourite authors.

Novels widen the doors of knowledge. They give us an insight into the complex ways of this world. Sometimes, we are able to resolve many difficult problems with the help of knowledge obtained from these novels. We are able to chalk out many schemes that could be very useful in our daily lives.

Fourthly, I love my country. I can sacrifice anything just for the honour of my country. If someone were to ask me to go to a foreign land and serve there (and get a handsome salary) I would be the first blunt young man to reject this offer. I am very much fond of the ways of Indian life, the food, the sunshine, home, friends, parents and other relatives. Further, if I were to go to a foreign country for some remunerative employment, I would complete my duties towards my motherland as she has given birth to me and brought me up.

Last but not the least, I love my sweet home. It has been rightly said. "East or West, home is the best." I live in a small house that does not provide all the modern facilities but it is no less than a paradise. I have visited my friends' homes. I find ultra-modern decorations. Those houses have dining rooms, sitting rooms and bedrooms and very rich and lavish food is served. In spite of all this, I don't like that shade of life, which is artificial.

I have selected the afore-mentioned five things that are dearest to me and are the essence of my life.　　●

12. MY MOST INTERESTING DREAM

Dreams are the byproducts of our sub-conscious state of mind. Dreams are of many kinds. But the dream, which I had last Sunday, was the most interesting dream of mine. In this dream, I was transported into a fairyland where beautiful belles were dancing and singing.

I dreamt that I had gone to Paris. There, I went into a night club. I saw many exciting scenes there. Twist, Ballroom and Leg-shaking were going on. As I was watching the spectacle of dance and drama, a beautiful girl looked at me. I was attracted by her rosy cheeks, alluring eyes and smiles on her face. I at once recollected the famous poem of Keats known as *La Belle Dame Sans Merci.* Her silent expression of love enthralled me. I was really captivated by her charm and sweetness. She was really making her silent expressions of love to me. I thought of responding to her love.

I talked to her and she passed very lovely and witty remarks upon me. Then both of us took a cup of coffee. We talked to our hearts' content. At the same time, I was recollecting the eternal lines of Shakespeare :

> *Love is not love that alters*
> *When it finds alterations,*
> *Or, bends with the remove to remove.*

Now, I was thinking whether her love was true or false. But I tried to be true to her. I sincerely expressed my love to her in the most unambiguous terms. We ultimately promised to marry and live as companions.

Soon the dance, drama and music programme came to an end. When the programme was concluded, she went somewhere, saying that she would be coming soon.

I kept waiting for her. But she did not turn up. I was longing for her love. I was thinking that I had been betrayed in love. As I was pondering over this heart-stricken subject, my eyes opened. I realised that I was enjoying the night life of Paris only in my dream.

In the dream, I really came across a woman who has been described by John Keats in his profound poem *La Belle Dame Sans Merci* i.e., "The Beautiful Woman without Mercy." The dream was interesting, exciting and intoxicating.   ●

13. INDIA OF MY DREAMS

Everyone in this world dreams. One always makes a plan about his future. So, I also have an India of my dreams.

It would be an India in which, there would be no racism, communalism and regionalism. First of all, I would root out communalism, whatever its shape or form may be. All such tendencies, which fan the forces of separatism and disruption, would be eliminated.

Secondly, I want India to be scientifically advanced, technologically better and agriculturally advanced. I would like to build an India where logic and scientific ideas, blind faith and fanaticism as well as crude emotionalism and coarse sentimentalism shall never rule. I would like to bring India at the apex of scientific and technological progress because modern age is an age of science and information technology. Every country, which wants to prosper and progress, must give due importance to science and information technology otherwise, she cannot create achieve good standards living for her citizens.

The India of my dreams would be an India that is self-sufficient in food. All the barren lands would be cultivated for achieving self-sufficiency in food-grains. Agriculture would be given special attention because agriculture is the backbone of Indian economy. Another Green Revolution would be brought about by launching intensive agricultural programmes and farmers would be asked to use better seeds and fertilisers as well as modern tools and implements.

Next, I would like the country to be highly industrialised. This is the age of industrialisation and in this age, the country is to be taken to the zenith of progress and prosperity.

I would also strengthen India's defence. The country would be so strong that no enemy would ever dare cast his covetous eyes on the sacred soil of India. Defence and security of the country would be of paramount importance. For achieving this objective, the country would be equipped with all the paraphernalia of modern defence because people worship military power in the present-day world. We have proved during the Kargil War that we are second to none but we would have to work harder for military supremacy.

Elimination of ignorance and illiteracy would be my next priorities because these are also banes. People would be educated on a mass-scale. Then, more pragmatic the system of democracy could be individual liberty and freedom would be defined and granted in letter and spirit.

Another thing, which I would like to see in India of my dreams, would be the abridgement of the gap between the rich and the poor. National income would be distributed rationally among the all sections of the society. Provision of food, housing and clothing to one and all would be given top priority in the India of my dreams. For achieving and accomplishing this, socialism would be the only remedy which, if practised sincerely, would really usher India into an era of economic equality.

If these measures are taken with utmost sincerity, India would really be counted among the most powerful countries of the world and would also guide those countries that are still slaves of big powers. It would be an India that Rabindra Nath Tagore described in his lines :

*"Where the mind is without fear and the
head is held high, where knowledge is free
Where the world has not been broken up into
fragments, by narrow domestic walls.*   ●

14. IF I WERE A MILLIONAIRE !

We often hear elderly people advising the young ones to
forget the past, ignore the future and care for the present. But
there is hardly any one who has no ambition for a higher
status than the present one. This constant struggle for higher
position sticks to man till the last day of his life. This is true
of every human being right from the man in the street to the
most celebrated personality of India. This struggle, in fact, is
essential for achieving the more pious objectives in life.

I belong to the middle-class stratum of the society. I can
never think of earning millions of Rupees. But God has His
own ways. Who knows, I might get a lottery ! And if I ever
get it, I cannot say whether I would be able to enjoy because
sometimes, man is so much overjoyed that he joins the great
majority. Let me suppose than I am fortunate to get a lottery
of millions of Rupees ! I shall try to spend it in the most
judicious manner so that I am able to derive maximum
pleasure out of it.

My colleagues advise me that first of all, I should try to
improve my living conditions. I should have a huge mansion
to live in, a car for the family and gadgets used for modern
living. But my concept of life is quite different. Instead of
improving my lot, I am much more interested in uplifting the
poor masses of the country.

India is a poor country. There are many people in India
who hardly get two square meals a day. How could they

enjoy the comforts and luxuries of life ? They are poorly fed and ill-clad. The largest number of these people is living in villages where the main occupation of the people is agriculture. In villages, the old bullock-carts are still used though the advanced countries have adopted mechanised farming. I shall offer them loans at a very nominal interest so as to enable them to purchase tractors, fertilisers and better seeds. This scheme would save the villagers from the village money-lenders and would also increase their agricultural production levels.

I shall invest a good portion of money in setting up a hospital with all the modern amenities. I shall also employ highly qualified doctors. This hospital would be run for the poor masses. The rich classes could donate generously for this noble cause. This will save people from the jaws of death.

Therefore, if I become a millionaire, my sole object would be to utilise this money for the greatest good of the greatest number of people. To help the poor, feed the hungry, nurse the sick and improve the plight of the people, would be my only major objectives.

Many people, particularly villagers, have no means or recreation. I shall spend a part of my wealth for providing means of recreation for the poor. I shall open various social and educational centres in the rural areas of the country.

I am disturbed to learn that there is no adequate provision for supporting orphans and widows. I would, therefore, open new centres for widows and orphans. They would work and earn their livelihood honourably. This would certainly protect the interests of our downtrodden masses.

There would be people who would jeer and mock at the utter foolishness of spending millions of Rupees in this manner. probably, they do not realise that a man gets spiritual happiness by helping the poor and this joy is much more than the sensual pleasures that one gets from the money he possesses. In case I become a millionaire, money spent in the aforesaid manner would give me solace and peace of mind.

●

15. MEMORIES OF CHILDHOOD

The memories of childhood have their own significance in one's life. As one grows up, one feels more and more attached with his childhood, the best period of a man's life. A child has no worries, anxieties or work. He is free from the dirty and filthy noise of worldly life. His motto of life remains "eat, drink and be merry." The charm of childhood cannot be forgotten. These memories leave an everlasting impression on one's life.

Same is the case with me. When I recollect the days of my childhood, I feel very much delighted; it was a pleasant period that I spent in high spirits.

During my childhood, I was carefree and had no worries at all. I used to wander like a deer in the open fields, enjoying the natural beauty in the pastures.

There are certain incidents that are still fresh in my memory. For instance, at the age of five, I got a severe attack of typhoid. In those days, medical science was not so much advanced. In the absence of proper diagnosis, I was reduced to a skeleton. After taking medicine for a sufficiently long period, I was cured. The doctor advised me to go to some hill-station. So, my father took me to Simla.

Once a juggler with two monkeys came to our street. He showed monkey's tricks which engaged our attention. He-monkey fell in love with the she-monkey. She-monkey refused to marry the he-monkey. He-monkey went to his father-in-law's house after wearing colourful dress. These were the pranks that attracted me. I fully appreciated the tricks shown by the juggler.

Another incident, which I still remember, is the swimming experience. It was a Sunday when I, along with my friends, went for a picnic to Okhla. Some boys were expert swimmers but unluckily, I did not know how to swim. My friends dived into the river and compelled me to do the same. Soon, I was caught by the current of water and was carried away swiftly. There was every possibility of my losing life but due to the valour of one of my friends, I was rescued from the current of water and was brought on the bank of the river. I was really very much grateful to him because he gave me a new lease of life.

The memory of the days spent during my childhood is still haunting my mind. Although I do wish that those days, full of pleasure, may come back, yet I know that it is a thing of the past. Time always flies on its wings. I cannot enjoy those days again.

It is this period that has often been praised by poets and writers. Recollecting past is to plunge ourselves in a state of melancholy. Wordsworth, the immortal poet of England and a great worshipper of Nature, describes his childhood period in his poems. Childhood, according to him, was full of pleasures, thrill and entertainment.

As I am growing in age, I feel greater attachment and attraction for those days that I had spent during my childhood. I know that my desire of enjoying childhood again can never be fulfilled because gone are the good old days when I was a child.

16. MY BEST FRIEND

The world appears to be gloomy in the absence of a true friend. Man, by nature, is a social animal. A man, who lives alone, is either an angel or a beast. Therefore, the need for a true and honest friends, is always prepotent in the mind of man. True friends, no doubt, are rare in this world.

Bobby is my best friend. He has been my classfellow since my early days. He comes of a very good and respectable family. His parents are well-to-do. Bobby always stands first in our class. Bobby is very much interested in games and debates. He is a good speaker and always bags prizes. He is one of the most popular boys in the school. Students like him very much because of his fine qualities and good character.

He possesses all the qualities of head and heart. He has a sweet temperament. He is like a mirror that reflects the merits and demerits of others. He gives a useful piece of advice to everyone. He loves all but hates none. He also shares the joys and sorrows of his friends.

A friend is the elixir of life and panacea for many ills. A friend is very useful at the time of adversity. Bobby really proves the proverb that "a friends in need is a friends indeed." But there are many persons in this world who are fairweather friends. When one's purse jingles with money, they flock around him; otherwise, run away.

My best friend is the embodiment of all the human virtues. Bobby never injures any one's feelings. He is a calm and quiet boy. He is very sympathetic towards the poor. He feeds the hungry and nurses the sick. He has a religious bent of mind. All of these noble acts of his make him my true, sincere and best friend. I have learnt a lot from him. For me, he is a sea of knowledge. Service of humanity, devotion to duty, respect for elders and love for youngers are his great ideals.

As a matter of fact, I am lucky that a person like Bobby is my best friend. For me, he is a source of inspiration and strength. These qualities have tempted me to call him my true friend. ●

17. MY AMBITION IN LIFE

People have dreams in their lives. Many aspire to be rich or to become business tycoons. Some persons dream of becoming leaders, politicians and social reformers. Some aspire to become the leading hooligans and anti-social elements of their localities or cities and this is a bad aspiration. There are others who have a craze for becoming poets, writers and novelists while most of us generally have a desire of becoming engineers, doctors and scientists of great repute. There are very few persons who are happy-go-lucky by nature and have no clear-cut aims in their lives.

I do not have very ambitious aims in my life. I do not wish to become a mill-owner or a multi-millionaire. The some object of my life is to lead a life of simplicity and goodness devoted to the service of humanity. The life of a professional leader or a politician would not suit me as most of such persons have become parasites on the society.

I was born of middle-class parents. From the very beginning, I have been passing through the struggles of life. I have seen cut-throat competition in most of the professions. Its consequences have been far-reaching; people are demoralised. Examples can be quoted in which, we can find the engineers accepting big bribes, lawyers rescuing guilty persons or murderers and doctors demanding money from the patients at crucial stages of surgical operation.

29

Then what do I want to be ? Indeed, from the core of my heart, I wish to become a teacher. The motto of this life, *'simple living and high thinking,'* inspires me to take up this profession. The noble ideals of the teachers in the ancient times are before me. I am fully aware of the difficult and hard life of a teacher. I know that a teacher is lotted to be poor. He leads a life of drudgery, busy in correcting exercise-books or answer books of the students. There are no stirring event in his life.

Inspite of these hardships, I would like to become a teacher. I have reasons and considerations for adopting this profession. Since my early childhood, I have the days of developed affection for the young children. In my view, they are delicate and beautiful like the petals of a flower. If feel that as a teacher, I can help the students in widening their outlook by giving them knowledge. I shall help the country by producing better citizens. Moreover, the company of the young children would also help me in remaining young and fresh in thoughts and outlook. Besides rendering all these important services, I shall also have the means of subsistence. I have a great faith in the life of a noble and an ideal teacher because *teachers are the custodians of the highest values,* according our former President, Dr S Radhakrishnan. ●

18. IF I WERE THE DEFENCE MINISTER !

"If wishes were horses, the beggars would ride," so runs a proverb. Everybody wishes to be the Prime Minister or a film hero. *Uneasy lies the head that wears the crown.* The life of a Prime Minister may appear to be very much luxurious and comfortable but if we have a closer look, it would be obvious that it is not so. Defence Minister is next in rank to the Prime Minister. I have an earnest desire to find a way for materialising my dreams regarding the defence of the country.

Our country is passing through a critical period. We are still confronted with many difficult tasks. So, every Indian ought to do his utmost to defend the Motherland. We have yet to deal with opponents like China and Pakistan. If ever I get a chance of becoming the Defence Minister of India, I shall put in my best efforts to make my country strong and prosperous. It would be my first and foremost duty to guard my country from all possible dangers and difficulties. For this purpose, I intend to pursue the following programme.

First of all, I shall raise the strength of Indian Army. Every physically fit youngman would be required to join the army where he shall be imparted training on modern training patterns. The persons would be fully equipped with modern, automatic and semiautomatic weapons of modern welfare.

Secondly, NCC training would be made mandatory in all the schools and colleges. All the students would be made to realise the importance of such training. They would encouraged to adopt Army as their career after completing their education. I shall popularise the slogan "Militarise the Nation." The student-batches would be sent to the villages where they would help illiterate villagers understand the various procedures of Civil Defence. Those students, who show interest in the tasks assigned to them, would be awarded the "Certificate of Merit." When these grown-ups seek employment in my Ministry, I shall give them preference.

Thirdly, besides raising the numerical strength, the whole Army would also be equipped with modern weapons. They would be fully trained in the techniques of modern warfare.

Automatic and semi-automatic weapons would be replaced with old type of weapons. Many more ordinance factories would be set up in our country. Jaguar, Mirage-2000, supersonic and other planes like MIG-29 and F-16 bombers would be manufactured in our country. I shall take concrete steps to achieve self-sufficiency in arms production so that we may not have to depend upon foreign assistance during war time. Self-reliance in defence is the most important function in the entire government. The Defence Ministry is responsible for resisting foreign aggressions and invasions and I shall ensure that it comes up to the mark.

Fourthly, I shall give maximum concessions to *Jawans*, The *Jawans* who are on the borders, should not be worried about the fate of their families in case they sacrifice their lives for their motherland. The bereaved families would not feel rejected or dejected. I shall offer them maximum concessions in the form of suitable employment to some of their members of their families, family pensions and handsome cash rewards in certain deserving cases. I would also like to revise the pay scales of the *Jawans*, especially soldiers who get very meagre salaries. The widows and families of *Jawans* and officers, who died during the Kargil war, have been given adequate compensations. I shall maintain this tradition.

Further, I shall endeavour to give a new look to the defence set up. For achieving all this, I may have to divert the maximum of the country's resources to defence. I know that the life of a Defence Minister is not a bed of roses. I shall consider myself to be the most fortunate person if I am able to find an opportunity that may enable me to achieve my long cherished dream. I shall make Defence Ministry the most prestigious and useful organ of the government. ●

19. MY HOBBY

The word 'Hobby' has been derived from "Hobby Horse," which is a stick fitted with a wooden horse and on which, small children ride for their amusement. So, hobby is a useful work that could be taken up during free time. Hobby means a useful work in which, one takes interest and drives pleasure by doing it in his spare time without any monetary benefit. This occupation is quite different from regular work. There are many hobbies like gardening, stamp-collection, coin-collection, photography, reading etc, that one adopts according to one's leisure hours and purse.

After a day' hard labour, not all persons can go to see the movie and visit clubs for entertainment. Hobby provides a cheap source of entertainment and amusement.

Gardening is my favourite hobby through which, I can see nature and enjoy it. Nature is a true and a dependant guide of man. Wordsworth, the poet, contends that nature never betrays anyone who loves her.

Ours is a big bungalow at Shanti Niketan in New Delhi. There is vast space for growing vegetation, fruits and flowers. have grown flower plants of rose, lily and sunflower. The sweet fragrance of the flowers serves as a tonic for my body and mind and thus helps me become stronger on physical and mental grounds. I have planted a few trees and plants of fruits also. There is an adequate growth of vegetables in our compound. So, we rarely purchase any vegetable from the market.

Gardening provides me with good exercise for the day. It keeps me healthy, happy and fresh for the day's labour at my work-place. Gardening is my sincere friend and inspires me whenever I am in a depressed mood. Whenever I cast a glance over my small garden and see the beautiful flowers, my heart blooms.

Life is a strife if we take rest. If we work, we shine and if we shine, the world gives us the credit. Moreover, an empty mind is a devil's workshop. It is better for everyone to lead a busy life. Struggle in life itself gives pleasure to man.

Hobby, is an interesting pursuit through which, one could derive pleasure, recreation and amusement during his free time. While pursuing a hobby, one gets pleasure, feels exalted and remains mentally elated. Hobby removes the monotony and melancholy of the mind. Further, hobbies have a great academic value as well.

20. THE HAPPIEST DAY OF MY LIFE

There is hardly any living being who has never gone through ups and downs in his life. In fact, life is full of bad as well as good incidents. Some of them may be forgotten with the passage of time whereas others leave an everlasting imprint on the mind. One feels delighted when one is favour with fortune but plunges into despair during misfortunes. In fact, a wise man is one who is neither overjoyed in prosperity nor takes adversity to heart.

Last year, I passed the Higher Secondary Examination. Although I had fared well in the examination, yet I was not so hopeful of getting a first class. I was very much anxious because the question of my career was involved in it. A day earlier, when the result was expected to be published in the local newspapers, I spent a restless night. I, along with my friends, got up early in the morning and went to catch the newspaper hawker on the way. Finally, he appeared, shouting aloud, the declaration of the Higher Secondary results. His voice were piercing my heart. I hurriedly bought the paper and started spotting out my roll number. All sorts of expressions were appearing on my face. It was a matter of immense surprise and pleasure to find that I stood second in my school, securing a first class. God fulfilled my desires. I felt grateful to Him. My other friends also passed, securing good marks. In order to celebrate our happiness, we chalked out a programme to go to some picnic spot. We decided to go to Okhla.

We reached Okhla, a lovely picnic resort, at 12 noon. There was a heavy cavalcade of people. The banks of the canal were occupied by the visitors. We identified a place under a banyan tree and sat there. We also took with us all the paraphernalia lunch. We had our lunch to our heart's content. Then, we listened to music. As we were lost in the sweet music of our transistor, we heard loud cries. I immediately rushed towards the canal and saw to my shock and surprise that a boy was drowning. He was crying for help.

I immediately jumped into the water and swam towards the drowning boy. After a great struggle, I dragged him towards the bank. He was in a very bad state. When I observed him carefully, I was surprised to know that he was an old classmate of mine. He was immediately given medical aid and after some time, he regained consciousness. I was delighted to see him recovering. My joy knew no bounds because I had saved the life of a boy who happened to be my old classmate.

This day was a day of great joy and happiness. Not only I secured second position, but also did a brave and noble act by saving a boy from going into the jaws of death. This day would go down as one of the happiest days of my life. ●

21. THE FUNNIEST INCIDENT

One Sunday morning, I received an invitation from a friend of mine, Sudhir. I had come back from the UK to my native place. So, he invited me to lunch. I got up early in the morning and started getting ready. My sister gave me a cup of tea early in the morning. Then, I took my bath and got ready. My sister then again asked me to take some snacks and tea but I refused to take it as I was more interested in reaching my friend's house. She insisted upon me to take a heavy breakfast but I ignored her request. I went out of my house and stood at the bus-stop. I boarded the bus. The conductor came and asked me to buy a ticket. I asked him to give me a ticket for Babar Lane. The conductor frowned upon me saying, "It is going in the reverse direction, you get down at the next stop and catch another bus." I was baffled for some time. Then, I alighted from the bus and again waited for the bus going to the Babar Lane.

I got the bus and reached 15, Babar Lane. But surprisingly, when I reached his house, I found the door locked. I was puzzled and thought whether I had come to the right place. After some time, a neighbour of my friend came and asked me, "Why are you standing here ? Do you want to meet someone?" I replied, "Yes, I want to see Mr Sudhir living in Quarter No 15." He immediately quibbled, "But he changed his house last Wednesday and has gone to R K Puram."

Frustrated, I came back to the bus stop. I was feeling hungry. After some time, it started drizzling. I was now in a fix as to what to do. My confusion was compounded by the torrential rains. I had refused to take morning breakfast in the hope that I would take it at my friend's house. At this state, my anger was mounting. I was cursing myself as well as my fate. But I controlled my anger. I made up my mind to meet Sudhir.

An idea hit my mind. I gave a ring at the Enquiry Office, R K Puram. The person on duty gave me his address. I made my journey to R K Puram and reached the quarter as I was told by the Enquiry Office. I rang the door bell. Tupan, a tiny tot (Sudhir's youngest brother) came out and greeted me with a "Hello uncle !" The moment I entered the drawing room, I saw the parents of Sudhir sitting on the sofa. They offered me a seat and I sat comfortably. As I was about to talk about invitation extended to me by Sudhir, Dolly (Sudhir's sister) came with tea. She was looking like a pretty and vivacious damsel. (Let it be known that I used to love this girl from my college days and had written many love letters to her, making a proposal for marriage). Now, the elderly mother of Sudhir began to talk very politely, "Look son, the invitation to tea was a joke. As you know, today is First of April — Fool's Day. But you are fortunate that your proposal of marriage has been accepted by all the members of our family." I was thrilled to hear these words coming from the august lips of Dolly's mother.

My joy knew no bounds. The facial expressions of Dolly were quite attractive. Her looks pleased me as she was making silent expressions of love. We had the tea to our heart's content. I rushed from their house in order to convey this happy news to my parents. This day, indeed, was the funniest and happiest day of my life.

22. THE DAY I WOULD LIKE TO FORGET

The Day, on which, India was partitioned, was a day of mixed feelings. It was marred by sadness as well as by happiness. People were happy because they were now free from the foreign rule but sad because their motherland was partitioned.

As I was living in the Sialkot district of West Pakistan, I saw some of the most tragic and painful events. Whenever I remember them, I shudder with fear. Mass migrations were the natural outcome of the partition. People living in one country were going to the other. In those days, the most tragic incidents like kidnapping, abductions, arson, murders, rapes, loot and bloodshed were witnessed.

I left my hearth and home on August 14, 1947 and reached Pasrur from my village Kalaswala with great difficulty. From Pasrur, I caught a train so that I might reach Derababa Nanak, a small town near the border. I got some space only for standing in the train. The train was packed to its capacity with the refugees. Many people were sitting on the roof of the train. We continued the journey slowly but in a steady manner. On the way, I saw one man murdering another with his sword. I was shocked to see this ghastly murder. In the meanwhile, our train reached a station on the banks of the river Ravi. It was night time. It was a perfectly dark night. The driver of the engine refused to start the train on the pertext that engine was out of order. It was a difficult time for me. The train was not moving. The raiders attacked the train mercilessly. I took some of my belongings and tried to cross the bridge on the river Ravi. As I was very tired, I rested for a while. People were rushing forth, screaming and crying. The families were disunited and separated.

I spent my night on the bridge of Ravi along with other people who were also passing that dark and dreadful night there. But as ill-luck would have it, it rained very heavily. Rivers and streams were flooded. The gurgling water was gushing forth on the plains. Nothing could be seen. Many persons became the victims of cold and fell ill. There was no conveyance. The fear was ruling my mind. Somehow, I ventured to walk through the water that was knee-deep onwards and moved in the direction of Derabada Nanak. As I was coming with some of my luggage, I was stopped by a stranger who snatched my belongings. Thank God, the stranger did not kill me. Later, I ran immediately in a frightened manner. I crossed the difficult terrains in a bid to reach Derababa Nanak where all the refugees were arriving. I had not taken any food for the last two days. I was feeling very hungry. Finally, I reached Derababa Nanak. I met a family that was in my neighbourhood at my home town. The members of that family offered me some eatables and I thanked them. But as there were heavy rains and dirt, an epidemic was spread in the area and I also became the victim of that epidemic. I had no money for buying medicines. I remembered God and somehow, escaped the jaws of death.

The aforementioned dreadful details of partition days always haunt my mind. When I recollect the grim instance of cold-blooded murders, mass killings and arson, I am shocked. But now, I have decided never to remember those days of misfortune. Indeed, I would like to forget that most unhappy and unfortunate day of my life.   ●

23. A HAPPY LIFE

Everyone in this world craves for a happy life. Happiness is just a state of mind. It is very difficult to define happiness. Sometimes, happiness is related to material glory and splendour. Sometimes, it is associated with the health of a man while to others, it lies in a sort of contentment with whatever one possesses.

People crave for happiness. Happiness to them is just a good and comfortable dream. The manner of living has various standards. Everyone, therefore, has his own concept of happiness. But one thing is very clear that every man is dissatisfied with his present state of affairs and condition. One always wants more and more of the materialistic assets. A poor man, living on the roadside, may be aspiring for a hut while a hutdweller may be aspiring for a house. A house owner may be aspiring for a beautiful bungalow and a bungalow-owner may be aspiring for a posh-residence and so on.

Thus, the question arises — where is the real human happiness and solace ? Generally speaking, material splendour and prosperity are considered to be the main factors leading to happiness. A wealthy man enjoys all the comforts, luxuries, amenities and facilities of life. But does he consider himself to be really happy? A rich man may be the master of millions but even then, he may be unhappy because he, normally, is a sick man. Being sick, he cannot enjoy all the pleasures of life. He considers himself to be a condemned and cursed man in this world. And when he finds himself amidst wealth, he is all the more troubled. His state of mind is not elevating. Rather, he is always in a mood of melancholy. We conclude that wealth is not the only criterion of a true happy life.

Take the life of a poor man. It is an admitted fact that poverty and happiness are diametrically opposed to each other. But there have been some instances when we find poor people quite happy and gay. Their minds are not corrupted by the sweeping changes of the times. Their lives are balanced and happy. They feel contented with their meagre resources and they believe in the following lines of Wordsworth :

"Be content with what you have
Little be it or much ..."

Such people are really happy. Their mental states are always calm. Otherwise, there is no end to the desires of human beings. Human desires are infinite; they multiply with the fortune. A millionaire longs to become a multi-millionaire and his vicious circle for acquiring riches does not end anywhere.

Moreover, this humanity is a strange lot. People always want what is not in their possession. So, their desire to acquire and possess leads to aspirations but their failure to achieve those aspirations brings frustration. Craze for more things and its unfulfilment leads to unhappiness and melancholy. This world is really a strange affair and has been aptly described by Shelly in the following words :

"We look before and after
And pine for what is not"

A happy life results from a state of mind. Health is also one of the most important factors that promote happiness. A healthy man can take strolls in the morning and can enjoy the fresh air of the fields and fragrance of the flowers by visiting a garden. A poor but healthy man can spend his time in sports and games and can resort to other entertainments and recreations that are cheap and easily accessible.

Therefore, we can conclude that the very secret of happiness lies somewhere else and not in the mere possession of huge wealth. A wealthy man always remains in a state of tension because he thinks that a thief or a dacoit might rob him. But ideal happiness is in a man who always does a right thing, never injures the hearts and minds of others and is a God-fearing person. One's actions and ambitions must be good. Good actions also lead to happiness. Contentment with the prevailing circumstances is another factor that promotes happiness. Thus Shakespeare was right when he wrote :

Nothing is good or bad but thinking makes it so."

Everything appears to be pleasant to a happy mind and unpleasant to a diseased mind. ●

24. THE CHOICE OF A PROFESSION

Everyone in this world has his own likes and dislikes. So is the case with choosing one's profession. There are many professions to choose from. But most of the people have got some pet profession that they like most. In the childhood, everyone talks of becoming a barrister, a doctor or an engineer but some like to become politicians, statesmen and professors. The brave and the courageous ones want to join the services for becoming officers in the army, navy and air force.

It is quite difficult to choose a profession. Upon a profession, depends the whole life of a man and so, one must have an aim in his life. An aimless life is just like a boat or the ship that is not aware of its destination or is a letter without an address. Hence, there arises the necessity of choosing a profession.

Although I am not fit enough at this age to choose a profession, yet I would like to take up teaching as a profession. Other professions have no future. But teaching is a noble profession and has a future.

I want to become a professor. Ours is still an illiterate country. So, to take the masses from the darkness to light, from ignorance to knowledge, from illiteracy to literacy, is really a pious task. That is why, I want to take up teaching as my profession.

Teaching has many advantages over other professions. First of all, it is free from all the corrupt practices prevent in other professions. It is an ideal and a noble profession in the sense that a teacher remains honest and studious in his profession. He gives the gems from his mind to his students. The words of wit and wisdom are far more valuable than all the riches and everyone can get benefit out of the same.

A professor remains in touch with various books. This keeps his knowledge up-to-date. He is the storehouse of knowledge and information. He is the picture of wisdom. A professor has to read books of eminent authors, philosophers and literary figures. So, his maturity is high. His ability to solve complex problems is enhanced.

Almost all the great men of the world started their life as teachers. Dr S Radhakrishnan, our ex-President, was a university professor. Acharya Kripalani was also a college teacher. Our late President, Zakir Hussain, was the Vice Chancellor of Aligarh Muslim University. Dr M M Joshi, our president HRD, Minister has also an academic background.

A teacher is the true builder of a nation. It is he who moulds the characters of tender children and creates in them, noble qualities of service, sacrifice and patriotism. A teacher is the pillar of nation's progress. It is he who guides the students in their most critical periods. He is the maker of their lives. That is why, I like this profession most. A teacher is kept in high esteem by everyone—students as well as the society.   ●

25. MY NEIGHBOUR

Last Sunday, we shifted our residence to a new government colony. This colony is inhabited by employees of the government. They belong to various departments and ministries. But my next door neighbours are really very nice. One of them is a Police inspector. He has a small family. His son is a college student. He is a very intelligent boy. He often tells me very interesting stories. The police inspector is also very gentle. His habits and temperaments are very fine. He considers himself to be the custodian of law and order. He never misuses his powers but always helps others. His wife is a woman of religious bent of mind. She is a God-fearing lady. She also extends deep cooperation and help to all.

The in front of ours belongs to a Principal of a school. He is an old man 55 years of age and is thoroughly gentle. His behaviour is very nice. He is highly respected by the inhabitants of the locality. He helps the deserving students by admitting them in his school. He gives fee concessions to the needy and poor people. He has a medium-sized family of two sons and a daughter. They are of a very helping nature. His daughter is my class-fellow. We go to school together. The Principal loves me very much. Sometimes, he gives us very interesting lectures. I am proud to be in the company of such a well-educated family.

The family that lives at the back of our house is a middle class family. But the members of this family are really very disgusting. They do not possess the decorum of civilised people. The head of the family is an Assistant in Central Government. His behaviour is rude. He has quarrelled with many people over trifles. His children are very naughty. They beat other younger children. Their mother is also a terrible lady. She often scolds her children. She being an uneducated lady, always creates hell in her house. Everyone in the locality is afraid of her. Most of the people are not on speaking terms with this family.

But a majority of my neighbours are my friends. They are social and of helping nature. I pass my time easily in their company. Neighbours are sometimes, more helpful than relatives. We should always create a climate of friendship among our neighbours. I should conclude by stating that I am lucky to have good neighbours. ●

26. HOME SWEET HOME

East or West, home is the best. It is a famous old saying, which is true to the hilt. I live in a small flat that was built by the DDA. My father owns it on hire-purchase basis and pays monthly instalments. When the house was allotted, it was only a one-room set. We were not born at that time. As the family grew in size, my father added one more room to meet the needs of the children.

It is a compact dwelling in which, we have all the facilities within the four walls. We have combined the bathroom and toilet and created a small kitchen. There are marble chips on the floor. We have covered the drawing-room with a wall-to-wall carpet. The showcase in the drawing room has been arranged very nicely in the centre. Whenever we visit some historical place, we bring some memento from there and place it in the show-case. We have arranged the drawing room in such a manner as would allow it to be changed into a guest room. I have a foldable study-table in a corner where I do my home work.

There is box-type double bed in the bed room. We have filled those boxes with our winter clothes. The almirah in the corner contains all our clothes that are used at present. We have a TV set in one corner. We never miss The News and *Chitrahar*. We can watch it with the help of remote control, lying in our beds.

Although it is a very small home, yet I get all the comforts of life in it.

27. MY FAMILY

I belong to my middle class family in which, the both the parents are working. My grandparents also stay with us. My grandfather retired from the army and draws a small sum as a pension. He is strict disciplinarian and would not allow anyone to sleep after 5.30 AM. All the children have to get ready for morning by 6 AM. He treats us as recruits in his training centre. He pulls us up very often and my parents have no choice before him. If you have to visit my house, you have to be properly dressed. You cannot sit in our drawing room with legs crossed. It is against the etiquettes. My grandmother is very submissive and gentle. She prepares breakfast and helps us in getting ready. Although she is past sixty, yet she is very active and hard-working. But for her, we would not have conducted our work outside the home. She takes adequate care of the home and keeps it neat, clean and shining.

My father works as an accountant in a private firm. He sleeps with a calculator in his pocket. He maintains an account book for the whole family. He would never go to sleep before preparing a balance sheet. When we are busy watching TV programmes, he can be seen taking everyone to task for not giving proper account of daily expenses. When my grandmother brings costly fruit, it is balanced by simple *chapatis* next day.

My mother is the finest lady in the world. She does not poke her nose in anything. She is working as a receptionist in a private firm. She has to get up very early in the morning. She is always smiling. When she returns home, smile returns to everyone's face. My elder brother is a student of senior secondary class. He is a very serious student and does not take part in games or other extracurricular activities. His mind is always concentrated on Physics, Chemistry and Mathamatics.

I am the youngest in the family. Although I am a student of Class X, yet the whole family treats me as a child. No one calls me by my proper name. I am *chhotu* for all of them. I really feel every awkard, when my parents call me *chhotu* in the presence of my friends. My friends have also started calling me by this nick-name. There is no solution to this problem because I cannot swap my status with anyone in the family.

Ours is a very happy family and I wish that it may prosper in all terms ! ●

28. MY FAVOURITE BOOK

Thousands of books are published every year and it is not easy to make a wise choice. I always take the suggestions made by my teachers and parents into account while choosing a book. Some days back, my uncle gave me one as a birthday gift as he knows my love for books. It has been written in English by C Rajagopalachari and has been published by Bharatiya Vidya Bhawan, Mumbai. I had heard that these books were meant only for elderly people and so, I hesitated in making a beginning. When I went through the first chapter, a fascinating story unfolded itself. The *Rishis* in the Himalayas had scared away the cow that was born in the form of the Ganges. King Satyavan married the daughter of a washerman and his son from the first wife took a pledge to remain a bachelor all his life. He came to be known as Bhishma Pitamah. The story was so eventful that it was very difficult to keep pace with the individual events. The battle between the Kauravas and Pandavas is so well-known that it need not be repeated. In the centre of the epic, stands *The Gita* that serves as lighthouse. It sheds light on the theme of the whole story. The language is so poetic that one floats in its divine stream. Lord Krishna tells us to do our duty and leave the fruit to God. We should forget the sense of attachment as it blurs our mind. We should strive for excellence in any type of work we do. This body is short-lived. Our soul is eternal. It never dies. It keeps on changing bodies just as we keep on changing clothes. Fire cannot burn the soul nor can the sword cut it. When death is a must, why should we be afraid of it ?

It was this "song celestial" that help Arjuna to forget his attachments and do his duty boldly and fearlessly. The author also tells us that the struggle always continues in our hearts. Whenever we are in doubt, whether we should do something or not, we should seek guidance from *The Gita*.

This book has changed the whole course of my life and I wish that it should be read by every one in India and abroad. The book is for those young people who have yet to begin their careers.

29. HOW I CELEBRATED MY BIRTHDAY ?

My birthday is a red letter day not only in my life, but also in the history of free India. I was born on January 26th, fifteen years ago. My mother had noted the exact time and got a horoscope prepared from a learned astrologer. But that is useful only for the parents. For me, it is the only day when I am made to feel important. I am busy in issuing invitation cards, arranging gems and decorating the drawing room. I have left certain things entirely to my sister. For example, it is for her to decorate the cards and write addresses in a very beautiful handwriting. She invites her friends also to join the party. My father has a very different notion about the celebration of my birthday. Last year, he had taken me to an orphanage and had made me contribute Rupees one hundred to their welfare fund. This year, he intends to take me to the school for the blind.

My friends start arriving at around 5 PM. I receive every one of them with warmth and make them sit comfortably in the drawing room that is beautifully decorated. They bring gifts for me, nicely packed in coloured wrappers. My uncle, who lives in Mumbai sends me a beautiful set of pens or a pair of jeans. This year again, I hope to get something nice from him.

When all the friends gather around, my mother brings the cake in the drawing room. The candles are lit on its corners. As my friends sing "Happy Birthday," I blow off the candles and use a knife to carve out small pieces of the cake. Everyone wishes me a prosperous future as he is served with a piece of cake. Some snacks are also served. My sister helps my mother in serving them to my friends. The gifts are piled up in one corner and we all get ready to play the games. Every game seems to be full of fun. They all roar with laughter. The lengthening shadows of the evening remind us that we have to wind up. Those friends, who come from far-off places, start taking leave. It is the turn of my father to drive me to a charity home, school for the disabled or a hospital in the city. He wants that I should remember all those people as my brothers and sisters and help them in their hour of need.

30. HOW I SPENT MY SUNDAY ?

I wish everyday was a Sunday. This day comes after waiting for six long days. We praise God who made this day especially for the students. I have not to get up at 5 AM and get ready for the school. My mother knows it and does not touch me before 7 AM. She is so sweet when she tells me that the breakfast is ready. I leave the bed with a heavy heart and spend maximum time in the bathroom. We have formed a small club of cricket players who assemble in the park to play the game. We have devised the wickets and also have the necessary gear for playing the game. We have also settled the boundary of the park as the boundary of our ground.

Mother calls me to take lunch and it is only when she herself appears at the scene that I go back home. I never miss' the lessons on cricket by Kapil Dev that are telecast from the New Delhi station of Doordarshan. I note down the points made by him and try to practise them while playing the game.

Our teachers load us with heavy homework. The parents check my school diary and do not allow me to go out till I have finished my assignments. I try to complete my homework as fast as possible. I never miss the Sunday movie on TV. It is the best source of enjoyment. Sometimes, I invite my friends to visit my house. We discuss our plans to organise a friendly match with other clubs. We also go to the park to see nature bathed in all its beauty. The park of our locality has won first prize in the annual competition and is one of the best maintained ones.

In the evening, when we sit for supper, the fear of getting up early in the next morning again grips my mind. I remind my mother to wake me up early so that I could finish the remaining homework. Before going to sleep, I wish a sad farewell to my dear Sunday and wish it to come again as soon as possible. A Sunday is an excellent holiday.

31. HOW I SPENT MY SUMMER VACATION ?

A fortnight before the summer break, we stopped taking interest in studies. Everyone of us made an ambitious plan to visit some place or the other. But man proposes and God disposes. On the very first day, my mother slipped in the kitchen and broke her ankle. Her whole leg was plastered and she was advised bed rest for three weeks. I had to prepare tea and cook food for the whole family. My friends came to enquire about her health and I had to serve them as well. I kept company with my mother, told her stories and tried to make her happy in every possible manner. My mother could not stand the moist air of the cooler and so, I had to perspire along with her. It was not easy to prepare her bed, serve her food and change her clothes. As no male member could help, I had to bear the burden. Whenever she was to be carried to the bathroom, I had to be very careful about the plaster on her leg.

Three weeks were over. We had to carry her to the hospital to get the plaster cut. There was a long line of patients and we had to wait in the verandah, sitting on the wooden bench. It was a really trying time for all the patients in the hospital. The patients were crying with pain. Some were being taken on the stretchers while others could walk only with great difficulty. The doctor told us that plaster was to be put on once again. I wish that it would have been my leg so that I could get bed for rest for whole day !

My friends wrote from Kashmir that they were having nice time. My friends described the pleasant weather and their trekking experience from Pehalgam to Glacier. I wished that I could fly like a bird and join them. One of my aunts came all the way from Mumbai to enquire about the health of my mother. Her younger son was also with her. So, I had to look after not only my mother and members of our own family but also my aunt and her naughty son.

Therefore, I had to look after my mother, my family and my guests during the summer vacation.

32. HOW I CAUGHT A PICK POCKET

I cannot say exactly weather he caught me or I caught him but I was called the hero of the day. It all happened when I was travelling in a local bus. It was packed to the capacity. Some commuters were also virtually hanging on the rails, I was trying to move forward to stand in a comfortable place. Suddenly, I saw a man putting his hands in the back pocket of another passenger. First of all, I grew nervous but the next moment, I alerted the passengers. They caught him red-handed. He struggled hard to get away from them. He showed his empty hands to plead innocence. I refuted him loudly and told everyone that I had seen him putting his hands in the back pocket of the other passenger. The pick-pocket caught me by the collar and challenged me to prove it. I struggled hard to get myself free but his grip was very tight. Some passengers spoke in his favour and called me a liar.

In the meanwhile, the driver changed the route and took the bus to the police station. I cursed my foolishness because that healthy man had started dragging me. I was in tears and sought help from other passengers.

The bus reached the police station. The smart policemen put a cordon round the bus. The driver reported the whole matter to the police. The sub-inspector caught hold of the pick-pocket and took him to the investigation room. I sat in the reporting room. The police checked the record and found out that he was the most notorious pickpocket of the area. He confessed many other crimes also.

The policeman offered me a glass of water. I washed my face and relaxed. Next day, my name was published in all the newspapers for the remarkable bravery I had shown for nabbing an anti-social element.

33. WHEN THE PARENTS ARE ANGRY

My parents are very gentle but they are not gods. They get angry sometimes but that is for a very short while. The reactions of my mother and father are of different types. Whereas my mother gets angry very often, my father is cool and calm. My mother is a working lady and has to work on two fronts. She has to cook food, clean the kitchen and wash the clothes. She has also to reach office in time. She gets tired and irritated. I know her mood and when she starts snubbing my father, I lock myself in the bedroom. When she cools down, I come out silently as if nothing had happened. She has the habit of nagging every one. I have got used to it. When mother works hard in the kitchen, my father sits in the *Pooja Room*, quite relaxed. He gets angry once in a year. When he is angry, he becomes the God of fire. His eyes burn, his muscles twitch and he is ready to give vent to his anger everywhere. The first victim of his anger is my elder brother. Pappa catches him by the ear and pulls it so hard that he starts crying. If the mother is around, she would also jump in the fray. She would save him at the risk of getting beaten herself. My turn came only once. I had secured a zero in Mathematics and added the figure eight, raising it to an enviable eighty.

My father was very happy to see the report card and promised to buy me a new bat. Suddenly, the bell of our telephone rang and my teacher spoke to my father. He had knowingly awarded me zero because he wanted to give me

53

tuition. I do not know what transpired between them. I heard my pappa saying that in the report book, the marks obtained were eighty. I wanted to jump over the wall or escape in any other direction. There was no help around. Mother had gone to the market, Elder brother was also not at home. I was caught by my father. He hanged the receiver and called me angrily. I was already in the bathroom and had decided not to open it till mother was back home. My father kicked the door angrily and it opened. I feel a burning sensation in my ear when I write these lines. No one could save me from his anger. He thrashed me mercilessly and I cried for mercy. My mother had to apply all types of ointments to soothe the swelling of my skin.

34. WHEN I MISSED THE SCHOOL BUS

It was a Saturday. I had seen the movie on the TV that was telecast from 11.30 PM to 1.30 AM. I went to sleep after 2 AM. My mother had prepared the breakfast and was taking her bath. She had thought that I was getting ready in my room. She was surprised when she saw me sleeping as she came out. She woke me up with great difficulty. I prepared myself hastily and rushed to the bus stop. There was no student waiting there. I realised at once that I would have to reach the school by the local bus. The buses were over-crowded and some commuters were hanging outside. It is very difficult to catch the rails inside an over crowded bus. As the bus stopped, I entered from the front door. The driver was nice. He did not object when I requested him to let me stand in a corner. The conductor asked me buy the ticket. I passed on a two-Rupee note through another passenger and requested him to give the same to the conductor. This note passed from passenger to passenger and reached the bus-conductor at last. He sent the ticket and a fifty-Paisa coin back in the same manner. At every stop, new passengers kept on entering the bus. I was badly squeezed. At last, my stop came and I jerked myself out. The stop was at least half a kilometre away from my school. I ran as fast as possible but the school prayer had already started. I was made to stand among the latecomers. When I told my teacher honestly that the last show of the movie was the main culprit, he excused me and allowed me to attend the classes. I learnt the lesson not to keep awake late in the night. As I had not taken bath, I kept scratching my skin and continued to feel sleepy all the time during the school hours.

35. WHEN I WAS CAUGHT IN SHOWERS WITHOUT AN UMBRELLA

It was the month of May. The school had re-opened after the examinations. I was dreaming of sitting in the higher class. My bag was full of new books. My uniform was brand new. I was walking briskly towards the school. Suddenly, there was a dark cloud in the sky. It soon spread and covered the Sun. Fast winds stared blowing. I started running towards the school. I was hardly a hundred metres away when it started pouring very hard. I ran towards a tree and stood under it for some time but the showers did not stop. The leaves of the tree were also full of raindrops. Soon, water drops started drenching me to the marrows. I tried to save my bag but to no avail. My shoes and socks were so full of water that I started feeling a numbness in my feet. At last, I took the risk and started running towards the school. My shoes threw mud at my back. When I reached the school building, I took shelter in the porch. I immediately opened my bag and tried to rescue my books and notebooks. There was cardboard wrapper of pastel chalks that were meant for the drawing period. These chalks had become pulp and splashed their whole colour on my books. It seemed as if they had played Holi with my books and notebooks.

I removed my shoes and socks and left them to dry up. I looked awkward. My hair was unkept and face bathed in rain drops. I could not attend any period. As soon as my clothes were dried up, I collected my books and notebooks and walked back home. My mother told me that Lord Indra (the god of rain) had welcomed me on my first day to the school.

36. WHEN I WAS A SMALL CHILD

I am the eldest child in my family and was born after seven years of marriage of my parents. You can very well imagine what a rare gem I am for them. I was fondled lavishly and single tear from my eye would bring ten from my mother's eye. When I started walking with the help of a baby-walker, my parents held a grand feast. Noises of every type fascinated me. When the balloon seller passed through our lane, I used to run after him. My mother would buy the balloon filled with grains. It made sweet noise when it was shaken. She also bought me beautiful toys that had many colourful and fascinating features. When I pressed the doll, she would squeak. When I was three years old, my birthday was celebrated with great pomp and show. My parents might have celebrated my first and second birthdays as well but those celebrations have not left any imprint in my memory. My relatives had brought beautiful toys, which had to be wound up.

When the toy car was left on the floor, it would run for some distance. When the joker was wound up, it would blow a trumpet. It was a strange world; my parents were ready to bring moon from the sky for the sake of my pleasure.

Once, a juggler, with two monkeys, came to our street. He showed monkey tricks that engaged my attention. He-monkey fell in love with she-monkey. She-monkey refused to marry he-monkey. He-monkey went to his father-in-law's house and wore a colourful dress. I cannot forget the scene at his in-law's house. I also liked the tricks shown by the juggler.

I was taken to the school when I was five years old. My parents had carried sweets to be distributed among the students. I was wearing a new dress and my mother had groomed me with great care. Both my parents left me there and walked back home. I shouted and cried but there was no help. My tears could not bring them back. The teacher talked gently and asked other students to be friendly towards me.

I grew up very fast. My friends grew in number and we started playing tricks with our neighbours. We used to enter into any house and press the button of call-bell. When the owner came out, we used to run away as fast as our legs could have carried us.

These are only the memories, the things of the past and now, the huge bag of books and heavy home-work has been left behind. ●

37. IF I WERE THE PRIME MINISTER !

If wishes were horses, beggars would ride. My case is no different. It is the most magnificent dream that could me forget my student life. The office of the PM seems so distant that it is beyond the each of ordinary persons. India has population of 1,000 million. So my chance of becoming the Prime Minister is one upon 1,000 million.

I have my own idea of what a Prime Minister should be. So, there is no harm in expressing my ideas. If fortune ever smiles on me, I can modify my views according to the situation.

My first target would be to eliminate black money and bank deposits of Indians in the foreign countries. When I find some people rolling in wealth and the others begging on the streets, my heart revolts. Is this the India of Gandhiji's dream? These people do not pay taxes and keep the money stocked in some secret places. This money is used for hoarding and smuggling the goods. We need foreign exchange so badly but it is being used for buying gold and luxuries.

I shall change the whole system of education. We produce battalions of young people for whom we cannot arrange jobs. They would naturally spread chaos and destruction. They would kill innocent people or burn their houses and assets. We should teach our students so that they could make useful things in the school workshops. They could also make them in the school laboratories. Little children can assemble small toys pens, watches and electronic goods. These things can be sold in the market. Their hard work give them confidence to do something in their lifetimes. They would prove to be useful citizens of our country. However, children would also be required to study in the morning schools or evening schools. The politicians have made a mess of the whole country. They seek votes in the name of caste, community and religion. They make different communities fight. The places of worship are used for storing arms and ammunitions and polluting the young minds. Religion is the personal affair of every citizen and it should not be used as an election device.

I shall develop friendship with the neighbouring countries. If America and Canada can keep their boundaries open, why can't we do so with Pakistan and China?

I shall invite the teams from all the nations to play in India and send our own teams to those nations. We shall not exchange bullets but balls in order to promote universal fraternity, peace and harmony. No person in India would be allowed to criticise our opponents and the same would also be expected by those nations. The money spent on the purchase of arms and ammunition would be spent for buying beautiful garments for small children. I shall make India a heaven on earth.   ●

38. IF I WIN A LOTTERY !

If there were dreams to sell,
what would you buy?

I would buy a beautiful bungalow in a posh colony and lead a peaceful and luxurious life. The lottery help us in realising our dreams. Even if I don't win anything, there is no harm in living in the dream world for some days. The world around us is full of haste and confusion. We spend the whole day working hard and what is the reward ? If one is a clerk, he would remain a clerk throughout his life. He can hardly think of turning a corner. We hear of so many fairies helping the human beings in their lives and making them millionaires overnight. If a woodcutter could be rewarded with a golden axe for his honesty, why can't the god of wealth smile on me in the form of this lottery ticket? We have "Jhun Jun Lottery Wala" round the corner of our lane who has displayed the photographs of those lucky winners who had purchased the tickets from him. It is another matter that the prize was never more than Rs one hundred. Who knows, I may be the person who would hit the Jackpot ? If that golden day comes, I shall go in a car to collect the prize money. How pleasant it would be to offer a hundred-Rupee note to the chauffeur and ask him to retain the change as I would no longer have small currency notes !

I shall deposit the whole money in my bank and shall issue cheques to my parents and sister. I would plan a holiday in Kashmir where I would stay in a beautiful *Shikara*. I shall watch the beauty of the Dal Lake with my own eyes. In the evening, I shall drive to the choicest picnic spots. I shall spend lavishly and shall give tips liberally to the waiters and attendants. I shall purchase the choicest gowns and beautiful clothes not only for myself, but also for my parents and sister. I shall tell my sister to make her own choice without thinking of the costs. I shall loosen the string of my purse for my parents and shall ask them to spend without any restrictions. It would be really my dream-world. I shall ask my parents to shift to a bungalow in a posh colony so that we could live there in the style of the millionaires. ●

39. THE PERSON I LIKE THE MOST

I have a many of friends who are dearer to me than my own life. It is very difficult to name the best choice out of them off-hand. My maximum time is spent in the company of Brijmohan whom I call Birju but others call him Mirchi. I do not know, what type of child they consider him to be but for me, he is sweeter than honey.

He is one of the best centre-forwards in the hockey team of our school. His only ambition is to bring India on the Olympic map once again in this game. He is an ace sprinter and when he chases the ball, no one can recover the same from him. He was the captain of the State Junior Team that participated in the National Games.

It is surprising to make out how he stands first in different subjects in the class. Most of the players occupy back-seats in our class and relax while the teacher writes something on the blackboard. He is very active and keeps on asking inquisitive questions.

Last year, he decided to take part in a Hindi play and he acted as the milkman so well that the spectators burst out with laughter. He had observed his milkman very closely and had noted all his actions before mimicking him on the stage.

You would not believe if I say that he is the best debater as well. How can a single person combine all these qualities ? He has learnt this art from his father. His father taught him to put his heart and soul in anything he did. He often tells me that we should be like Arjuna who did not see anything but the eye of the fish when he sort the decisive arrow. We cannot achieve much because our minds are divided most of the time. When we study, we should study and forget everything about the games. When we play, our mind should not see anything but the ball. This is the secret of the success of my friend.

I wish that I could also follow in his foot-steps ! ●

39. THE PERSON I HATE MOST

It has been said that man's body is the temple of God. I don't agree with this view. There are some human beings who are worse than devils. They can shoot down innocent bus passengers or attack the peaceful citizens. They can throw bombs anywhere and blow up buildings and factories in no time. It is not so easy to build but it does not take much time to destroy. Such people are a curse for the entire humanity. Many innocent, who use religion as their opium, are joining the ranks of the terrorist organisations. When asked why they are doing so, they reply that they are doing this to save their culture. They have never read any book on religion nor have they anything to do with culture.

One of my classfellows was caught by the police. He was found planting a bomb in a local bus. He was never regular in the class and always occupied a backseat. He never completed his homework and was always found sleeping in the class. When the teacher checked him, he denied that he was sleeping. He could invent lies at the spur of the moment and never admitted his fault.

Once, he had to pay some money to the manager of the canteen. He threatened the manager with a dagger. The matter was reported to the Principal and the boy was rusticated. His parents came and apologised on his behalf. He remained adamant and refused to admit his fault.

I do not know what happened to him afterwards. I was surprised to see his photograph in the newspapers. When I read what he had done, I really felt ashamed that he as my former classmate. He had brought bad name to the school. The police came to the school to enquire about his background. We told the police officer how he was expelled from the school.

He would be tried in the court and is likely to be prosecuted. Hence, he has earned a bad name for his parents, relatives and our school. ●

PART III

School's Surroundings and Examinations

41. OUR SCHOOL

The name of our school is DAV Higher Secondary School. It is situated on the Chitragupta Road, New Delhi.

The building of our school is very impressive. It is made of stones and bricks. It has 35 rooms. The rooms are airy. Every room has ventilators. There is a big library as well. The library has a good stock of books. Some of the books are very interesting. There are books that increase one's wisdom, intelligence and commonsense. The school has a big laboratory. It has been equipped with the necessary apparatus and scientific instruments.

The school has six classes. Every class has been divided into four sections. There are 1,000 boys in the school. It has a staff of 45 members. The staff members are capable and efficient. The Principal of the school is a reputed man. He is very popular among the staff and the students alike. He keeps a strict eye upon the students. The school office is managed by one clerk and one cashier. All are hardworking.

The school has two playgrounds — one is a tennis courtyard and the other one is a cricket ground. A swimming pool and a nice cafeteria are also located in our school. It has also a beautiful garden where students relax and play during the recess period.

Our school is progressing in all the fields. In academic field it has made a mark. Its students secure positions in the board examinations. Even in games, sports and tournaments, it has made much progress. Our school has won many trophies, shields and medals in such extracurricular activities.

In debates also, the students of our school secure good positions. It is considered to be one of the best schools in Delhi. Its reputation is very good. All of us would be really proud of our *alma-mater*.

42. A FAREWELL PARTY

The day, when I was free from my school for appearing in the Senior Secondary examinations, would be remembered by me throughout my life. As ours was the outgoing class, it was given a farewell by the student class XII. The Principal fixed the responsibility for making arrangements. Then, farewell party was given on Sunday.

When I arrived at the school at 3 PM. I saw that all arrangements had been made by the host students. The school hall was beautifully decorated with charts, posters, flowers and placards. The main table, on which, the Principal and the Inspector of Schools were to be seated, was beautifully decorated with flowerpots. There were many chairs for the outgoing students, staff and the students of class XI.

The party began at 4 PM. For about one hour, we ate to our heart's content, chatted and laughed without restrictions.

The party came to an end at 5 PM. The farewell function started after the party was over. Mr Anil Kumar, a student of class XI, made a moving and an emotional farewell speech in which, he mentioned our long and deep association with the school as well as with their class. His speech, which was full of praise and appreciation for our outgoing class, was delivered in a befitting manner. His farewell speech was punctuated with humorous remarks and pleasantries. Anil Kumar also prayed for our success in our future. His presentation and theme were really the most touching.

After his speech, I, on behalf of my class, thanked the host students and got blessings from my teachers and the honourable Principal. In my speech, I lauded the good arrangements made by the host and accepted their good wishes and feelings for all of us. When I was delivering the speech, I was deriving a mixed pleasure. I was feeling sad because of the separation from my old and august institution in whose lap, I had obtained education and training of my mind and body. For me, my school was an embodiment of knowledge and learning whose sacred atmosphere would always be part of my memory. For me, this was not merely a school that imparted knowledge but was a cradle of decent culture and civilisation.

In the end, the principal, whose association with the school is as old as the history of our school, made an impassioned speech. In his farewell message, he gave us some pieces of advice, to be followed by us throughout our lives. He made a fervent appeal to build mind and character on sound lines. He stressed upon us to inculcate a spirit of service and sacrifice as well as of patriotism and nationalism. After his encouraging speech, the function came to end.

We parted after taking the blessings of our teachers and good wishes of our friends. While going, we felt sad. We shall always be grateful to our institution where we spent the most formative periods of our lives. ●

43. STUDENT'S UNREST

One of the greatest problems that our country has been facing since the seventies is the problem of growing indiscipline among the students. The unrest among the students is confined not only to India, but also it has become a global phenomenon. In India, students' unrest has assumed alarming proportions. This, if not checked, would eat into the very fabric of our national entity. The prevalence of the mood of despondency and dejection among the students is nothing but a reflection of general dissatisfaction and discontentment prevailing among the masses.

Why our students are resorting to the acts of violence and rowdyism, needs a serious study. We hear about students going on rampage and arson, stone throwing and brickbatting. Their actions result in the ruthless repression by the police personnel who make them the targets of their bullets and sticks. We hear closure of the universities, *gheraos* of Vice Chancellors and beating of professors by the students. All this is really a sorry state of affairs. And behind this orgy of violence, let loose by the students, is a plethora of grievances and demands of the students. The inability of the authorities — both public and academic — results in the indulgence of the students in the acts of hooliganism, strikes and demonstrations.

The community of students complains that higher tuition fees, which their parents can't afford to pay, are charged from them. They also complain about ill-equipped libraries and laboratories, improper admission facilities, overcrowded class rooms, inadequate and inefficient staff, wrong medium of instruction (in a foreign language) that they cannot understand, absence of vocational education policy and cold teacher-pupil relationships. All of these causes are responsible for diverting the attention of the students from their primary objectives.

Most of the students fail in English that is a foreign language. As the late Dr Ramdhari Singh 'Dinkar' once remarked, "We are killing our students at the cross of English language. As 60 to 70 percent of failure in the examinations are due to English, this aspect demands a serious national debate. Moreover, authorities must pay attention to the legitimate demands of the students.

Students are the pillars of a country's progress. They have a tremendous reservoir of energy and if it is channelised in a proper direction, it could work miracles. However, if it is misdirected and frittered away, it could spell disaster. The answer to the violent expressions of the students is not bullet or *lathi-charge*. They have to be tackled in a careful manner. We cannot use the same stick for crushing *Goondas* and students. Students are the bedrock of our country's progress. Only a proper redressal of their grievances could put an end to the vicious circle of students' unrest.   ❂

44. MY SCHOOL LIFE

School life is one of the most important periods in the life of a man. It is this period during which, one learns the basic principles of behaviour, speech and etiquettes. School life, in fact, is a period of learning and training in all the aspects of personality of a man. One gets training for the maintaining physical fitness, increasing one's mental powers, learning the proper mode of behaviour and understanding the basic concepts of life. School life is a period for the formation of character, mind and body on sound lines.

But there are some students who hold a different view regarding school life. To them, the warnings of the teachers, the strict attitude of the parents, the compulsions for completing homework and the regular attendance in schools are some of the unhappy aspects of this period. They do not feel free in their schools and wish to be like the birds that are quite free from this business. The students do not like the strict discipline that is to be followed while studying in a school. These students curse their school days.

But my school life is really an ideal one. It is ideal in the sense that this is a period of the training of our minds. The impressions, which one gets during school life, remain throughout life even if they are good, bad or indifferent. My school life prepares me to develop good habits as well as right and rational thinking. It makes me duty-bound and obedient. Respect for teachers and elders is my abiding faith. I obey all my school teachers and parents and this is also one of the good habits that was developed by me during the school life.

During school days, I developed an interest in playing games, staging dramas, debating and other extra-curricular activities.

I am a good debator and speaker, athlete and sportsman and at the same time, I hold positions in the class in academic terms also. All the qualities of head and heart have earned for me a profound love and respect from my teachers and friends. My teachers encourage me very much and help me in all possible ways. I am in the good books of all the teachers as well as of the Principal because I have won many medals, cups, trophies, shields and certificates for my extraordinary display of abilities in examinations, athletics, debates and theatre.

Wordsworth has said, "As a twig is bent, so the tree will grow." This is very much true in the case of tender and delicate students. The minds of students are just like photographic plates; whatever impressions are left on them, would be retained by them. The good ideas, — like love the motherland, devotion to duty, obedience towards elders, service to the nation, helping the poor and the needy, nursing the sick, feeding the hungry etc — are inculcated in the students during their school days.

Broadly speaking, school life is not only a period for learning, reading of books or playing, but also it is a period of time during which, all the good habits are acquired, bad habits are shunned, good conduct, fair play and sound thinking are developed. Further, the healthy ideas of patriotism and nationalism are imbibed by the students during this period.

My school life shall prepare for me, a sound and firm foundation upon which, the building of my life is going to be erected. My mistakes and failures would guide me in my future life. I do not feel discouraged and disheartened because for me, the failures are the stepping stones towards success. My school life is a good and great experience and experience is the best teacher. I shall always adore my school days. ●

45. THE DAY BEFORE AN EXAMINATION

The day before an examination is interesting in many ways. On this day, the examinees are in a different mood. Everyone is in a state of uncertainty as to what would be the questions in the examination. Everyone tries his best to prepare himself for the crucial hours.

The candidates for the examination put heart and soul into their studies. They prepare the subject in which, they are required to take test. Preparing the questions, notes and points of important questions is the normal but gruelling routine of all the examinees. A bundle of books is read by the examinees in order to get good marks in the examination. But even then, they are not very sure about their success.

The parents of the examinees take care of them. Everyone wishes success to them in the examination. Examinees are helped by all; everything is given ready-made to them so that their time may not be wasted.

During the night before the examination, much care is taken. The students revise their courses and try to recollect the questions. They also make guesses. They study very carefully during the nights. They do not study until late in the night because they want to have some sleep; otherwise, they may get confused during the examination.

Examinees, who care too much for their examination, look upon everything with contempt. They do not like to eat anything, see anything or hear anything. Their minds become weary. For them, everything bears a sad look because they think of the examination only.

The examinees also prepare their paraphernalia for appearing in the examination. A pen, an inkpot and tools for drawing and painting are put in order. When they go to sleep at night, they set the alarm so that they could get up at right time and revise their notes for the last time.

A day before an examination is a day not of elevated spirits and delightful moods but it is a day of the disturbed mind. One does not feel like enjoying. A melancholy prevails upon the students.

No one in this world likes to be examined. Even Christ said "Do not put me to test." It is this thing that makes the examinees a little sad, however, intelligent they might be. ●

46. MY EXPERIENCES IN THE EXAMINATION HALL

It is interesting to pen a few lines on the experience that I had in the examination hall. My first university examination was held in the year 1999.

I read a lot on the night preceding the examination day. I revised my entire course, though my father warned me against the consequences of studying late in the night. I did not pay any heed to his advice.

I went to the examination hall almost at the right time. The moment I was climbing the stairs, the first bell rang. I rushed to the hall and searched for the seat that was supposed to have my roll number. Within five minutes, all the examinees took their respective seas. My heart was beating at a fast pace. I began to feel nervous. The superintendent of the examination read instructions aloud to the students. He also warned the students against the objectionable papers and slips that could be of any help to the examinees. So, many students searched their pockets and threw away all the slips related to the examination. They retained their bus passes, money and roll numbers. The Superintendent also warned the candidates not to use any other unfair means for answering the questions.

He then broke the official seal of the envelope containing the question papers. At this time, there was a pin-drop silence in the hall. I became all the more nervous. Then, the supervisors distributed the question papers to the examinees. As I received the question paper, I felt confused. I began to read it but could not understand the questions, I made a second attempt at reading the questions. This time, I understood all the questions and some of them seemed to be easy to me. Other examinees were seen looking hither and thither. Some of them were busy in writing while others were gazing at the ceiling of the examination hall. Some were whispering and talking. An examinee and the supervisor pointed his accusing finger towards them. Both were expelled from the hall. This instance was an eye-opener to others who were trying to copy.

As the first bell rang, I was already solving the questions. I did the easy questions first and then, attempted the difficult ones. After some time, one examinee fell from his seat. He became unconscious. Attention was diverted towards him. Soon after this incident, the doctor came and gave him medical aid. He came to his senses but the doctor advised him not to exert any more. So, he left the examination hall without completing his paper.

There was another bell. Now, only half an hour was left. I completed my paper and re-read the whole of the answer sheet. While reading I corrected many mistakes that otherwise would have made me lose marks. I stitched all the extra-sheets with my original answer book. Then, there was the final and last ring. The superintendent of the hall announced that no one would write anything from that moment onwards. Soon, the invigilators collected the answer books. I was feeling tired at that time. Finally, I came out of the examination hall. This interesting and unique experience shall always be remembered and recollected by me in my life. I learnt a lot about the precautions to be taken and instructions to be followed during the period of examination.

47. EXAMINATION FEVER

Even the saints say, "God ! do not put me to test." A test saps the energies of a person, generates mental agony and makes him incapable of thinking in a proper and logical manner. Examinees shudder at the thought of the examination and fear of failure makes them unhappy. Evil dreams haunt the students and the dose of admonition given to them regularly disturbs them.

Before the examination, the students suspend pleasure-oriented activities. They do not go to the playground. They also cancel their picnic schedules and forget about going for the latest movies. They are busy with their books. They go on reading while sipping a cup of tea. They go on revising while lying in their beds. They discuss questions, talk about books and dream about answers. Some perch on the trees while others sit in a remote corner. Some others stick themselves to chairs.

The examination fever touches the highest point on the night before the examination. One gets disturbed sleep. Students get up early in the morning and even the atheists pray. In front of the examination hall, one feels that everything has drained out of his brain. A friend says, "This question is sure to be set." Another says, "Have you prepared these questions?" The student feels disturbed and turns the pages of notes or books in a hasty manner. He tries to move his eyes over the answers.

As soon as he takes his seat in the examination hall, he prays to God and revises the questions. If the question paper is difficult, glasses of water are ordered. An easy question paper may make the choice of questions difficult. As he settles down to answering the questions, he might feel that most of what he had learned has evaporated from his brain.

Even after the examination, the fever still haunts the student. He tells his friend, "I was a bit confused" or "I could not do justice to some of the questions." He counts his marks daily and thinks that he would get a second class. He remains in this type of suspense till the *Judgement Day* arrives. He tries to find his roll number in the newspaper. This movement is very troublesome because failure would invite taunting remarks of the friends, neighbours and relatives. Even if he gets through, he would be heard saying, "There is something wrong with the examiner. Perhaps my answer sheets were replaced with those of a weak student." Examination fever is in fact, a painful experience for every student.　●

48. PRIZE DISTRIBUTION FUNCTION IN MY SCHOOL

Prize Distribution Function is important for the efficient working of a school. It comes only once a year. This generates new enthusiasm in the students. A strong link is established with the parents of the students. This function is really very thrilling and worth a visit.

This year, the prize distribution function attracted hall-packed audience consisting of parents and invitees. This prize-giving function of the school was held on the fifteenth January. The Director of Education was invited to grace the occasion as the chief guest. The preparations for the function started a month earlier. The school building was whitewashed. The school hall, where the function was to be held, was beautifully decorated with pictures and charts. On the appointed day, a beautiful table and some chairs were placed on the stage. The carpets were spread to accommodate the children and in the remaining part of the hall, chairs had been arranged. The front rows were reserved for teachers and invitees. The function was supposed to start at 4 PM. By 3 : 45 PM, the hall was jam-packed with the audience. The visitors were very much impressed by the arrangements that the students had made. In one corner, there was a table where the prizes and trophies had been arranged. Now, all of us were eagerly waiting for the arrival of the chief guest.

In the nick of time, the Director of Education came in his car. He was accorded a warm welcome by the Principal and the senior members of the staff. The school band was played in his honour as he entered the hall; all the students and other audience stood up as a mark of respect. The Director of Education was profusely garlanded by the Principal and by some senior members of the staff. As soon as the chief guest occupied his seat, there was pin-drop silence in the Hall.

The principal broke the ice by giving a brief introduction of the life-sketch of the Chief Guest. Later, he read the Annual Report of the school, giving an account of the past achievements of the school. At the same time, he requested the Chief Guest to enhance the annual grant that was quite insufficient in view of the students' interest in manifold activities. The Principal instructed the President of the Literary Club to begin with the cultural programme. Some students sang some melodious songs. "Prince and the Wood Cutter" of *Six One Act Plays*, a prescribed book, was staged next. The participants got thunderous applause from the audience for their wonderful talents that they displayed in acting and presentation. The students, who took part in this play, seemed to be well-prepared. Some folk-dances added charm to the show.

The Chief Guest, who presided over the function, gave away the prizes to the prize-winners and shook hands with all of them. The President delivered a short speech wherein he praised the performance of the students and encouraged them to participate still more enthusiastically. He also admired the sense of discipline imbibed by the students during the entire function. Then, the Principal got up and thanked the President for his kind visit to the school.

Finally, the function came to an end with the singing of the National Anthem. The following day was declared to be a holiday by the Principal.

49. AN EDUCATIONAL TOUR

Our History teacher always talked about Ajanta and Ellora caves as our great relics of the past. We requested him to plan a tour to these places and he readily agreed. As the school closed for the summer break, a group of twenty students of our class left for Aurangabad. We hired our own bus to go to Ellora that is hardly fifteen kilometers from there. It is an old city that has been excavated by the Department of Archaeology. The Hindu temples present a fascinating sight. There are statues of Hindu Gods and Godesses everywhere. It is surprising how the architects of those times could plan such as beautiful city ! The rooms are constructed in such a manner as would ensure that cross-ventilation and hence, no need of fans. The idols of bull and *Shiva Linga* are masterpieces of art. Although the city is more than two thousand years old, yet the construction is stable and durable. Ajanta is also situated in the same district but it is quite far-off from the district head-quarters. It represents the rise of Buddhism in India. The caves were carved out of solid rocks on the banks of a waterfall. The artisans and architects spent a lifetime in planning and constructing the divine city. The Department of Archaeology provides decorations and well-trained guides. They throw light on the subtle aspects of every statue. For example, we were taken to a cave in which, there was a huge statue of Lord Buddha. When light was thrown from the front, he looked sad. When it was thrown from other angles, the mood of the Lord changed accordingly. The decorations on the wall are in different colours. Those colours were taken directly from the flowers and leaves of the trees. It is surprising that those paintings are still fresh on the walls of the cave. We asked the guide how did the artisans work in the caves. He pointed out that the reflection of the solar rays on the water-falls were divided according to their needs.

The monuments remind us of the greatness of man who can create under all circumstances. He can work wonders, if he is inspired to execute a job.

The sad aspect was that Lord Buddha had decreed against the worship of statues. His whole religion was based on teachings against idol worship. His own followers raised his statues and started worshipping them. ●

50. INDISCIPLINE AMONG STUDENTS

One of the greatest problems haunting our country today is the problem of growing indiscipline among the students. The unrest amongst the students is not only confined to India, but also it is spread all over the world. If not checked well in time, it could eat into the vitals of national health. The unrest amongst the students is only a reflection of the despair prevalent in the society. We hear about students going on rampage and arson in the news and we also read newspapers that give gory accounts of such incidents. They indulge in stone-throwing and brick-batting. The police comes in action and makes them the targets of their bullets and *Lathis*. When the authorities cannot control them, they indulge in violence and hooliganism.

The students feel that the education given to them in the schools or colleges is useless. They cannot get jobs or make use of their knowledge in any other sphere. Although they work hard, yet those students, who are weak in studies, are those who indulge in illegal practices such as copying. People with recommendations or resources bag all the good jobs. The politicians have also started taking interest in the students of senior secondary schools. If they have to organise a rally or a demonstration, they lure the school students to join them. They are treated there nicely. So, the students start feeling that the best way to get respect is to become a camp follower of a known politician.

The teachers also do not take much interest in teaching the students. They are paid so meagerly that they have to supplement their income with tuitions or by taking up some part-time jobs. When the students do not get the care and education in the schools, they start picking up cheap methods to get importance. The parents are busy in earning bread and butter for their families. They have little time to listen to their problems. The children move about in the world as confused young individuals, just groping in the dark.

The government has implemented new education policy that was declared in 1991. The students will be taught crafts and useful vocations so that they could earn while they learned. The pay scales of the teachers are also being revised so that better people could join the profession. It would take some time before we could see the results of the new education policy. ●

51. COPYING IN THE EXAMINATION

Copying has become so widespread in the examinations that the authorities find it very difficult to control it. The students consider it their birth-right. They use every method to cheat the invigilator and if they are caught, they shed crocodile tears. They beg before the supervisors but some bullies threaten them of dire consequences.

Their creative brain could be admired in the new methods they devise. The girls do not want to be left behind. Sometimes, copying is organised on a mass scale. As soon as the students receive the question paper, they note down the questions on a piece of paper and throw it out of the window. Their friends, who are outside, write down the answers and struggle to send them back to the students. They bribe the peon and the sweeper who bring these slips for them. They also go to the bathroom and collect the material from there. When they are caught, at first, they try to beg for an apology. If this method fails, then they show the dagger to the invigilator. Some states have passed very strict laws to punish these students. This habit should stop otherwise, it would bring a very bad name to the academic institutions. ●

52. A SCENE IN THE EXAMINATION HALL

The scene in the examination hall can be described better either by the invigilators or by the superintendent. The examinees have little time to stand and stare. If they look up, the invigilator looks at them with suspicious eyes. Time is too precious for one to look right and left.

When I entered the hall, I was a bundle of nerves. My whole body was trembling and perspiring. I was face to face with fate in the form of a question paper. Time moves very fast. The students took their seats. Some of them prayed to their gods for help. Others just kept looking right and left, waiting for the invigilators to deliver them the answer books.

The superintendent stood up and read out the instructions. We were also asked to search our pockets for any material that could be useful to us in the examination. I searched myself completely and found a letter in my rear pocket. My friend Raghu had send my best wishes for the examination. I deposited it with the invigilator.

The second bell rang and the question papers were distributed among the students. Everyone was feeling nervous. I read the question paper and found some questions that had been revised by me a day earlier. I prayed to God and started writing the answers.

Suddenly, there was a noise outside. One of the candidates had thrown the slip having questions (from the question paper) outside and his friend had run away with them. The invigilator made the boy stand up and carried out complete search. The boy took out the slip and swallowed it. The piece of paper stuck in his throat and he started gasping for breath. The peon offered him a glass of water and he gulped everything down. Some slips were found pasted on the soles of his shoes. the superintendent issued him a second answer book and his first answer-book was taken away.

Again, there was some noise outside. The flying squad had come. Some candidates threw the objectionable papers away from their seats. The flying squad did a thorough checking and caught four students using unfair means. Those students were weeping, crying and pleading for mercy.

I heaved a sigh of relief when the examination time was over. I did not know when three hours actually passed. The invigilator ordered us to stop writing. I had just finished the last question.

I thanked God that it was all over ●

53. WHEN THE LAST BELL GOES

Can one ever think of a music that is sweeter than that of the last bell? The whole school gets a thrill. It seems as if the gates of the prison have been opened and the inmates are lining up to leave it as soon as is possible.

All the periods after the recess are full of boredom. The gloom reaches its height in the last period. Even the teachers know it; they also wait for getting rid of the students. But for the students, every minute hangs heavily on the heads of the students. They keep on looking at the needles (hands) of the watch. When there are only five minutes left, they start packing up. Their eyes are on the blackboard but their hands are busy in packing up their bags. Their brain stops working and they are mere robots. The sound of the last bell fills them with sheer joy. One can hear their noise and shouts. Just like the bus passengers, every one wants to come out first. The teachers try to control them at the staircase. They shout at them to line up. The students obey and forget the orders immediately afterwards. As soon as they reach the school compound, their chatter and gossip grow louder. It seems as if they were turning their back on the school forever. Within five minutes, the whole mad rush is over and the school wears a dreary look. ●

54. RECESS PERIOD IN THE SCHOOL

It is the only period that is greeted by the students with shouts of joy. They rush out of the rooms and start running in every direction. Some students open their lunch boxes in the classroom itself. They sit in small groups so that they could enjoy their meals with gossip and sweet talks. They combine their snacks and *chappatis* so that they could have a better choice. Everyone praises his own mother for expert cooking. They have to finish it as soon as possible so that they could wash it down with a hot or cold beverage. During the rest of the time, they go and recline in the lawns. Some sports-lovers do not waste their time during the lunch hour. With the, ringing of the bell, they run to the playgrounds and pick up their sports gear. They know that the playgrounds are not enough for everyone. The person, who reaches first, would be able to do his best. They occupy backseats in the classrooms and munch their lunch stealthily. Sometimes, they can be seen eating it on their way to the ground.

The busiest place during the recess period is the school canteen. Every one shouts over the head of the other and wants to get the snack or the cold drink first. The ice-cream vendor has a hayday. The shop is strewn with wrappers and wooden spoons. The students, who purchase fast foods, do not wait to get aside. They take it from the shop straight to the mouth. The sweet smell of sweets attracts them like bees to the honey. There are few students who go to the reading room or the school library. They are serious students who do not want to waste a single minute of their precious time. When the second bell rings to announce the end of the recess period, the students make their ways to the classrooms. One can see gloom writ large on their faces. They get themselves ready to attend the last periods.　　　　　　●

55. THE BACK BENCHERS

The back-benchers in a class make a group of their own. They sit in the class but are not a part of the class. They have the best of both the worlds. When the teacher is reading out the lesson, they are dozing in their seats. When they are asked to solve the questions, they are busy making the cartoons. They judge the teacher properly and act accordingly. There are some teachers who always ask questions from the back-benchers. They stand up sheepishly in their seats. First of all, they pose as if they have not heard or understood the question. As a matter of fact, they are prompting some students to tell them the answers. They use all the methods for finding an answer to the question. For example, they would touch the other one with their toes or pass their hands under their seats. Their friends are always obliging. They never tell the teachers what is going on at the back of the class. Some of them are very good cartoonists. When they pose that they are writing the answers, they are actually drawing the cartoons. They pass on slips from one corner to another and sometimes, carry on glossy magazines. The sportsmen among them do not disturb anyone. They feel tired after playing the games and use their seats to relax or sleep, if possible. They always try to chose their seats behind a tall student so that he can work as their shield. When the lecture becomes dull beyond tolerance, they open their comics or novels. If they find that the teacher is observing them, they pass it on to other benches. Some students bring apples or other fruits. When the teacher is busy writing on the blackboard, they have their bite without making any noise. If the recess is to begin after a long time period, they open their lunch boxes and starting tasting the snacks. They have their own code of conduct. If ever they are caught, they would never name their friends. Ask them to mimick any teacher and they would show their talents. Some of them express their art of drawing by spoiling the walls of the schools especially in the toilets.

56. AN IDEAL STUDENT

An ideal student is one who is fully conscious of his duties and responsibilities. He paves the way for the younger generations. The students of today are the leaders of tomorrow. A national can progress if the students have high ideals before them. A student, who scores high marks, is not necessarily an ideal student. He may set a new record in the school but could prove to be a total failure in his real life. An ideal student believes in simple living and high thinking. He is fearless and bold enough to face the trials and tribulations of life.

An ideal student lives in accordance with the strict rules of conduct and discipline. This is the time of life when the foundation of character is laid. It has been said that if wealth is lost, nothing is lost; if health is lost, something lost; and if character is lost, everything is lost. A student without any sense of discipline, is like a ship without a rudder. It sails adrift and never reaches the harbour. He must follow the rules of the school and ought to obey the orders of his teachers.

He should select his friends intelligently and wisely. He must be fully conscious to ensure that no evil tempts him. He knows very well that a single rotten apple spoils the whole basket.

An ideal student tries to understand how much he owes to his parents. He realises that he owes a heavy debt to his parents. He should never forget to look after them when he enters his adult life.

He is a servant of the humanity. He should share the worries and other problems with the members of his family. He should also take keen interest in social service. He should be active in finding out solutions to various problems prevalent in the society.

Our country needs such students as have muscles of iron and nerves of steel. They should be able to dive deep into the secrets and mysteries of the universe. They should be determined to do their duty even at the risk of their lives.

Such students alone can help the nation in achieving prosperity for the country. ●

57. OUR SCHOOL CANTEEN

All the corridors of the school should lead to canteen but unfortunately, it is in one corner of the school. It has a small window through which, the contractor supplies us snacks, tea and cold drinks. Our principal has allowed a stall of Gaylord ice-cream to be incorporated into the canteen. There are two other counters for books, stationery and beverages. It is only the parents who visit the stationery counter. The students go there only under compulsion. Their most favourite spot is the ice-cream corner. The students flock round it and buy the ice-creams that are available in different colours and sizes. Their mouth waters at the sight of the ice-cream and they want to break the queue to have it first. The second favourite counter is that of beverages. They wash down their lunches with some cola or a cup of tea. They sip it slowly so that it could last for the whole period. As the bottle starts showing its bottom, their speed also decreases. They gulp down the last drop with a heavy heart as if it were the end of their friendship with the bottle.

The third counter, to attract a small crowd, is the place where the students get snacks. Toffees and chocolates are in great demand. Some students, who miss their lunch box at home, take *bread-pakoras*, slices or cakes. Some teachers also make a beeline at this counter. Everyone is in a hurry. There is a rule of "first come, first get" but the students do not follow it. They always hand over money to the students who are just nearer the counter and ask them to purchase the snacks for them. As the recess period is over, they leave their disneyland with a heavy heart. The students wend their way to the classrooms. One can see gloom writ large on their faces. They get themselves ready to attend the last periods.

58. IF I WERE THE PRINCIPAL OF MY SCHOOL !

I have my own views about becoming the Principal of my school. I feel that the principal of the school should also be elected from the students. When we live in a democracy, why should we deny this right to the students? There should be a Students' Council elected by the students themselves. Every class should send its own representative. These class representatives should form a Parliament. The Principal should be made responsible to them. The students are never consulted in the appointment of the teachers. I shall ask a candidate to teach the class only if the students would. Only those teachers, who can satisfy the students, would be selected.

The students would look after the discipline and cleanliness in the school themselves. They shall punish the latecomers and would tell their parents to send them in time. One student from each class would be on duty. He would check the cleanliness of the students. He would also see to it that no one roams about the corridors. Another would be on duty in the reception hall. He would attend to the visitors and the telephone calls.

There would be very few teaching periods. They would end before the recess. The students would take part in games, sports and co-curricular activities. They would make more use of library. In fact, the teachers would guide them only in solving their difficulties. They would inspire the students to read new books.

There would be no physical punishment. If a student misbehaves, he shall be suspended from the games and other school activities.

The clubs and societies would not be mere showpieces for the visitors. They would function actively and shall stress on self-learning. Each and every student would be expected to take part in drama and group songs. I shall lay stress on manual labour. Each student would have to work in the garden or the workshop. The students would earn while they learn.

No teachers would be allowed to take up tuitions. Many students need help and they would be guided during the school hours.

I got this chance last year for one day. The students managed the school themselves on the Children's Day, *ie*, November 14th and I was made the Principal.

I wish to get this opportunity once again and that too, permanently.
       ●

PART IV

Visits

59. A VISIT TO A ZOO

Last Sunday it was very cloudy. I, along with my friends, visited the zoo. As we reached near the main gate of the zoo, we saw a huge crowd. Some were buying entrance tickets, some were gossiping and chatting while others were relaxing under the shady trees.

We entered the zoological garden and came across a beautiful lake in which some water-birds — like ducks — were swimming. Looking at the white ducks on the smooth surface of water is a charming delight. As we moved, we came to the enclosure in which, flying birds (fowls) were kept. They ranged from sparrows, eagles and parrots to pigeons of various colours. The birds were chirping. It was an enchanting music. We enjoyed it very much.

In the next enclosure, there were lions and leopards, tigers and tigeresses whose roars were deafening. We approached the net. A lion rushed towards us and we were frightened. Their fierce looks were frightening for us. After seeing we came across a garden in which, stags and deer were frisking about. These animals were really very smart and beautiful. In one of the corners of the garden, there was a huge tree on which, monkeys and baboons were jumping. Their tricks and pranks were very pleasing. Some people threw foodgrains to them and they immediately jumped down the trees in order to eat them. Some children were also seen making faces at them.

Our next halt was at an aquarium in which, we were most interested. A large number of the aquatic birds were kept there. There were fish of many species and colours. The see them fidgeting in water was really a delightful spectacle. There were many other aquatic animals. Just by the side of this enclosure, we came across polar bears who looked sad and deserted.

It was the cage of the black bear that attracted a mammoth gathering. The bear was playing many tricks, which thrilled the spectators. Some people offered him eatables, which he gulped at once.

The zoological park is so vast that it is very difficult to describe all the departments and enclosures fully. When we took complete round of the zoo, we relaxed for some time in a cool and beautiful garden inside the zoo. The fragrance of the flowers was tremendously soothing. Then, we had some snacks and drinks, which refreshed us much. It was evening and the Sun was setting. We came out of the zoo like many other visitors. We boarded the bus while casting our last and lingering look on the zoo that is surrounded on one side by the old but majestic wall of the old fort, which added to the beauty and grandeur of the zoo. I shall always remember my thrilling experiences in the zoo. ●

60. A VISIT TO A CINEMA SHOW

Cinema today forms one of the most important means of mass communication, instruction and a source of entertainment and amusement.

Last Sunday, I happened to visit Plaza theater where *Shaheed* was being screened. As I saw the posters pasted on the wall outside the theatre, my craze to watch this movie increased all the more. The posters showed Bhagat Singh in many moods, sometimes, in prison and sometimes, kissing the gallows. I purchased a ticket and entered into the cinema hall. The entire hall was packed to its full capacity. When I entered, the newsreel was being shown. Soon, the movie started.

From the very beginning to the end, the picture was lively, inspiring and thought-provoking. Bhagat Singh, the great martyr of India, was shown in his most buoyant moods, performing heroic deeds and playing courageous roles. How he faced the tyranny and cruelty of the British government, is really a story of agony. But his unalloyed patriotism withstood all the cruelties and tortures of Britishers. In the film, Bhagat Singh has been portrayed as a strong and staunch nationalist for whom the freedom of motherland was the mission of his life. The cruelties of British regime were borne by Bhagat Singh and his friends — Rajguru and Sukhdev. While in prison, he was shown as a free and fearless son of India, determined to undergo all the troubles, trials and tortures, in order to win freedom for his motherland.

Towards the end Bhagat Singh alone with Sukhdev and Rajguru was sentenced to death. All the three sons of India were hanged. This was perhaps the most moving and touching scene. How these patriots of India kissed the gallows with patience and passion, courage and conviction, is inexplicable. The entire story is infused with the spirit of patriotism and nationalism. Bhagat Singh's role is unique and marvellous. The courage and convictions of Bhagat Singh and his acts of bravery, gallantry and poise would be the most inspiring acts for the coming generations. The story, broadly speaking, depicts the struggle of Indian independence and the part played by Bhagat Singh from the winning freedom from British rule. ●

61. A VISIT TO A MUSEUM

A museum is a treasure-chest of antiquities. In it, are kept all such articles and diggings as reflect a country's culture and civilisation, her historical panorama, modes and manners, its religions and relics and finally, her art and architecture. A museum is the miniature reflection of a country's ancient periods and gives a vivid picture of the customs, conventions and traditions of the nation.

In New Delhi, I had a golden opportunity to visit the historic and famous National Museum. The building of the museum is majestic and sturdy and has many departments that cover various subjects and periods of history. As I entered the ground floor, I saw a number of articles, images, sculptures and rock-engraved scriptures and many other things of great interest and value. The entire museum has been divided into many compartments like anthrological division, archaeological division and display selection etc.

Then, I moved to the first floor where, among other things, charts, paintings and murals were kept. Manuscripts in various languages were on display. There were ancient dresses, robes and weapons. In one corners there is the numismatics section. In this section, coins of different periods have been kept. In other halls, one finds historic Ajanta and Ellora paintings with the lovers in a mood of dalliance. Just by the side of these, there is a vivid depiction of the lives of Lord Rama, Lord Krishna and Lord Budha through charts, scriptures. By having a look into this section, one really discovers India.

On the second floor, one finds the remains of Indus Valley Civilisation. The excavations from Harappa and Mohenjodaro, broken pitchers, beads, toys, stones and skulls throw light on the civilisation of those times and one comes to the conclusion how advanced that civilisation was!

The third floor houses the military equipment. There are weapons like swords and sheaths, spears and pruning hooks; shields and helmets; various dresses of the Generals and Commanders of ancient times. After seeing this part of the museum, I was thrilled because all this ancient military equipment of our past heroes and heroines inspired me.

Broadly speaking, the entire museum was a treasure-house of India's great men and morals, historical facts, laurels and legends that are connected with the whole gamut of India's life and literature — whether they are poets or prose writers, dancers or dramatists, songsters or sculptors, scientists or galaxy-gazers, lawgivers or lexicographers and musicians or doctors.

For me, the visit to the museum was a thrilling experience and what I saw and observed in the museum is a part of the richest experiences of my life. I was deeply moved to see this vast storehouse of India's ancient glory. This visit has left an ideliable impression on my mind. ●

62. A VISIT TO AN EXHIBITION

I am very fond of visiting exhibitions. Exhibitions are of various types. But the exhibition, which I saw a few months ago at Vigyan Bhavan, was the most impressive. In this exhibition, were displayed articles of various types. But mainly, it was an exhibition of books, paintings, graphics and clay models. Almost all the halls of Vigyan Bhawan were full with the displayed articles.

As I entered the main gate, I saw a huge statue made up of clay. This was a very grand statue. For me, it was really a piece of art. Then, I entered into one of the halls where books were displayed. There were books on almost all subjects. Books on science, technology and engineering were displayed in one of the corners. The books on subjects like history, sociology, political science, economics and literature were displayed in the other corner. There were huge volumes on almost all the branches of sciences and humanities. The works of Shakespeare attracted much larger crowds. Some of his works like *Macbeth, Hamlet* and *Othello* were selling like hot cakes.

The hall in which, clay models were displayed, was also a centre of attraction. The clay models included pitchers, kettles, glasses, dishes, saucers as well as figures of men and women. These clay models looked very beautiful. The children were really delighted to see these toys of clay.

This exhibition increased my knowledge. I was really impressed to see the various exhibits. This exhibition continued for a fortnight. It attracted lakhs of visitors. This was, as a matter of fact, an exhibition organised on an international scale. Many countries like the USA, Russia, England, Germany, France, Japan, Nepal, Sri Lanka etc participated in this exhibition. They displayed their best abilities in sciences and humanities. Some of their top artists and painters were also present during the exhibition days. This exhibition has left an everlasting impression on my mind.   ●

63. A VISIT TO A HOSPITAL

A visit to a hospital is an experience in itself. During the last summer, one of my friends met with an accident. He was admitted in the Safdarjang Hospital. Once, I paid a visit to him. In this manner, I also visited the whole of the hospital.

As I entered the hospital, I saw people coming and going. I went to the enquiry office and enquired about the wards. First of all, I visited the surgical ward. I saw patients lying silently on their beds. Some of the patients had their arms and legs bandaged and plastered. I also saw how a nurse and a doctor were attending to them. These two persons were very sympathetic towards the patients. The doctor was directing the nurse to give them necessary medicines. His way of talking was itself very consoling. A peaceful atmosphere prevailed upon the whole ward.

Then, I went to the medical ward. I saw some of the patients lying on their beds very pensively. From their faces, I guessed their pathetic plights. They all seemed to be disgusted with their diseases. In the meanwhile, the doctor took a round of that ward. The other members of the staff were also accompanying him. The doctor was enquiring about the welfare of the patients one by one.

He listened very sympathetically to the agonies of the patients. He was also giving injections to some of the patients. To others, he gave dosages of medicines or mixtures.

Then, I turned towards the operation theatre. Outside the theatre, I saw patients to be operated upon lying on the stretchers. The corridor presented a very serious and quiet look.

Some of the people, after recovering from their diseases, were sitting in the lawns of the hospital. They were playing cards and chess. They were enjoying themselves on the grassy lawns while some of the people were going home after recovering completely from their illnesses. They were in delightful moods.

The entire hospital presented a very gloomy look to me. The plight of the patients and the seriousness of the prevailing atmosphere touched me deeply. The behaviour of the doctors and nurses was worthy of commendations. They acted most wisely and ably while handling the problems of the patients. The patients, in turn, were also happy with their sympathetic behaviour.

Finally, I came out of the hospital. There was a world of difference between the atmosphere that prevailed outside and inside the hospital.   ●

64. A VISIT TO A FAIR

Every year, a fair is held near our village. The fair is held on the occasion o an annual cattle show. This cattle show is arranged by the whole state of Punjab. In this fair, cattle from all the corners of Punjab are brought by their owners. The cattle of the best breeds are brought there. People flock in large numbers to the place of the fair to see the variety of animals. Cows, buffaloes, bulls, oxen and other animals are brought by their masters.

As this fair attracts the people from all the neighbouring villages and states, many other items of public interest are also displayed there. When I reached the spot, I noticed many things. First of all, there was one bazaar where shopkeepers were selling articles of daily usage. In one corner, there sat a juggler. The juggler was amusing people with his clever tricks. His feats were really marvellous. His mannerisms were amazing and stunning. At one time, he cut the belly of a small boy that amazed and shocked every spectator.

As I moved further, I saw a merry-go-round. On this merry-go-round, many boys, girls, men and women were having joy rides. There was a great rush of people on the merry-go-round.

Then, I moved to another side. Here, some wrestling bouts had been organised. The renowned wrestlers of the adjoining areas had come here to participate in the wrestling. It was an interesting scene to see them tugging, pushing and grappling with each other. After seeing it for some time, I moved away.

From a distance, I saw a circle of people. When I went near it, I saw a snake charmer surrounded by spectators. The snake charmer was playing on his flute pipe. The pipe was giving out a very melodious tune. Before his flute, a serpent was dancing. The serpent seemed to me completely hypnotised by the sweet sound of the flute. It as an interesting sight and was enjoyed by one and all.

The fair was arranged on a grand scale. Many people had come to buy and sell their cattle, some of which, fetched very high prices. Many farmers brought bulls of good breeds. The cattle were exhibited nicely. Every fair-goer was buying something or the other. Some destitute, lame, crippled and handicapped men and women were begging for alms. Passers by were giving them a Rupee or two out of charity. There were many *sadhus* who had come to visit this fair. These *sadhus* were chanting some *mantras* and pious hymns. Some were giving lengthy discourses. The religious-minded people sat before them, listening to religious speeches with great attention.

I enjoyed this fair very much. It was enthralling for me to see this fair. A flood of humanity was all that I could see there. In the evening, the rush began to disappear. After going through the whole fair, I also made my way for home in the evening. I felt very tired on that day but I enjoyed this delightful fair to my heart's content. ●

65. A VISIT TO A CIRCUS SHOW

Last month, I happened to see a circus in my town. It was the famous Kamla Circus. The proprietors of the circus got a big *maidan* on rent outside the town. This spot was covered with many canopies. Some were meant for the animals while others were for the workers and a huge *shamiana* was meant for the circus show.

As I went there, I saw huge gates having the photographs of tigers, elephants and other animals. The entire place was glittering with lights. I entered the arena. There were many seats. All the seats were packed. Men, women and children were anxiously waiting for the show to start. Soon, the show commenced.

The first item to be presented was gymnastics. This performance was given by girls. All the girls did marvellous exercises like swings, exchange of swings and walking on a rope.

The second item was a dance by a troupe of girls. They all danced to the accompaniment of a band. This dance performance was highly appreciated by spectators.

Then came elephants. One elephant stood on its hind legs. Another elephant walked over a plank that was placed on the chest of a man while one of the elephant cycled on its own.

Another item was that of lions and the lion-tamer. All the lions obeyed the commands of their human master. The item showing a lion and lamb drinking water from the same tub was also shown.

The show came to an end at 10 PM. It was a thrilling circus show. Almost all the spectators were pleased with this show. The memories of those scenes are still afresh in my mind.

66. A VISIT TO A VILLAGE

When someone from Delhi visits a village, it seems as if he were on to a different planet. Life moves so fast in a city that the residents feel hard to keep pace with it. The automobiles spread smoke everywhere. Everyone seems to be running from place to place. He may use a car a motorcycle or a DTC bus. Animals and birds seem to have disappeared or migrated to some other lands.

It was my first visit to a village that is not far away from Delhi. Only one bus goes there in the morning and returns in the evening. The passengers had not only put milk-drums in the bus, but also they had carried huge bags. Some of them were sitting on the roof. As we passed through the link roads, there were green fields all around. The farmers had sown the winter crop and were watering the plants carefully. I had never come across so much of green space anywhere in the city.

The bus stopped near a pond that was giving out a stinking smell. I covered my nose with handkerchief. We were supposed to reach the school. The lane was covered with mud. As we started, some cows and buffaloes came from behind. They ran into one another and could have trampled me but I was saved due to my alertness.

An old man was sitting on a cot, smoking *hookah*. Some children were playing around him. It looked as if life had come to a standstill. When I requested a villager to guide me to the school, he asked a small boy to take me there. There was a small building with only two rooms. The students were sitting on coir mats. They were writing on the wooden plates called *takhties*. There was dullness all round. I could not hear noise of any kind except that of barking of a few dogs.

There were a few well-dressed young men who told me that they were employed in the city. They had come there to visit their relatives. I was told that there were no shops or medical facilities in the village.

I have decided that I shall work for the improvment of these villages when I grow up. ●

67. A VISIT TO A HILL STATION

Our school organised a tour to Simla during the summer vacation under the guidance of our physical education teacher. A group of twenty students left for Kalka by mail train. There is a metre gauge line from Kalka to Shimla. It is a hilly tract of sixty kilometres that the train covers in about eight hours. The train winds its way on the zigzag lines very slowly. It has a small engine and has only eight or nine ompartments. One can easily catch the running train. The mountains were bathed in the glory of the rising Sun and everything looked majestic. The trees were so high that they seemed to be receiving messages straight from the heavens. There was greenery everywhere. We had left the scorching heat of the plains far behind and felt like wearing woollen and warm clothes.

The teacher had booked rooms for us in the Grand Hotel that is located on the Cart Road near the bus stand. It is also known as Thakur Hotel. We had to bolt the doors and windows very carefully because sometimes, the clouds enter the rooms and wet the beddings and clothes. When we sat on the ridge, the clouds passed by us and made us cool and drenched.

Simla is one of the most beautiful hill stations and the British had made it the summer capital of the Government of India. The Governors' Lodge has been converted into the Centre of Advanced studies. Now, it is the capital of the state of Himachal Pradesh. It has become overcrowded and one does not enjoy those lovely hours on the Scandal point or on the Ridge.

There is a steep height that takes us from the ridge of Jakhu. It is the mountain peak surrounded by very tall trees. It is said that Hanuman had carried Sanjeevani for Lakshman from there. There are monkeys all around and look at the tourists with angry eyes. One has to carry grams to please them. There is a skating ground on the Maal Road where young people enjoy skating. There are some beautiful places around Simla that attract every tourist. There is a snow-skating at Kufri that is barely ten kilometres from there.

The days passed so fast that we forgot that we had to go back. The manager of the hotel reminded us that our booking days were over. As we drove back to Kalka, we wished that we could have stayed there for a few days more.

68. A VISIT TO AN HISTORICAL BUILDING (THE TAJ MAHAL)

A visit to some historical monument is a fascinating adventure Last winter, I happened to visit the Taj Mahal. Taj Mahal according to a greater thinker, *"is a drop of love on the rosy cheeks of time"*. Tagore called it, *"A Dream in Marble"* while others held the view that it is *"Poem in Marble"* and *"Symphony in Stone."*

As I reached Agra, I rushed to the Taj Mahal. This majestic piece of art and architecture was built by Shah Jahan, the Mughul Emperor, in the memory of his beloved wife, Mumtaz Mahal. This historical monument is a monument of love between Shah Jahan and Mumtaz Mahal.

As one enters the premises of this building, one is greeted by the sky-high cypress trees that stand on both the sides of the main path. This path leads to the main mausoleum. There are beautiful gardens and flower-bearing trees around this majestic historical buildings.

The main building stands on a platform. On the four corners of the platform, there stand four towers acting like four sentinels of this central crown of glory. Inside the tomb, is the graveyard of Shah Jahan's wife. At the back of the Taj, runs the sacred river Yamuna. The reflection of the Taj Mahal in the still waters of Yamuna on a moon-lit night is an exquisite sight. Thousands of people visit this great work of art. The entire building, which is made up of white marble, shines like a dream in a moon-lit night.

I visited each and every part of this superb piece of art and was deeply delighted to see it as a work of profound skill and art. Almost all the foreign visitors visit this monumental structure. It is said that crores of rupees were spent and a many labourers were employed in order to construct this tombstone. The Taj Mahal took 31 years to complete. After t had been completed, the hands of the artisans and the labourers, who built it, were chopped off so that they might not be able to build another Taj Mahal.

Throughout all these centuries, the Taj Mahal has withstood all the vagaries of time and weather but still, it has preserved its ancient glory and splendour. Many a poet, thinker and writer has showered encomium on this historical building. It is also hoped that in the years to come, it would continue to be ranked among the finest wonders of the world. ●

PART V

Scenes, Sights and Journeys

69. TRAVELLING, AS A HOBBY

"Travel in the youngest sort," says Bacon, "is a part of education; in the elder, a part of experience." Some may think otherwise; to them, visiting churches and monasteries, castles and fortifications, antiques and ruins as well as libraries and colleges is a sheer wastage of time. They may further say that one could read the accounts of these or watch the movies that cover the important places of the world. They forget that the touch of reality — living and breathing contact — gives a different type of sensation and satisfaction.

Travelling may be an expensive hobby but it compensates for the financial loss. If a traveller has interest in life and its manifestations, he can explore a lot to keep himself absorbed and happy. A student of sociology can gather much from the customs and rituals of life of the people living in the different regions of the world. A student of history can discover a vivid account of history in the historical monuments. An engineer can enrich his knowledge by looking at the engineering feats at different places. In fact, one can find everything that satisfies his intellectual and sensuous cravings.

As a hobby, travelling keeps us busy during leisure time; it is the best method to utilise time. Till a person breaks from the dull routine, physically and mentally, cannot find satisfaction; travelling helps us to achieve this break. At a new place, one is curious to know and eager to gather information. He gets thrills and surprises that keep his interests alive.

While travelling, one comes across a large number of people. In case one has psychological bent of mind, one increases one's experience and power to understand others. Understandings human nature is perhaps, the best part of education. Travelling satisfies all the demands of a good hobby; it is absorbing, educative and refreshing for the mind and the body.
●

70. THE NICEST PLACE I HAVE SEEN

Kashmir is the nicest place I have ever seen. I happened to visit Kashmir valley this year. The moment I crossed the boundary of the valley, I was wonder-struck to see the ravishing beautify of the "Paradise on Earth." Some rightly call it the "Switzerland of India." Indeed, Kashmir valley is one of the most bewitching and beautiful valleys of the world.

It is situated in the middle of the mighty Himalayas. Kashmir is the home of deities and bounties, fruits and flowers and finally flora and fauna. At the same time, there are many historical monuments, picturesque spots, enchanting landscapes and green forests. Apart from the fact that it is the most lucid expression of God on earth, Kashmir is also a land of temples and taverns. It is the home of various gods and goddesses as well as an abode of saints and sages. Its winding rivers, huge lakes, mighty waterfalls, snow-clad mountains, long cypress tree lines and delightful gardens render this place the name "a Mecca of beauty."

Some of the places of historical interest are the monuments of great importance and significance. The Nishat Bagh, Chandanwari, Verinag, Anantnag, Chashma Shahi, Nagin Lake and Shalimar Gardens are places for every visitor to see. The scene of Dal Lake with houseboats and their reflection in the still waters of the lake, present a beautiful spectacle. The mighty cataracts, producing music of their own, haunt our minds. The caves of Amaranth, where the temple of Lord Shiva is situated, is really a marvellous place to visit. It is situated at a height of nearly 15,000 feet. Besides this, there are other places of religious interest and shrines of historical importance. Every year, thousands of people make pilgrimage to these ancient and religious shrines of India.

Kashmir is one of the best natural spots of India. Its exquisite scenery, superb sights, green fields and long trees of deodar and cypress add to the beauty and grandeur of this God-gifted paradise on earth. The entire valley is enthralling. That is why, a large number of foreigners come to this place.

Over and above these things, Kashmir valley is endowed with some of the best hill stations like Pahalgam, Gulmarg, Sonmarg and Khilanmarg. These hill stations are really fascinating and are good health resorts. Khilanmarg is the last place where tree-line ends in Kashmir.

On the whole, the entire valley, with its cultural hues, narrow ravines and gorges as well as hills and dales make it a heavenly abode on earth. The whole Kashmir valley, as a matter of fact, is an embodiment of the beauty of Nature. ●

71. WAITING FOR A BUS

In every big city, there is a local arrangement for bus service. It offers cheap transport as well as it leads to economy in time and energy. It connects various parts of the city. It is very sad to note that the bus service in Delhi is gaining noteriety as it has proved to be an utter failure while coping with the demands of the citizens of Delhi. Usually, people say that bus service in Delhi is the worst.

The city of Delhi is expanding rapidly. From distant places, the people come to Delhi to attend offices. They often have to change more than two buses. In the absence of an efficient bus service, many people take more than two hours to reach their offices. A man does not feel fatigued during the entire day-working in the office but he certainly feels tired when he has to wait for the bus for more than an hour or even more.

Last Sunday, I was waiting at Bangla Sahib Stop for bus No 580 to go to Malviya Nagar. There was a long queue. I adjusted myself in the queue. In order to kill time, some of the passengers were busy in chatting, smoking or gossiping. Women were knitting whereas young boys were cracking jokes with one another. Some gentlemen were busy going through the newspapers or novels.

On account of the long waiting time, the eyes of the would be passengers were fixed in the direction from where, a bus came but the conductor whistled and the bus did not stop. Two more buses came but not more than six passengers could get in. All the passengers were cursing the DTC.

It was very hot. The passengers were perspiring and the small children were crying. Soon, a special bus came. We thanked God and got into the bus. Unluckily, when the bus reached Safdarjang Aerodrome, its engine failed. All the passengers were asked to get down and wait for another bus. Again, I stood waiting for the bus. Soon, a taxi came. I got into it as I had become impatient.

Waiting for a bus is really a grave problem in Delhi and it is quite agonising for all the passengers. No doubt, the authorities are taking steps to lessen the woes of the commuters but so far, no tangible results have come out.

Waiting for a bus means wasting a lot of time and energy which, otherwise, could be put to better use. So, the people responsible for inter-state transport must improve its efficiency and punctuality. The bus service has already been privatised but the DTC remains operational (as a government organ) in the city of Delhi and around its neighbouring states. ●

72. AN INDIAN TEMPLE

Foreigners often remark that India is a land of temples, taverns, shrines and sacred place. With the history of India, are interwined many stories that are religious, legendary and social. Right from Kashmir to Kerala, we come across temples of many gods and goddesses.

One of the biggest temples of India is also known as Lakshmi Narayan Temple (Birla Mandir) that is situated in Delhi. This temple was built by Shri GD Birla.

As we approach the temple, we see a majestic and magnificent construction. It covers a wide area having the front wall artistically built with gates in it. At the back of this temple, lie the hilly mounds. The trees give it very natural and fascinating look.

The entire temple has been built with marble. Inside the temple, there is the statue of Lord Krishna that lies in the central precincts. There are engravings and murals on the walls of an inner temple that depict the stories of *The Ramayana* and *The Mahabharata*. There are also green lawns inside the temple and some parks have many swings and slides which, the children enjoy. The figures of cow, camel, bear and many other animals, carved in stone, have been placed. The fountains and water coming out of tiger's mouth attract people.

On one side of the temple *kirtan* without break goes on for the whole day and night. People going to the temple listen to it with full attention. Devotees, saints and sages are seen reciting the hymns of *The Bhagwad Gita*.

The Lakshmi Narayan Temple wears a grand and decent look on the days of Janam Ashtami and Ram Navami ie, the birthdays of Lord Krishna and Lord Rama, respectively. Thousands of visitors visit this temple on these days. There is a great rush of people during these days. The temple-tops are illuminated with electric bulbs and it renders an exquisite sight. *Pujas* are performed. This sacred place hums with activity during these festivals. The entire temple is lit-up with electric bulbs and lights on the day of Deepawali. If we visit this temple on Deepawali when it is decorated with glittering lights and adorned by the flowers and other decorative things, we derive great mental satisfaction and solace.

73. A DISAPPOINTING JOURNEY

Bacon said that travelling is a kind of education among the younger people. Perhaps, he had a journey in his mind as it gives more experience and enables one to develop more courage. Hazllitt, in one of his essays, says that a journey becomes enjoyable if one hopes to get a good meal and good rest after a tiring journey and adds that travelling hopefully gives the maximum happiness. Perhaps, he had no experience of a journey that could have been more instructive.

It was a day of disappointments and being an optimist, I did not attach much importance to bad omens. First of all, the taxi I hired for the station rattled noisily and emitted more smoke than an ordinary vehicle does. But I had limited time at my disposal. So, I decided to travel by it. After a short distance, it was panting like an extremely tired giant and came to a sudden stop. It was the first disappointment. Somehow, I reached the station in a tonga but found a long queue for the tickets. There were only a few minutes for the train to leave but there was no hope of reaching the ticket window. This was the second disappointment. I decided to travel without ticket and pay the fine during Journey.

Boarding the train was itself an ordeal. Despite my healthy body, I was pushed like a shuttlecock and my luggage was mercilessly trampled upon. However, I managed to wriggle into a corner. There, I found some persons smoking cigarettes. As I could neither stand that smell nor could budge an inch, I covered my nose with my handkerchief but the bad smell choked me.

As expected, the ticket checker came and I willingly told him about my inability to buy the ticket. He looked at me with strange eyes and all the passengers started staring at me. The ticket checker was not going to allow me to travel but I protested and told him that if a passenger was prepared to pay the fine, he should be allowed to travel. After much discussion, I convinced him and heaved a sigh of relief.

As I reached my destination, I was thanking God. I was thinking that I would meet my uncle and aunt with a broad smile and their hospitality would make me forget the ordeals of the journey. I was dreaming of it while the rickshaw-puller was pulling the vehicle in a half-sleepy manner. To my great disappointment, I found that my uncle and aunt had gone to Simla for a month and the house was locked. This was the greatest disappointment. I did not have much money to return. I do not want to recall this disappointing journey further because it makes me extremely sad. ●

74. A JOURNEY BY TRAIN IN WINTER

A journey by train is an interesting experience. In the winter of 1999, I happened to attend the marriage of one of my friends. My friend was living at Amritsar. I got a seat reserved in the first-class compartment from Delhi to Amritsar in Flying Mail.

When the train crossed the platform, it began to attain fast speed. Soon, it ran very fast and after some time, it reached Panipat. I was carrying some novels, tit-bits, magazines and a newspaper with me. For some time, I read but my mind felt bored due to reading. I gazed outside. A peep through the window of the train lent me a charming sight. I saw lush green fields, trees, groves and forests from the window of the running train. I also saw farmers ploughing the fields. Then my train reached Ambala at 4.50 PM. Here, I had my evening tea at the tea-stall on the railway platform. There was a lot of rush. The hawkers and vendors were selling the foodstuffs. Soon, the train whistled. I got into my compartment and the train left the station.

From Ambala, a couple from abroad boarded my compartment. The couple was very polite in behaviour. I enquired from them about their country. The man at once quipped that he belonged to Norway. Then, both the husband and wife began to narrate the facts about Norwegians. They also compared the same with the facts and information about India. His wife spoke highly of Indian womanhood. She praised the beauty and behaviour of Indian women. She also praised the culture, civilisation and places of historical and religious interests in India. Both were deeply impressed by the grandeur of Punjab. Its folklores and festivals were highly appreciated by them. This chat with the foreign couple was interesting for me.

It was night. There was darkness outside. The chilling wind began to blow. My train was nearing its destination. The train halted at Jalandhar. The engine was also changed there. The train then steamed off and ran at its full throttle. The piercing wind was penetrating through the open window panes. At 9 PM the train reached Amritsar. The platform was lit up with lights. I got down from the train. I met my friend at the railway station who had come to receive me. We then, both drove to his home. It was a pleasant journey by train in winter. It added to my experience and knowledge. ●

75. AN HOUR AT THE RAILWAY PLATFORM

A railway platform is a world in itself. The rich and the poor, educated and illiterate as well as young and old have one aim - waiting for the train. Some talk of business; others of household affairs, still others of courts and colleges but the departure of arrival of their trains haunts the minds of all. The only subject that is of some interest to everyone is the time during the arrival or departure of the train.

Life at the railway platform seems to move at a very quick pace. People rush here and there; some check up time of arrival or of departure of the trains while others to buy tickets or eatables. Some others move around the railway station and try to locate their kith and kin. Coolies and TTEs move at slow pace; it is a matter of routine for them.

A variety of goods lies scattered all over the platform. There are shining bags, dirty trunks, huge bundles, new toys and what not? It seems as if some helicopters had dropped these goods. Ladies sit on their luggage while men stand as guards.

Children are patted, kissed, beaten or snubbed. A child, crying for a shining toy, is put off with an excuse. Another becoming a nuisance is beaten up and still others are hugged affectionately. Dressed neatly, many of them seem to be uncomfortable in their new shoes or new dresses. From some places, one can hear cries of the children.

To make this confusion more confounded, there are quarrels as well. Passengers are found quarreling with the porters over wages. They quarrel among themselves over petty matters. But these quarrels do not assume serious dimensions.

In contrast to this, there are some loud laughters. Young people are seen cracking jokes. Subordinates, who have come to see their boss off, cut jokes either to please him or at his expense.

Hawkers do not attract many customers. They hawk their goods, shouting loudly as if by force of habit. These hawkers do not indulge in much of salesmanship.

As the train steams in, everyone moves briskly. Hawkers shout loudly. People see their friends and relatives off with folded hands but heavy hearts. They garland the persons as if they were going to the battlefield. Equally emotional is the meeting of those who come to receive their near and dear ones. The announcements from the loudspeakers divert the attention but for a short period of time. What a great stage of life is the railway platform. ●

76. A WALK BY THE COUNTRYSIDE

It is a matter of great pleasure to have a walk by a countryside, especially for those people who live in noisy cities and to visit such places. The countryside has its own charms. A walk here removes the boredom and monotony of the life of cities. Countryside presents sights, scenes and sounds that are very pleasant and delightful. One feels elated and happy by having a walk through the countryside.

Such a walk helps us discover nature in her jovial beauty. Lush-green fields, dancing plants, the vast and wide landscape, with farmers ploughing it, rural women working on the wells, villagers singing folk songs in the open fields, the tinkling of the bells tied to the necks of bulls, cows and buffaloes etc, are the sights to enjoy.

The dense groves of the trees and the sweet sound of the chirping sparrows renders melodious music. All this is so enchanting that we envy the peace of the countryside.

The cool and fresh air, which we get in the countryside, is not available in the cities and towns. Smoky and dusty atmosphere in the cities makes life difficult there. The artificial life of the cities is nothing as compared to the serene, calm, quiet and peaceful life of the countryside. The blooming flowers, the green trees and women carrying pitchers on their heads can only be seen by having a walk through the countryside.

There goes a quotation, "God made the country and man made the town." Even God resides in the countryside because the purity and simplicity of the countryside is more congenial than the humdrum life of cities and towns. In the countryside, we find nature in its various moods and thoughts. Nature is the teacher, healer and mother of man.

Thus, a walk in a countryside is really pleasant because we breathe the pure and fresh air and see the objects of nature that are very pleasing and delightful and that elevate our spirits as well as refresh our minds. ●

77. A WALK IN MOONLIT NIGHT

The moon is the queen of night and a splendour among starry heavens.

A walk in a moonlit night is really a refreshing and fascinating experience. Strolling in a moonlit night is pleasant and delightful in ways more than one.

Walking in moonlit night does not only remove the weariness and boredom of the hectic day, but also it elevates our spirit, enlivens our soul and refreshes our mind. The atmosphere during a moonlit night is surcharged with calmness and quietness if we walk through the countryside, which is away from humdrum, noise and clamour of cities. Moreover, the cool air, the cool and soothing beams of the moon, kissing each and every object of nature, present a charming sight. One really feels thrilled and relieved. One feels a sense of joy. There comes the freedom of mind, thoughts and ideas.

A moonlit night delights our heart and soul. The tranquil surroundings in a countryside or distant landscapes presents a lovely sight. The moon shines like a light house to guide us in the dark night. And in such a night, away from the din and dust of cities, when we are in the company of our dearest friends, cutting jokes and chatting with them are very alluring pleasures. The stars in the presence of the moon make the moon the guardian of all the stars.

The entire nature is clothed in the shining silvery robes of the moonlit night. Every object appears to be cheerful and mirthful. The flowers emitting sweet fragrance, the petals dancing to the tune of soothing and cool wind and the trees whispering in the breeze really render a fascinating spectacle.

The green fields, flowers and fruits dance in a coherent rhythm because of the pleasant wind and moonlight.

Indeed, a moonlit night is a feast for our eyes. The superb sights, scenes and sounds of nature are enhancing. To play, sing and talk would be some of the coveted pleasures of a moonlit night.

The memories of a moon-lit night are still fresh in my mind and are still haunting my mind. A walk in a moonlit night is a good experience because we come close to mother nature. ●

78. HIKING

The word 'Hiking' means a "journey on foot." So, hiking means to walk or to tramp. And such walkers and trampers are found everywhere in the world. Some men are extraordinarily great hikers. Their only interest hiking. They climb up the hills and mountains, along the banks of a river and through the fields. Therefore, there are many places for hiking. But the question arises — what are the benefits of hiking? Has hiking got any merit? Is it a good physical exercise?

First of all, hiking is a kind of physical exercise. While walking, the various limbs of our body move. Our legs, arms and other parts of the body are in motion. Therefore, it provides good physical exercise that keeps us physically fit.

Hiking through the countryside gives us a feeling of being independent. There is independence of the mind as well. We are away from the noise and din of the city life. While walking through a countryside, which is very calm and quiet, we get mental peace. We walk as we wish. No discipline and etiquette required to be observed. We can chat and gossip freely and for a long period of time. Moreover, while hiking, we can give a free vent to our emotions and feelings. Our suppressed thoughts can be expressed during our hiking tours.

The third advantage of hiking is that we can inhale plenty of fresh air. The air of the gardens and hills, the open places and meadows is loaded with the sweet fragrance of the flowers and is without any dirt or filth. The cool and fresh breeze revitalises our life and limbs.

Another merit, which walking tours provide to us, is that we can enjoy the scenes, sights and sounds of nature. We can see nature in various moods and colours. We can see the gurgling waters of a river, hear the sweet music of a waterfall, see the lush-green meadows and pastures and can gaze at the bewitching mountains and hilltops, covered with densely grown trees and plants of various types. The beauty of nature thrills us. Indeed, fervour and zest are inducted in our life.

Hiking enables us to feel fresh, healthy and sturdy. Hiking is a medicine for some patients while it is a good exercise for most of us. After walking through a countryside, one has more appetite and thus enjoys one's meal. Hiking wards off dullness and boredom of life. It drives away our sad thoughts.

While on a hiking trip, one enjoys all the beauties and bounties of nature. The entire nature, clothed in green garments, is enjoyed by us. One enjoys these to his heart's content. Nature appears before us a great teacher, healer and consoler. It gives us moral lesson, "Books in running brooks and sermons in stone."

79. FLYING IN AN AEROPLANE

This summer, I happened to visit Kathmandu. I decided to go by an aeroplane. I got my seat booked a week in advance of my departure by Royal Nepal Airlines. My plane took off from palam Airport at ten AM in the morning. Before the take-off, everything was checked and passengers tied their belts. When the plane started moving on the runway, there was a terrific noise. But soon, the plane ran on the runway and in no time, it started flying. This was my first air trip. As the plane was flying, I was feeling a little giddy. My ears seemed to be swelling. But after some time, I began to feel normal.

Now the aeroplane was flying at a fast speed. I looked downwards and saw big cities and towns that seemed to be like small toys. The landscapes appeared to be very attractive. Some forests and trees looked like tiny plants. Even the great rivers appeared to be small drains of water. As I was gazing, the air hostess came and offered me a cup of coffee and some snacks. I enjoyed their refreshment very much. The sight of the travellers in the aeroplane is worth mentioning. While some passengers were dozing and snoring, others were feeling giddy and uneasy. Some passengers were just glancing over the magazines and other periodicals while others were engrossed in reading novels. Some passengers were chatting and gossiping with one another.

At 11.30 AM our plane made a brief halt at the Patna airport. We had some refreshments again. Some bought newspapers and novels. The plane then finally took off for Kathmandu, the capital of Nepal. As the aeroplane was flying, I saw many wonderful scenes and sights on the way. Peeping through the cockpit and looking over the landscapes below

117

were really charming. The moment, our plane flew over the mountainous regions of Nepal, the scenery became all the more attractive and pleasing. The majestic hills, the mighty waterfalls, the narrow ravines and gorges, the deep groves, the green vegetation grown over the hills, the cypress trees and other densely grown forests rendered a beautiful view. The Kathmandu valley presented all the more charming spectacle. Having an aerial view of the city of Kathmandu surrounded by hills, towers and turrets, pagodas and *stupas*, is a marvellous experience. When our plane landed at the Kathmandu airport at about 2 PM, the whole city was bathing in the silvery sunshine.

I came out of the aeroplane and had a cup of coffee at the restaurant at the airport and then, I left the aerodrome. I hired a taxi and drove to my friend's house. ●

80. A DROWNING TRAGEDY

It was the month of July. A fair was being held on the banks of the lake near my town. The lake was flooded due to heavy rains. I, along with my friends, went to see the fair as well as to bathe in the lake.

There was a great rush of people. On the banks of the lake, there were many stalls and hawkers. The bathers also kept their belongings on the bank. There was a great hustle and bustle. Most of the people were taking bath in the lake. I also took off my clothes and jumped into the cool and clear waters of the lake. Hardly had I swum for a few minutes, when I heard the cries of a drowning man. I swam towards the drowning man. When I saw him, he was in a precarious condition. Sometimes, he went under water while at other times, he again came to the surface of the water. Many swimmers swam towards the deep waters of the lake in which, the man was trapped. The drowning man was caught in a whirlpool.

People tried their best to rescue the man but in their earlier attempts, they failed to catch hold of the drowning man. By this time, there was a huge crowd on the banks of the lake. In no time, an expert diver dived into the lake and after searching for some time under the surface of water, he brought the man out. The man was in an unconscious state. He was made to lie on the side of the bank. He has taken to the nearby dispensary where he was given artificial respiration and medicines. Everybody was worried about the victim.

The parents of the man also arrived at the dispensary. They were all shocked to hear the news. The parents burst into tears upon seeing the precarious condition of their son. Everyone was praying to God for saving his life.

Even after administering oxygen for one hour, he did not regain but there seemed to be no signs of improvement. People, friends and relatives were also standing silently and solemnly, waiting for the man to recover. Despite the best efforts put in by the doctor and his assistants, there was no sign of improvement; rather his condition deteriorated from bad to worse. Soon, the doctor pronounced him dead.

Upon hearing this sad and tragic news, everyone related to the deceased cried while his parents wept bitterly. This was the worst ever drowning tragedy that I happened to witness with my own eyes. ●

81. A RAILWAY ACCIDENT

During the last few months, there have been many railway accidents. The losses incurred due to these accidents are immense. In July, there occurred a serious accident between

Frontier Mail and Bombay Express near Ratlam Station. It occurred during the early hours of the morning.

As the two trains collided with each other, there was deafening sound. Everybody was paralysed to hear the dreadful noise. Soon, it was discovered with great shock and dismay that the trains had collided. People immediately woke up and rushed to the ill-fated spot.

The scene at the accident spot was most tragic and pathetic. The engine of the Frontier Mail, after striking against the Bombay Express engine forged deep into the compartments of Bombay Express. Both the trains were equally damaged. The passengers of trains were in a state of shock. Some died because of the serious injuries while some passengers were sandwiched in the windows of the trains. There were also heard loud and piercing cries of children, men and women. Some had lost their legs and arms while others were bleeding profusely. It was spectacle that was difficult to see with the naked eyes. The luggage lay broken and scattered. The belongings of the passengers were lying strewn around the site of the accident.

Medical aid was immediately rushed for the injured and wounded passengers. Vans and ambulances came to the rescue. First aid was also given to the victims of this ill-fated collision. Some passengers were carried to the hospital in the ambulance while others, who were not so seriously wounded, were bandaged there and then. Food and medicines were also brought by the people living near the site of the railway accident. It was a terrible sight as there was only a pile of the dead and there were only few survivors. People came to identify their kith and kin, friends and relatives. The entire spot was full of victims, doctors, nurses, social workers and the relatives of the victims. It was the most soul-piercing and heart-throbbing scene.

Later, people enquired about the cause of the accident. It was learnt that the signal man gave wrong signals. It was one of the most pathetic and disastrous accidents in the history of Indian Railways.

82. AN INDIAN VILLAGE

India is predominantly a land of villages. A major portion of Indian population resides in villages because agriculture is the main occupation of Indian people. Today, there are more than six lakh villages in India.

An Indian village reflects the real picture of India. An Indian village, as a matter of fact, is the very epitome of India's progress after the attainment of independence. The government of free India paid much attention to the lifting of the standards of Indian villagers. An Indian village is still confronted with various problems that range from the lack of education to improper sanitation. No doubt, during the last eight Five Year Plans, much has been done to uplift Indian villages. However, the majority of them are still afflicted by the evils like ignorance and illiteracy. An Indian villager is a rough diamond. He still sticks to the old superstitions, customs and conventions era have become obsolete and irrelevant in this modern era of science and technology.

An Indian village, in the truest sense, is still made up of huts with thatched roof and *kuccha* mud. We are still having unmetalled roads, leading to and coming from the village. Its surroundings are green because of the crops and other vegetation. The streets are usually narrow and dirty due to the open drainage system that gives out foul smell. During the rainy season, the entire village, because of poor insanitary conditions, gives out a very foul smell.

121

Outside the village, there is a pond where cattle drink water. There are some big and shady trees on the outskirts of the village where village people, farmers and others take rest during their leisure hours. Under these shady trees, they hold discussions, smoke and enjoy tit-bits and talks. Some take their lunch under these trees.

Outside the village, there is also a well from which, villagers draw water for drinking. The scene at the village well in the mornings and in the evenings is worth watching. The village belles, dressed in their lovely and multi-coloured costumes with pitchers on their heads, come to take water from the well. To watch them chatting and talking while coming and going is an alluring sight. The village women are still victims of the customary veil.

There is also a school in the village. This school consists of two or three rooms where only one teacher teaches all the classes. The students of the school are ill-clad and rough. They sit on the floor. So, they become all the more dirty.

An Indian village lacks various amenities like the police station, the post office, the health-centre and the rural dispensary. So, all of these features make an Indian village a rough and tough place. Further, many bad characters and ruffians move about scot free. Anyhow, there is a watchman who keeps a vigil over the village and reports all the matters to the *panchayat*.

But every dark cloud has silver lining. Indian villages have some merits as well. People enjoy the free air. The open fields with lush-green crop, present a beautiful sight. The diet is very nourishing. Milk, curd and other foods are abundantly available. The villagers have sound health. They live in the bosom of nature. The cool and fresh breeze of the morning, the scenes of sunrise and sunset with the farmers going to their fields along with their cattle and the tinkling of the bells tied round the necks of the cattle producing charming music are the sights, scenes and sounds that are very attractive and enchanting. But an Indian village needs improvements in many fields. After herculean efforts on the part of the villagers and the administration, it could become an ideal dwelling place. ●

83. A RIVER IN FLOOD

During the rainy season, almost all the rivers in India are full up to the brim. Some of the rivers are so flooded that they create a havoc. During the month of August, I happened to go to visit my uncle. He lives at Dhilwan, a village on the banks of the river Beas. There are torrential rains during that month. Once, it rained for thirty-six hours continuously. The villagers were at a great inconvenience due to the rains. One day, when I woke up, I heard the cries of the people. The people were crying for safety. In the meantime, I heard that the bridge on the Beas river near Dhilwan was carried away by the torrential rains.

As I was listening to the cries of the people, a farmer came and broke the news that gurgling water of Beas river were hurtling towards our village. Soon, I saw it submerging the streets and the roads. The forceful currents of the water carried with them animals — cows, buffaloes and dogs. Many trees were also uprooted and were carried away by the strong currents of the water.

Within two hours, the flood water entered the houses. I saw from the house top that the plight of the village was pathetic. Many houses had collapsed. Walls made up of mud were also washed away by the powerful currents of water.

The entire village was so inundated by the water that it appeared as if it were an island in the sea. There was water and water everywhere.

The flood caused a great harm to the property and the animal life of the village. Many houses collapsed and huts were submerged under water. People were rendered homeless. For the rescue of the flood victims, boats were arranged by Indian Navy. These boats carried away the flood victims. Parched grams clothes and garments were distributed by various welfare organisations as well as by the government. The people were badly harmed by this flood. Loss of life and property was worth millions of Rupees.

Some old village men said that this was the worst ever flood in their living memories. Such a great toll of property and animal wealth had never been taken by floods. Some of the after-effects of floods were all the more harmful. Many diseases broke out because of the flood in the village. ●

84. A HOUSE ON FIRE

One day, as I was returning from the playground, I saw a house on fire on the way. I rushed towards the burning house. When I reached there, I saw many people outside the house. Some of them were pouring buckets of water on the fire while others were throwing sand and dust. It was a horrible scene.

The house was double storeyed one. Some of the inmates of the house were in the rooms on the first floor. They were crying as they were surrounded by the flames. The fire was spreading. Some of the inmates came out of the house with burns and injuries (blisters). But those, who were on the top floor, could not get out.

In the meanwhile, the fire brigade arrived. The neighbours had tried their level best to extinguish the fire but they could not. The staff of the fire brigade fought bravely with the fierce flames. Water pipes were laid and the fire brigade officials made an effort to control the fire. One of the officials set a staircase that led to the windows of the upper storey. He took a great risk. He brought out the inmates and came down through the stairs amidst flames. The moment he got down along with two inmates, he fell down unconscious. The inmates whom he had rescued had severe burn injuries. They were immediately rushed to the nearest hospital in a serious condition.

The fire did a great damage to the house, clothes, furniture and other valuable articles were reduced to ashes. The fire brigade brought the fire under control after one hour of long efforts. When the flames were controlled, the house was found to be badly damaged. All the wooden materials were reduced to ashes. The kitchen, from where the fire started, was presenting a dismal picture. The dining room, the drawing room and the store were seriously damaged.

But thank God! After that there was no loss of human life. After enquiry, it was found that the bursting of stove in the kitchen was the cause of the fire. The sufferers were given compensation by the municipal authorities later on.

85. A BUSY STREET SCENE

I live in a crowded locality of the area and the crowd presents the scene of "a human sea" in the evening. People return from the offices and students are back from their schools. Housewives come out to purchase vegetables, fruits and other domestic items. Some young boys and girls dress themselves in their best and go out for shopping.

There is maximum crowd in the vegetable market. The ladies move from stall to stall and bargain for each and every item. They are also very careful about short-weighing by the vendors and keep an eye on the weighing machines. The shopkeepers have a sweet tongue and try to satisfy their customers through sweet talk.

The confectioner's shop is another place of attraction. Little children guide their parents to the shop and force them to buy the sweets of their choice. The girls always go in for *chat pokaris* whereas the boys prefer *gulab jamuns* or *jalebis*. The street hawkers pedal their wares very nicely. The balloon sellers carry whole bunches of inflated balloons to attract small children. The toy-sellers set their stalls on the pavements. The newspaper vendors sell the evening newspapers in a very nice manner. They shout out the sensational news but keep the paper folded. As soon as the customers makes the payment, he is surprised to read different head-lines. Small children cannot control their games. They throw the ball and run to pick it up. It is very difficult for the cyclists and scooterists to apply brakes and save them. Kite flying is another activity. When the kite rises high up in the sky, the eyes of the kite flier are glued to the kite. He does not care for the crowd around and could be injured in an incident.

The whole atmosphere is spoiled by the beggars and the cows. The beggars use every technique to win the sympathy of the old ladies. They apply different colours to their bodies. Some of them are dressed in rags. Many of them do not have arms or legs.

The cows and calves are considered to be sacred by the Hindus. They roam about the streets, eating everything and looking angrily at the bystanders. Sometimes, they start crossing horns in the street. In short, every street has an interesting life of its own and could be enjoyed by the people who live there. ●

86. A MORNING WALK

It is not easy to leave the bed early in the morning. I normally go to sleep when the TV studio closes down for the night. The proverb, "early to bed and early to rise" seems to be very old. My father is a very hard taskmaster. He make me wake up early in the morning and starts teaching me Mathematics. Once, I reminded him of the advantages of morning walk. So, he asked me to dress up in shorts and get ready for a morning walk.

Our locality is very famous for its parks. I was surprised to see so many people having a walk in the park. Cool breeze was blowing. The green leaves of the trees were whispering along with the wind. The birds had left their nests and were flying away in every direction. The sunrise was a glorious scene. It was pleasant to see the first rays of the Sun touching the earth. Initially, the Sun looked like an orange-coloured but gradually, it covered itself with beautiful beams.

In one corner of the park, children were playing with a small ball. Some young boys were running in a circle. There were others who were practising various exercises. In another corner, a *yoga* teacher was teaching *yoga* exercises. The learners were raising their hands and legs in a balanced manner. He asked them to laugh. All of them laughed so loudly that I could not control my own laughter.

A flag was fluttering in one corner. Some young and old persons saluted the flag and sang a patriotic song. All of them were wearing white shirts and *khaki* shorts. They all belonged to the RSS and were learning martial arts.

My father asked me to make two rounds of the whole park. It was thrilling to run a few steps but it was not easy for me to complete two rounds. After running for a few steps, I returned to my father and told him that there was little time left for the study of Mathematics. I was between two devils, learning Mathematics and running a race. My father agreed and we returned home. ●

87. FIRE IN A MULTI-STOREYED BUILDING

The school had been closed for summer vacations. I was playing cards with my friends under a *Jamun* tree, near India Gate. Suddenly, I heard the screeching whistle of the fire brigades. As I looked back, I saw clouds of smoke rising out of a high building on Kasturba Gandhi Marg. All my friends left the game then and there and rushed towards the buildings. There was a deafening noise all around. The firemen, the policemen and the members of the public were trying their level best to extend a helping hand. Some people had climbed up the roof of the top storey of the building. It was so hot that one could not keep his feet on the roof. The tiles were hot and were adding to the scorching heat of the day.

There were some people who were trapped on the sixth floor of the building. As the flames swept nearer them, they grew panicky. One of them jumped through the window and died instantly. His dead body was carried by an ambulance.

There is a building adjoining Ansal Bhawan. Some young persons brought the crane in between both the buildings and made a rope bridge. They took the risk themselves to test its strength. When they were satisfied, they helped the trapped persons to walk over the bridge to the safety. The first person to cross was a lady who had become a nervous wreck. More than seventy persons crossed to the other side and their lives were saved. It is surprising that five young persons, who build the bridge halled from different communities and religions.

The Lieutenant Governor of Delhi was there to have a look at the fire-fighting operation. The police officer ordered to send a helicopter to save the people trapped on the top. A helicopter flew above the building and landed on the building. It saved about ten persons but the wafts of wind made the flames spread all the more. The scheme of air rescue was abandoned and the firemen again started fighting the flames with courage and dedication. The employees of an English daily connected the water hoses with those of their own building. The flames were controlled after three hours. The offices on the sixth floor of the building were burnt to ashes. There were only three casualties. More than fifty persons were admitted to the hospital and were discharged after first aid. I helped the firemen to get water for their hoses. It was a terrible scene that I shall never be able to forget.   ●

88. WHEN THERE WAS COMPLETE BLACKOUT

It was the first day of April. I had my English paper next day. It is a foreign language and chases us like a ghost everywhere. The more we try to learn it properly, the more mistakes we commit. I had marked every important question to be revised at night. The electricity board played April Fool with us by declaring a complete blackout. I was sweating all over but the failure of light made the things horrible as I had to revise my syllabus. I became nervous and started crying. Mother brought a candle and consoled me. She said that God would certainly help me and I should not lose heart. I am not fond of reading in candle-light. There was smoke all around. The flames flickered and I had to draw the book closer to my eyes. The heat and suffocation were becoming unbearable. I had made a fan with a piece of card-board but I could not use it. The flame would go out with the first whiff of the wind.

I thought of moving under the street light as it was the only source that could be tapped. When I opened my book under the pole of the street light, a scooter passed by. I started looking towards the drivers. I could not concentrate on the book at all. My mother advised me to go to sleep and promised to wake me up when the electricity supply was restored. It was like a camel sleeping with the whole burden tied on its back. Who could think of sleeping under these circumstances ? I closed my eyes as an obedient son but sleep did not obey me. The figure of the paper-setter still haunted me. The question papers appeared before me and frightened me out of my wits.

Electricity supply was restored at around 2 AM. My mother tried to wake me up but I was already lost in nightmares. My mother told me later that I was murmuring all the sentences and paragraphs of my syllabus in the bed till the morning. One can easily imagine my fate in the ensuing examination. ●

89. A JOURNEY IN AN OVERCROWDED BUS

It was a Sunday morning. I decided to visit my friend, Ajay who lives in Shahdara. The place is quite far off from my residence in Ashok Vihar and the autorickshaw would have charged at least Rupees hundred. So, I thought of taking a little trouble in a DTC bus to cover the whole distance at the cost of Rupees eight only. As I reached the bus stop, I saw a huge crowd swelling on the road. They all made a dash when they saw a bus coming. The buses were packed to the capacity and some **passengers** were hanging on to its the gates. The lucky ones managed to put their toe on the footholds and left everything else to God. There is no need of pushing ourselves inside. It is done with full force by those who board the bus after us. It was Sunday. So, everyone was trying to get the maximum out of the all-route ticket that cost only Rs 4. The private buses had observed a holiday. The crowd was swelling every minute. As I boarded the bus, the fellow commuters pushed me in. There were only 50 seats in the bus but more than hundred persons were travelling in it. The number of passengers standing in the corridors was in no way less than those occupying the seats. There were eight seats reserved for the ladies but they were occupied by young men. The old women were standing in the corridor and were requesting the boys to vacate the seats. The boys had turned their faces aside and were behaving as if they were deeply engrossed in the scenes outside. It was not easy to get to the exit door. One had to do some tight rope walking as if it were a circus show.

My stop was coming nearer. I started pushing my way ahead. Suddenly, I felt someone touching my purse. I tried to grab him but he had already slipped. I looked around foolishly because not only the money, but also the ticket was in the same purse.

I shouted loudly and called on the driver to take the bus to the police station. He kept on driving till my stop came. He told me that I would not gain anything because the pickpocket might have got down from the bus immediately. I had learnt a new lesson of my life by boarding a DTC bus.

●

PART VI

Matches

90. A FOOTBALL MATCH

Matches are an essential part of sports and games. Matches give rise to competitive spirit and sportsmanship. Moreover, sports matches are a kind of get-together where players, apart from playing and displaying their physical stamina, exchange ideas and information and have free and frank discussions among themselves.

Recently, I got an opportunity to witness a football match that was played between Khalsa Higher Secondary School, Qudian and DAV Higher Secondary School, Delhi. The match was played at the playgrounds of SN College. The entire ground was swept clear and then, decorated. There were chairs on one sides were open for the spectators. Both the teams were in their high spirits. They were dressed most smartly and neatly. Both seemed to be equally strong. The spectators were expecting a well-contested and lively game. The ground and its surroundings were jampacked by the public. The match started at 5 PM sharp. The DAV team won the toss and chose the favourable side. Soon, the referee blew the whistle and the match started. They were hopeful of scoring the goal. During the first few minutes, the DAV team dominated. They penetrated into the defences of their rival team but could not score any goal. Anyhow, their splendid performance puzzled the Khalsa Higher Secondary School team and the latter resorted to rough game *ie*, kicking ball at random. But the captain did not lose heart and encouraged his team. So, the team was re-invigorated. The Khalsa team soon recovered their lost position and in the heat of the moment, they scored a goal. There was thunderous applause when the goal was scored. The whole team was cheered by their supporters. But at the same time, the right half of DAV team was badly injured and the Captain had to play the double role throughout the entire game. Soon, the referee blew a long whistle and first half was declared to be over.

Then, the players took some rest and refreshments. There was a loud noise in the playground as the supporters of both the teams rushed to their respective sides in order to cheer them and encourage them.

Again, the referee whistled and the match started. Now, the DAV team girded up its loins and played with caution. The goalkeeper of DAV team also became very alert. In the first few moments, the Khalsa team put pressure on the DAV team; their left half made three hits one after another in the goal of DAV but the goalkeeper of DAV team showed his extraordinary skill by kicking the goal back. Then, in the heat of the game, the DAV side took the ball to their rival side and within no time, their left half gave a pass to right half and the right-half kicked the ball straight in to the goal and the goal was scored. Now, it became a drawn gam, which delighted the DAV team also and this served to boost their morale. There were loud cheers from their supporters.

Now, the game was passing through a critical stage. Each side was trying its best to score a goal but soon, the time was over and the exciting finale was synchronised with the scoring of a goal by Khalsa team over DAV team. This was a surprising feat that created a great sensation. The winning team received deafening cheers from its supporters while the other spectators admired the courage and sporting spirit shown by both the teams. It was really an exciting match and the spectators appeared to have enjoyed it very much.   ●

91. A CRICKET MATCH

Last Sunday, I, along with two of my friends, went to see the final match of the Sahara cup between India and Sri Lanka.

The venue, Ferozeshah Kotla grounds, was jampacked with enthusiastic fans. The match, scheduled to start at 9 AM, started with Azharuddin winning the toss for India and electing to bat.

India got to a fine start with Sachin Tendulkar and Saurav Ganguly scoring runs with ease. With fans cheering from all the sides, India reached 100 in just 11 overs.

But soon, the Sri Lankan bowlers got the better of the Indian team and Sachin and Saurav were run out in no time. Next, was the turn of Azharuddin who got out, trying to hit a sixer. The middle order batsman Ajay Jadeja and Vinod Kambli took the score to 225. After Jadeja was clean bowled by Muralidharan, three more batsmen lost their wickets to some truly remarkable bowling by Sri Lankans. The saving grace was a marvelous 53 by Srinath. India ended the innings at 297.

During the lunch break, almost everybody could be heard guessing about the outcome of the match.

Sri Lanka started with ace batsman Sanath Jayasurya and Arvinda De Silva hitting boundaries one after the other. But soon, the Sri Lankan batsman fell to some excellent bowling by Anil Kumble and Srinath who again claimed the show by taking 5 wickets by giving only 23 runs. The innings ended at 282 with all the batsman out and 10 balls to spare.

India won the trophy and Srinath was deservingly declared the man of the match.

The ecstatic crowd rushed to the ground to congratulate the Indian team. The police had to resort to light *lathicharge* to disperse the crowd.

I went back home with the everlasting memories of the memorable match that I am sure to remember for many years to come.   ●

92. A HOCKEY MATCH

Last Sunday, I saw a very interesting hockey match. It was played between the Khalsa School and Guru Har Krishan Public School. Mr Dhyan Chand and Balbir Singh acted as referees. It was played at Ram Lila Grounds.

A large number of students and teachers had come to see the match. The referee gave long whistles and the captains of both the teams forward. A coin was tossed in the air. The Khalsas won the toss and chose their favourable side.

Both the teams were in their proper uniforms. The Khalsa players of had blue shirts and white shorts while the players of Guru Har Krishan Public School had white shirts and white shorts.

The match started at 3 PM. It was quite brisk from the very beginning. The Khalsas pressed hard but could not score a goal. They got two short corners but failed to score. Their centre forward rushed at an amazing speed. But he was checked by the full-backs of the competitors. The ball was passed and re-passed like a shuttlecock. Neither side could score a goal. So, the first half was eventless.

After the half-time interval, the teams changed their sides. The game began again. The players of Guru Har Krishan Public School got a short corner and scored a goal. There were shouts of joy from the supporters of Guru Har Kishan Public School and also, from the spectators. Sticks went up in the air. But during the next few minutes, the Khalsas scored an equaliser. Shouts of joy from the Khalsa side dominated the sky. The game became more interesting. The Khalsas rushed forward. Their captain played very nicely. He ran with the ball into the D and hit it hard. But the goalkeeper of rivals was very active and alert. He checked the ball and therefore, foiled all the attempts of the rival team. The spectators raised shouts of joy.

Now, the time was almost over. Each side tried it hard to win the game. But all their efforts came to a naught. The referes blew long whistles and declared that the game was over.

They were given extra time to play. Now, each side tried hard to score a goal. But neither team could succeed. Thus the match ended in a draw. It was really a well-contested match. ●

PART VII

Science and Technology

93. COMPUTERS TODAY

A Computer is an electronic device that is used to perform repetitive calculations at very high speeds. The computer acts as a data processing device and also stores large amounts of data. This data could be text, pictures, voice, numbers, photographs and other types of information that are used by humans in their day-to-day operations. Life cannot be imagined without computers. In fact, the new millennium is the era of computers and its associated techniques, commonly known as Information Technology (IT).

Computers help the school children learn new techniques of study, graphic designs, games and other useful educational applications. They help the college students in preparing reports. They help the office executives in accounts, software development, sales invoicing and manufacturing. They help the libraries in the efficient management of their operations. They run the factories and equipment. They control the satellites and nuclear weapons. They help the young and the old surf through the Internet sites. They are, in fact, indispensable as every operation of human life is incomplete and inefficient without them.

As school-going students, we must learn computers. Computers are available in various configurations. For learning computer operations a computer with 166 MHz speed (known as the CPU speed), a HDD of 1.2 MB storage capacity and a RAM of 32 MB is needed. These elementary computers would help the school students learn LOGO, BASIC, Windows 95 (the operating system in usage now a days), games, various lectures related to the syllabi and Internet operations.

Although Indian society, industry and polity are gearing up for adoption of computers, yet we are far behind the Western nations in terms of computer literacy. In the USA, out of every 2 students, one has a computer. In India, out of every two hundred students, only one has a computer. Further, out of every 4 students in the USA, every two students have an access to Internet whereas in India, out of every fifty students, only one has a remote access to Internet.

A student would do well to learn the basics of computer operations. In his or her school, he or she can join evening classes for getting advanced level training. Computers are easy to learn and are student-friendly machines. They improve the efficiency of the student and make him more knowledgeable. They help him or her in his or her education, mental development and entertainment.

In the times to come, all the students would either have their own computers or would have a free access to them. Computerisation in banks is complete and most of the factories, offices, colleges and schools have advanced computer systems. The latest processing speed of the computer is 533 MHz but this computer is costly. A good computer, which would serve the purpose of the student, costs Rs 30,000 only. And this cost would come down in the years to come.

Students should adopt computers in their educational teaming and for their mental development. Computer software is a promising field and the students can build their careers in this field. Moreover, intelligent programmers are also in great demand in the USA, the UK, Canada, Australia and New Zealand. If the students work hard in the field of computers, they would have good careers in the latter parts of their lives. ●

94. INTERNET

Internet is a network of computer systems that have been connected to each other through satellites, telephone lines and optical cables. These computers can have access to a large volume of precious and useful information. Initially, Internet operations were confined only to the USA but this new technology has spread its wings around the globe during the last 10 years.

Internet operations began in 1986 when the US Department of Defence connected some computers through optical cable networks. These networks also used satellites for transmission of data to far-off places. Later, some American Universities also entered the Internet arena. The main systems, called the Internet servers, were located in the USA. Now, Internet is a global phenomenon. Every student can have an access to Internet through his computer system, a telephone line and a modem. The Internet service must be provided by a government organisation (like VSNL, MTNL etc) or by a private firm, which is known as an Internet services Provider (ISP).

The key to success of Internet is the information. The better the quality, the more usage of Internet operations. And this would lead to "hooking on" of more number of users on the Internet highway. Internet uses a special type of software, which has been developed in HTML, JAVA, VB and SGML. However, a student need not be worried about these programs as Internet surfing is very easy. It is a possible to surf through Internet with the help of Windows 98 software and Netscape Navigator Software and either of these two would have to be 'loaded' in the computer of the student.

Internet has given the most exciting mode of communication to all - the E-mail. We can send an E-mail (the short form of Electronic Mailing System) to all the corners of the world. The cost per page of E-mail is only 30 paise. Further, Internet, as already stated, can be used to collect information from various storage areas of the servers, called the websites. This information could relate to education, medicine, literature, software, computers, business, entertainment, friendship and leisure. Internet is also used for carrying out business operations and that set of operations is known as Electronic Commerce (E-com).

All the newspapers, magazines and journals of the world are available on Internet. Even our own *Doordarshan* is available on this information superhighway. Therefore, possibilities an Internet are endless. The student can enhance his knowledge about the world in a matter of few hours while he is hooked on to Internet.

Some students have mischievous intentions. They waste time on sending false E-mails. Some others try to view those websites that are not meant for them. This is a bad tendency and must be checked. Internet must be used for development and not for decay.

MTNL has offered internet connections far as low as Rs. 2500 per annum. This cost would be reduced further. The cost of the computer system, modem and other associated hardware is also likely to come down. The Internet user must have a telephone line that would connect his computer to an ISP. In India, this facility is being provided by the local networks have not been designed and made functional but Internet would be available in all the cities and townships of the country by 2002 AD. In four major cities, Internet services are available with ease and at very low prices.

Internet is the technology of future. In the times to come, offices would be managed at distant places through Internet. The advantages of Internet are low cost, large volumes of information, high speed of access and good quality of entertainment. Its disadvantages are faulty telephone networks, useless information for students and wastage of time while surfing through various websites. Students can create and maintain their own websites but for that, they would have to learn Internet programming. They can learn Internet operations and software and could be successful Internet programmes in the times to come. By the end of 1998, there were only 1,20,000 Internet connections in India. The students must learn Internet operations and must try to collect only the useful information. The new century would usher mankind into a new era of Information Technology (IT) and Internet is the blackbone of this exciting era. ●

95. STUDENTS AND INFORMATION TECHNOLOGY

The students of the twenty-first century would find Information Technology (IT) to be very useful tool for developing themselves. Computers, Internet and IT are closely related. The new millennium would essentially belong to the efficient and competent citizens of the world. Hence, the students would do well to get themselves trained in this vital area.

Students can use IT by learning computer operations. Computers are quite efficient devices. These could be used to learn the syllabi taught in the schools and colleges. Mathematics, sciences, drawing, fine arts, painting, history, civics and other vital subjects could be learned with the help of educational Compact Disks (CDs). The teachers could also guide the students in the context.

Further, computers are also useful for entertainment and leisure. High-quality games could be played on the computers. And if the monitors of the computers are large and coloured, they would certainly enjoy the thrill of computer games. These games (like car races) would also develop the skills and concentration of the students. Moreover, the students can play these games at home during any time of the day (or night), without bothering other members of the family.

Some students, whose parents have Internet access, would be able to surf through various websites of Internet Information about every topic is available on Internet. The student should surf through good websites so that only good-quality and useful information is collected by him or her. If he or she just 'wanders' through the Internet sites, he or she would waste his time as well as Internet time and would incur expenses in terms of telephone bills. There are many educational websites, available on Internet. At some websites, the information and articles could be downloaded as well (which means that the information could be printed on paper if the student has an access to a printer as well).

IT is the name of the game in the times to come Information is knowledge and knowledge, as the studen knows, is power. Earlier, during the eighties and the seventies, information was not available. But now a days, it is in abundance. The student, like a swan, has to pick the right type of information and use it for his educational needs. This is not an easy task as a lot of information and data being circulated on Internet and computers are not of much value for the students.

Other tools of IT include cellular phones, E-mail (through Internet operations), fax machines, telephones, magazines (related to computers sports and education), yellow pages, music cassettes, books, CDs, encyclopaedias and newspapers. All these tools would help the students in gaining more knowledge. And a student, who has knowledge, would certainly be able to make a good career in his life. IT is here to help the students in building their careers. They have to utilise this technology for their improvement in academic fields. They would also be able to learn more about this world, its citizens and the environment. The world is a small village, thanks to IT. In this changed world, students could be more aware about their capabilities, career goals and the society they live in. Welcome to the era of IT. We wish you all the best in your endeavours in this new "superage of information and achievements." ●

96. TELEVISION IN DAILY LIFE

Small screen has become so popular that people have stopped visiting the cinema halls. It provides the cheapest entertainment for the whole family in a very relaxed manner. There is no need of dressing up, putting on socks and shoes and washing the face with the best soaps. We can stretch ourselves in our beds in our night dresses and can switch on the TV with the help of a remote control.

TV has become the medium of entertainment, education and advertisement. It is for us to choose the programmes of our liking. In the morning, there is a programme of exercises. If we are able create some open space around the TV the whole family can watch the TV with comfort. It should never be watched by sitting close to it; the effect on our eyes could be serious in that event.

The national programme is the most interesting for the viewers of every taste. A play about the history of a refugee family from Punjab became so popular that people missed their appointments to view this programme. It was not only popular in India, but also in the neighbouring countries like Pakistan and Bangladesh. The programmes keep on changing and offer a variety of entertainment. Doordashan Channels have hard time satisfying people of every taste. India is a vast country and people of each region and religion want programmes of their own choice.

On Sunday, the telecast begins early and continues till late in the night. The old people never miss the *Ramayana* and sometimes, insist on the youngsters to join them. Some questions are advertised in all the newspapers and the readers are asked to send their replies within a specific period. Those, who gave correct replies, are selected and are called to the TV studios. The competition would continue for the whole year and we can learn much about the history and culture of our country through such programmes.

Now a days, the cable TV boom is at its peak. Private channels like Citi Cable, Zee Cinema, Star TV Network and Sony Network are very popular as they offer a variety of entertaining programmes. There are nearly 100 channels to choose from.

There are also programmes for the youth and the students from various schools and colleges take part in them. In sum, TV is proving to be a wonderful source of entertainment and education. ●

97. SCIENCE IS A CURSE

The nuclear bombs in the possession of the USA, Russia, France The UK, India, Pakistan and China are powerful enough to blow up the world within no time. The star wars programme will carry the struggle in the space and would pollute the whole atmosphere so badly that no form of life of any type would be able to survive. Scientists are busy making further advances in the field of armaments and the day is not very far off when by switching on one button, the whole humanity would become a thing of the past. The animals in the oceans may survive and may make another effort towards the evolution of news species on the earth. When billions of people are dying of starvation, more than fifty percent of the budget is being spent on defence outlays. Take the example of India. It is one of the poorest countries of the world. Our neighbour — Pakistan — is getting arms from the USA, France, Iran and Saudi Arabia. We have also to gear up our defence and spend more on our defence forces. More than forty percent of our budget has been earmarked for defence. Same is the case with Pakistan. The government of that country is busy making a nuclear device, though their military regime can hardly afford the mammoth expenditures on the same. The cost of one bomb would cross a thousand crore Rupees. The common man in that country is also ill-clad and ill-fed. In Iran and Iraq, a terrible war was fought. The whole wealth of both these countries was consumed by the fires of war. The nuclear power plants pose a very serious danger. In

Russia, the Chernobyl plant spread radiation all around and the neighbouring countries also felt the shock. The radiation level is already so high that some animals have already started dying due to it.

The smoke and pollution spewed by big industries is spoiling the whole atmosphere. In Bhopal, thousands of people were killed due to the leakage of poisonous gas. In Switzerland, a private company let out the pollutants in the river and the whole marine life of the river was wiped out. Ultimately, all this poisonous material reaches the ocean and kills fish of every type.

The whole work is done by machines. One machine can work for thousands of persons. Unemployment is increasing at a very fast rate. Even those people, who work in the factories, sit idle for whole day. We have forgotten manual labour that could keep us physically fit. We cannot walk even for a kilometre because we depend more and more upon automobiles. The result in that most of us suffer from diseases of various types. We cannot enjoy a healthy, vigorous and busy life. Science started as our servant but is becoming or master at a fast pace. It is getting on our nerves and that day is not far off when the entire humanity would suffer a great deal on account of the evils of science. Man himself can undo this damage, if he wakes up to the occasion. ●

98. ARE SCIENTIFIC INVENTIONS MAKING US HAPPIER ?

One of the most popular questions, which is often asked, is, "Are scientific inventions making us happier?"

Science gas given us such comforts as were unimaginable a few years ago. Today, we switch on the radio and listen to the music. We have electricity, telephone, television, washing machines, refrigerators, air conditioning plants, satellites, cellular phones, fast trains, aircraft and the most modern medicine systems. All of these things have made the life of a man very comfortable. The shower baths, electric fans, cinemas, cars, trams and jumbos are among other scientific inventions and discoveries that have increased the happiness levels of man.

Science has made travelling easy and efficient. The world has become smaller for us. But those exciting adventures and romances, which travelling bestowed upon us during the past, have disappeared. Modern travelling is a dull business.

Those people, who live in big cities, are previleged in some respects but suffer in many other ways. The city people do not have any leisure. Their life is so busy and mechanical that they do not have any time to stand and stare. Their lives have become artificial and devoid of all charms and delight.

As modern age is an age of science, men have become mean, calculative and mechanical. Science in advancing and it is thwarting our civilisation. In the kingdom of science, the words like love, affection and sentiments are quite alien. So, what is the use of science for man if he gains the whole world but loses his soul ? Spiritualism is on the wane while materialism is on the rise. Philosophy, culture and poetry are fading from human life because of the rapid advancements of science.

Again, on the destructive side, science has invented weapons that are most dreadful and disastrous. The inventions of laser beams, neutron bomb and hydrogen bomb have increased the chances of human destruction. Therefore, if these weapons are put to use, they would spell disaster for the entire mankind.

Therefore, the opinion remains divided on the subject. No one claims that science is complete happiness or an impending curse. While a scientist makes inventions, a politician misuses them. In sum, the wrong application of scientific inventions by the politicians sounds the alarm. In this respect, science has de-humanised us. Now a days, we have better drugs and surgical instruments but men are becoming weak in terms of physique and mind. What an irony of fate it is! Today, we have a sensitive 'ear,' a sensitive 'lung' and a sensitive 'liver' due to fast speeds, smoky atmosphere and dusty roads. So, science makes mankind happy by its latest achievements but it also makes us unhappy when it shows its destructive power. Science can be used for getting happiness but the mad mind of the man and particularly, that of the politician misuses the discoveries of science. ●

99. LATEST ACHIEVEMENTS OF SCIENCE

Science has invented many things. The achievements of science are too many to be counted. Some of the latest achievements of science are really wonderful. They are quite remarkable discoveries.

Science has given to humanity, many comforts and facilities. By providing humanity with air conditioners, science has made heat and cold ineffective while the television has delighted the viewers around the globe. On the television, we can see the scenes and sights of other countries. A person sitting in India can see the happenings in the USA. It is really one of the latest triumphs of science. And now, digital TVs have entered our lives. The invention of X-ray has enabled people to know about their internal injuries. X-ray has brought a revolution in the field of medicine and health

Further, plastic surgery is a wonderful invention. An ugly person can be converted into a beautiful one with the help of plastic surgery.

The invention of the rockets and satellites has amazed mankind. The rockets and satellites have reached other planets. The latest achievements of science have not only enabled man to have pleasure trips to other planets, but also they have solved the problem of interplanetary communication. Now, we can also study the density of composition of the upper layers of our atmosphere. Further, these inventions have made space travel easy. The USA has landed its probe on the Mars. There are also plans to build a space station above our earth.

The intention of wonderful drugs like penicillin, streptomycin and chloromycin has conquered many diseases. The most incurable diseases can be cured by these latest inventions.

While the latest triumphs of science have revolutionised life, its triumphs in the event of war are no less amazing. Science has made war very dangerous and destructive. Science has given to us gas warfare, bacteriological warfare and atomic weapons. This can destroy and kill human beings. The invention of other weapons of war like the atom bomb, the hydrogen bomb, missiles, neutron bomb, nerve gas, guns and ammunition etc, has endangered the very life and existence of human beings.

Therefore, science has progressed in both the domains — constructive as well as destructive. The latest triumphs of science try to remove the evils of diseases and deaths. These have also increased the threat to human life. The latest triumphs and victories of science need to be properly utilised, otherwise, they could bring death and destruction for the human race.

100. THE WONDERS OF SCIENCE

Twentieth century is the age of science. Science has progressed by leaps and bounds. It has brought about many revolutions in the life of a man. Rather, science has changed the very life and living style of a man. It has transformed the very face of the earth. Science has bestowed upon humanity great and far-reaching inventions and discoveries. It has blessed mankind with such instruments and have earned a name and reverence science.

The wonders of science are too many to be enumerated but still, some wonders are worth mentioning. The entire growth and advancement of science is really a vast subject. But some of the wonders, which science has provided to the human race, are decidedly remarkable.

In the field of health and hygiene, science has created many wonders. Penicillin, streptomycin and other drugs have proved to be miraculous drugs. Many fatal and chronic diseases have been overcome by science. It has conquered death and disease. It has prolonged the life span of man. Plastic surgery can transform an ugly woman into a beauty queen. X-rays can detect the defects in the bodies of living beings.

In the field of transport and communication, the advancement of science is amazing. The inventions like electric trains, aeroplanes and ships are well known to all and sundry. The marvels of science have converted this massive globe into a beautiful and high technology village that is full of all comforts and luxuries. In one day, we can visit many cities of the world. Distance and time have ceased to hold any barrier in this age of science and technology.

Atomic energy is one of the most wonderful blessings of science. This energy not only promises to satisfy the immense needs of this energy-hungry civilisation but also, it can work miracles because it is more powerful than other sources of energy. Atomic energy can run mills, factories and great industrial and technological establishments. Further atomic explosions can also be used for levelling mountains and digging canals.

Science has glorified machines. It has increased their efficiencies, though this has led to some unemployment and environmental pollution hazards. The usage of tractor; agricultural instruments, chemicals and insecticides has increased the average output. By applying scientific methods in agriculture, the yields of farms have been multiplied.

On the whole, the wonders of science are countless. Science has taught us to swim like fish in water and to fly like birds in air. It has given man comforts and facilities like telephone, television, fans, computers, air conditioned cars and buildings. In the field of science, the difference between summer and winter is negligible. Science can be used to eliminate poverty, clean slums, increase production in the farms as well as in factories and for other constructive purposes. All these are, as a matter of fact, the wonders of science.

101. TECHNOLOGY CREATES MORE PROBLEMS THAN IT COULD SOLVE

Technology is the knowledge of the process and techniques that transforms the abstract ideas of scientists and mathematicians into a concrete reality. It is the knowhow that enables us to extract the raw materials and then, convert them into fuel, steel, chemicals, plastics and food. Technology is also concerned with perfection of industrial processes, mass production and automation. The advancing technology implies pollution, the exhaustion of natural resources and the lack of workers' satisfaction in automated factories. Hence, technology is a two-edged weapon.

The chemical industry has grown a lot during the nineteenth and twentieth centuries. It turned natural rubber into a material that is to be used on an industrial scale. New discoveries like plastic, artificial fibres and synthetics were made. Dynamos and electric motors gave fillip to technological development. Henry Ford, the American industrialist, added a new dimension to industrial technology. These developments in technology led to serious problems of unemployment, squandering of material resources and social dislocation of humans.

Biotechnology and the manipulation of man's own body, made spectacular advances after the Second World War. An array of drugs to combat diseases was produced. By saving life, if contributed towards the population explosion. Transquillisers, stimulants and psychotherapeutic drugs for controlling mental processes assumed great importance. No doubt, they helped the medical profession but they also created a grave social crisis when they became generally available.

Computers have opened up new vistas. These can make any number of calculations; simulations of particular hypothetical situations can be produced and studied. These have created the problem of unemployment. Sometimes, mechanical calculations may do harm to other people and nations. Space technology poses a great danger to the world if it is used for polluting the environment.

Technology has made man mechanical in outlook, ruthless in attitude, materialistic in thinking and cold and calculative in behaviour. So, technology has created psychological, social and other human problems. ●

PART VIII

Functions, Festivals and Celebrations

102. DEEPAWALI FESTIVAL

Deepawali is one of the most celebrated festivals of Hindus. It is celebrated with great enthusiasm throughout India. With this festivals are associated many lores and legends. It marks the victory of Rama over Ravana. As a matter of fact, this festival the symbol of victory of the forces of virtue over the evil forces.

On the day of Deepawali, there are hectic activities all over the country. People invite their nearest and dearest ones. On this festival, sweets are made and distributed among friends and relatives. People indulge in fun and frolic on the day of Deepawali.

New clothes are worn by the young and the old as well as by high and low. Children and teenagers are dressed in their most glittering and dazzling dresses. At the same time, during night, fireworks and crackers are also let off. The bright flames of the fireworks present an exquisite sight in the dark night.

The festival wears a lovely look. Everyone is well dressed, gay and mirthful. Some celebrate the day in the most enthusiastic manner. Some indulge in gambling. Gambling, according to gamblers form a part of Deepawali festival and whosoever does not gamble, becomes a donkey during his next life. At night, the people illumine their houses, with lights, *diyas*, candles and tubelights. They eat, drink and enjoy the evening with crackers. The cities and towns are immersed in light and sounds of the fireworks. Apart from houses, public buildings and government offices are also lit up. The scene of that evening is very enchanting.

Many Hindus perform *Lakshmi Pooja* before celebrating Deepawali. The Hindus worship Lakshmi the Goddess of wealth — on this day. They say prayers so that Goddess Lakshmi may visit their houses.

Deepawali festival is the festival of the whole country. It is celebrated in every nook and corner of the country. So, this festival also creates a sense of oneness among the people. It becomes the symbol of unity. India has been celebrating this festival for thousands of years and continues to celebrate it even today. All Indians love this festival.

103. REPUBLIC DAY CELEBRATIONS

January twenty-sixth is a red letter day in the history of our nation. It was on this day that our own Constitution came into force and our country became a secular and democratic republic. It reminds us of the day when the Congress Party took a historic pledge to win freedom for the country from the foreign rule.

The preparations start at least one month in advance. The seating arrangements are made in the lawns near India Gate.

There are VIP seats and ordinary seats. The tickets are made available from different places in the city.

One platoon from every regiment of the armed forces takes part in the parade. In the same manner, the sailors and airmen are drawn from the Indian Navy and Indian Air Force. The country proudly displays her might through the guns, tanks, ships and fighter aircraft. The function starts early in the morning. The Prime Minister lays a wreath at the *Amar Jawan Jyoti*. He pays homage to the martyrs who laid down their lives to save the nation during various wars. At exactly 8 AM the President reaches the *Raj Path* and he is received by the Prime Minister and the Defence Minister. The President is also the Supreme Commander of our armed forces.

The march begins with the heroes of the earlier wars. All those members of the armed forces who won the highest gallantry awards *ie*, *Param Vir Chakra*, lead the march. Then, come the young boys and girls who have won bravery awards for the year.

The soldiers march briskly. The band plays martial tunes. As they pass the saluting base, they turn their eyes towards the President. The Commanding Officer salutes and marches on. The members of the paramilitary forces also take part in the march.

At last come the *Jhankis* of various states in which, Indian they display the life of people. The cultural troupes also perform the folk dances. The students drawn from various schools of Delhi come at the end. They put up a very beautiful show in the form of dances and national songs with action. The whole programmes is telecast on the TV. On January 28th, there is beating of retreat. The soldiers taking part in the parade march back to their barracks. It is one of the most charming displays put up by our armed forces every year.

●

104. INDEPENDENCE DAY CELEBRATIONS IN MY TOWN

August the fifteenth is celebrated as the Independence Day of India. Since 1947, India has been celebrating and would continue to celebrate this day every year. This reminds us of our gain of freedom from the foreign rule. On this day, the British left India and handed over the reins of the government to the national government of free India. This day marks the triumphs of those Indian nationalists and patriots who struggled hard and sacrificed their lives for the freedom of their motherland.

This year also, the Independence Day was celebrated in my town. Early in the morning, there were processions and *prabhat pheries*. People sang in that calm atmosphere of the dawn. These songs were reminiscent of the brave deeds of Indian heroes. People were in their cheerful moods.

Then, at 8 AM the national flag was hoisted at the committee grounds. People came to witness this ceremony. The flag was unfurled by a local dignitary who is the Health Minister in the Punjab government. After hoisting the flag, the visiting dignitary gave a powerful speech in which, he described the progress of Indian planning during the last fifty years. His speech was to the point and inspiring. He also paid glowing tributes to the Indian matyres. He encouraged the people for undergoing further hardships in order to preserve the freedom of the country. At last, the National Anthem was played. The people dispersed after the National Anthem.

Independence Day celebrations are of great importance. On this day, flags flutter on the top of all government offices. Night illuminations are also arranged. The buildings are lit up with electric bulbs that create charming sight.

On the whole, there was a great enthusiasm among the people. All were in their high spirits. Parties were thrown away and invitations were extended.

People also took a pledge to safeguard the freedom of the nation. This day, indeed, is one of the most important days in the history of free India. It is celebrated in every town and city of India with great fervour. ●

PART IX

Personalities

105. MAHATMA GANDHI

Mahatma Gandhi, the magic man of Asia, an apostle of non-violence and preacher of truth, was born on October 2, 1869 in Gujarat. He belonged to a well-to-do family. He passed his Entrance Examination when he was 17 years old. He remained very shy and regular during his schooling. He also went to England to study law and became a barrister. Then, he returned to India and began to practise at the Bombay High Court. But he was not very much interested in the legal profession. So, he joined the struggle for Indian independence.

He also went to South Africa. There, he made his best efforts to improve the lot of Indians. He underwent all the sufferings but remained steadfast in his convictions.

After returning from South Africa, Gandhiji entered Indian politics. He could not bear the miserable plight of Indian masses suffering and starving under the British rule. In order to uproot the Britishers from the Indian soil, Mahatma Gandhi sacrificed everything.

His entire life is a saga of sufferings and sacrifices. Freedom was the breath of Gandhiji's life. In 1919, he started a non-violent and peaceful movement. Hindu Muslim unity, removal of untouchability and usage of *Swadeshi* goods were his life-long missions.

Mahatma Gandhi was a man of sound and sterling character. In fact, he has a noble soul. He wore very simple dress and took simple food. He was not only a man of word, but also of action. What he preached was practised by him. His approach to various problems was nonviolent. He was a God-fearing person. He was a cynosure of all the eyes. He hated communalism in every shape or form. He was a friend of all and enemy of none. He was universally loved and liked.

The part played by Mahatma Gandhi on the stage of Indian politics is unforgettable. In those stormy days of the struggle for Indian Independence, Gandhiji suffered and was imprisoned several times but the freedom of his motherland remained his cherished goal. He guided the Congress policies, launched "Quit India Movement" and was imprisoned many times.

His entire life was a life of service, sacrifice, devotion and dedication. This saintly statesman, thinker, writer and orator of India still shines like a star on the horizon of Indian polity.

His tragic death on January 30, 1948, plunged the entire nation into gloom. He was assassinated by Nathu Ram Godse. His death was the greatest blow to the forces of peace and democracy. The memorable words of Lord Mountbatten are worth quoting, "India, indeed the world, will not see the like of him perhaps for centuries." His death left a great vacuum in the life of the nation. The whole world still reveres and respects this veteran of the twentieth century who has left indelible mark on the sands of time. ●

106. MY FAVOURITE LEADER
(SHRI LAL BAHADUR SHASTRI)

There is no end to the choice of a favourite leader but as far as I am concerned, Shri Lal Bahadur Shastri is my favourite leader. He was born on October 2, 1904, at Mughalsarai, a town of UP. He belonged to a lower middle class family. He was born and brought up in the cradle of poverty.

Shri Lal Bahadur Shastri got his early education at Kashi Vidyapeeth. It was the place where he drank the rich springs of Indian culture and civilisation. He moulded his living according to the Indian way of life.

After completing his education, Shri Lal Bahadur Shastri turned to the poor condition of his countrymen under the British rule. He could not tolerate the sufferings of his countrymen. He was deeply moved by the starvation and nakedness of his countrymen. Compelled by these circumstances, he joined Indian politics. He came in contact with great Indian national leaders like Nehru, Gandhi, Patel and Subhas Chandra Bose. He worked hard and fought bravely in order to get his country liberated from the foreign rule. He became the member of the Servants of the People's Society. He joined Congress and worked with its leaders who were organising the national movement.

When India got her freedom, Shri Lal Bahadur Shastri handled difficult tasks. He held important office in the Indian National Congress and became Union Minister several times. As a minister, whether of Railways, Commerce and Industry or Home Affairs, Shri Lal Bahadur Shastri discharged his duties efficiently and satisfactorily.

After the death of Shri Jawaharlal Nehru, Shri Shastri became second Prime Minister of free India. So, he rose to the topmost position of the land. The tenure of his Prime Ministership from June, 1964, till his death (January 11, 1966) at Tashkent would go down in Indian history as a decisive period. It was this period during which, he had to face many grave crises like food, famine and above all, of Pakistan's attack on India. But he emerged triumphant from all these ordeals and trials. In the days of Indo-Pakistan war of September, 1965, he gave the country a brave and dedicated leadership.

Shri Shastri was a thorough democrat and staunch nationalist. He was a protagonist of *Bharatiya Sankskriti*. He was a man of the people. He was a blend of firmness, flexibility, patience and perseverance. He possessed the courage of Patel as well as the Gandhian temper. He possessed all the qualities of the head and the heart. He was an astute politician, an honest statesman, a noted thinker and a powerful orator. He won the war but died for peace. Keeping his ideals of democracy and secularism alive would perhaps be the best tribute that could be paid to the memory of this renowned patriot and a noble son of India. ●

107. AN INDIAN HERO (SHIVAJI)

The history of India is replete with the stories of innumerable heroes and gallants. Their deeds of bravery, gallantry, chivalry and heroism have left indelible marks on the face of time. Shivaji is one of those Indian heroes who have been acknowledged as one of the most worthy and remarkable personalities. He was born in 1627. His father — Shahji — was a small *jagirdar*. His mother — Jija Bai — was a very pious and intelligent woman. She moulded the early life of Shivaji in such a manner as to ensure that he could dazzle like a star in the later period. She infused in him the burning love for his motherland. Right from the beginning, Shivaji had shown himself to be a fearless, brave and kind soldier. That is why, he is called the "Defender of the Hindu religion."

His boyhood proved the saying of Wordswoth, "Child is the father of man." He was very promising, shrewd, intelligent and patriotic right from his childhood. As a matter of fact, his mother was his first teacher who directed the early life and decisions of Shivaji in a manner that he came to be known as a fearless fighter, a brave soldier and great patriot of India. He could not tolerate his countrymen being oppressed under the tyranny of Muslim rule. So, he collected some chieftains, jagirdars (landlords) and others in order to liberate his countrymen from the oppression of the Muslim rule. He conquered the State of Bijapur and other Mughal territories. Aurangzeb could not tolerate this and so, he sent Shaista Khan to fight against him. Shivaji gave Shaista Khan a crushing defeat.

Shivaji being a shrewd politician and an intelligent statesman, proved more than a match for the tactics of Aurangzeb. Aurangzeb's attempt to imprison him failed. Shivaji also sensed the mischief of Afzal Khan and murdered him before he could attack Shivaji. Aurangzeb once made Shivaji a prisoner in Delhi but he, with his intelligence, thought of a plan and escaped from the prison with the help of the security guards in a basket of sweets.

All that Shivaji grabbed during battles were distributed equally among the poor. During battles, Shivaji observed all the cannons of morality and decency of behaviour; he did not touch children, women and old persons. Rather, they were protected by him. This shows Shivaji's secular outlook and a generous heart. Even Khafti Khan, Aurangzeb's court historian wrote, "Shivaji is a hellish dog. But he has certain qualities. He is most secular and generous." Mauser Germaine, the French envoy at the time of Shivaji, also paid tributes to the secular greatness and humanitarianism of Shivaji.

Shivaji would go down in Indian history as the defender and saviour of Hindu religion. He gave the enemies of Hindu religion a hard blow and established *Maratha Raj*. But after his death in 1680, the entire citadel of Shivaji began to disintegrate because of the quarrels and conflicts among chiefs and *jagirdars* (landlords). But for Shivaji, Aurangzeb would have destroyed the entire Hindu religion. The entire Hindu community is proud of this valiant son of India whose deeds of chivalry and bravery have inspired the millions of Indian youths. Shivaji has become an immortal hero in the history of India.

108. DIANA, THE PRINCES OF WALES

On February 24, 1981, in the white and gold ballroom of Buckingham Palace, as the notes of the National Anthem died away, Lord Chamberlain came at the centre stage and said that the Queen had commanded him to make a special announcement. Lord Maclean, in a manner that befits royalty, announced, "It is with great pleasure that the Queen and the Duke of Edinburgh announce the betrothal of their beloved son, the Prince of Wales, to Lady Diana Spencer, daughter of Earl Spencer and the Honourable Mrs Shand Kydd." This was indeed an illustrious moment in the history of the British royalty as Lady Diana was chosen by the exclusive royal family of Britain to be the future Queen of England.

On July 29, 1981, a midst the pomp, glamour and much litter Lady Diana walked down the aisle of St Paul's Cathedral with Prince Charles, the heir apparent to the British throne. Lady Diana became Her Royal Highness the Princess of Wales. It was a fairy tale wedding that struck the very picture of romance. The world applauded and cheered as the starry-eyed nineteen year old princess with a warm style and stunning looks waved to them as her royal carriage passed through the heavily packed streets of London. She was an instant success.

Diana was the third daughter of the eighth Earl. He held a position as Viscount Althrop, King George VI's equerry between 1950 and 1952 and an equerry to the Queen for two years after her accession in 1952. It was in 1954 that he married the Honourable Frances Ruth Burke Roche, the younger daughter of the fourth Baron Fermoy. Diana was the couple's third daughter. She was born at Park House, in a rambling Victorian mansion, in the grounds of the Sandringham Estate, the Royal Family's house. It was only till the age of seven that Diana enjoyed a happy childhood. Matrimonial strife between her parents ended in a divorce at this time. She was then, sent to a boarding school. In 1975, after the death of her grandfather, her father inherited the title and became the eighth Earl Spencer. They moved to Althrop, in Northamptonshire. Diana became 'Lady' Diana. Two years later, her father remarried and Diana went off to a finishing school in Switzerland. She felt homesick and was back before the year was over. It was in 1977, at a shooting party, that she met Prince Charles for the first time. Little did they know that destiny had more plans for them than were afforded by this casual meeting. After this, Prince Charles started taking more than a casual interest in this unaffected eighteen year old girl. She was a marked contrast to the more worldly girls in her circles.

At first, their marriage seemed to be happy enough. Within a span of three years, Diana gave birth to two sons — Prince

William of Wales and Prince Andrew. The four of them presented a picture of a happy family. Princess Diana had all that the future Queen of England must possess. She became an obsession with the media. Her gorgeous looks of a model, matched by a warm elegance, became a perfect story for the media across the globe. She was always in the news, sometimes as "Shy Di," sometimes as "Disco Di" and at other times, as "Caring Di" or "Crusading Di." So powerful was her appeal with the masses that many times, her charisma and charm overshadowed that of the more sober Prince Charles. Her fanfare was phenomenal and she gained a tremendous amount of applause when she associated herself with unfashionable and controversial issues like leprosy and AIDS. She soon gained the stature of a model lady of the twentieth century. She became an icon.

Unfortunately, this idyllic state did not last long. Hints of a strenuous relations between the couple became apparent. In December, 1990, separation of the royal couple was announced by the Prime Minister in the House of Commons and in 1996, they were divorced. Diana's title of Her Royal Highness was taken away from her and she came to be addressed as merely Diana — the Princess of Wales. This move by the royal household earned them a poor reputation as the world opinion was with their very own Diana. In a candid BBC interview, she said that what she wanted most was not to be the Queen of England but the Queen of people's hearts. And that she definitely was.

It would, indeed, be difficult to delineate the causes of the failure of this marriage that started with so much of hope and optimism. The formality of the monarchy, which Diana found stifling, together with the hounding media, are surmised to be two major causes of the failure of this marriage of the century. Prince Charles, trained to keep the proverbial tight upper lip, could not perhaps understand the spontaneousness of the girl he had married. They were two different kinds of people who were tied together in a set of circumstances that were made painful by fate.

The divorce could not rob Diana of the charm that she was endowed with. Her popularity never waned, though there were articles every now and then about some clandestine romance that she was supposed to be having. But all was quelled when Prince Charles too confessed of having a relationship with his companion of many years — Camilla Parker-Bowles. The public opinion as always was on the side of Princess Diana. For the public, she was a lone brave mother of the royal household, trying desperately to bring the much needed contemporaries into the portals of the British monarchy. People identified and sympathised with her.

Although she was no longer the wife of the heir apparent to the British Throne, yet Diana had a significant role to play as the mother of the future heirs of her country. She decided to forge a new bond with the public that gave her so much adulation. She concentrated on the causes that needed her attention. Her association with the AIDS Trust, Leprosy Mission, Cancer Hospitals and the British Red Cross won her many laurels. She was a symbol of refreshing new royalty who even shied away from wearing gloves while shaking hands !

When (on August 30th, 1997) the world heard of Diana's death in a car crash at Paris, there was gloom that spread across all the corners of the world. There was a common outpour of grief as people participated in what seemed to be a global loss. It was history in the making. Millions around the world mourned the snatching away of a person who was so young and irreplaceable. Ironically, it was on this fateful day that Diana had truly found personal happiness. In that evening, her companion and friend Dodi al-Fayed, the eldest son of the owner of Harrod's had presented Diana with a fabulous diamond studded ring that commemorated the beginning of a new life with him. Diana put in on the third finger of her right hand. She was on the threshold of a new life when Dodi and she were killed in the car crash in Paris.

Diana's tragic death put an end to an era that had just started to take shape. It reinforced the finality of death and the contrasting elusiveness of life. People from all over the world thronged the iron gates of the Kingston Palace, the official residence of the Princess and paid their heartfelt tributes with flowers and messages. Even 45 condolence books were not sufficient for recording the monumental grief of these people who mourned her death.

After her death, Diana has joined the enviable group of those people who, in their short but meaningful lives, have left a great and gloomy void. Diana's close friend and famous singer Elton John's first line of his song, "A Candle in the Wind" poignantly captures the essence of Diana's impact on the world. While bidding farewell, he says, "Goodbye England's Rose." With the death of Diana, a contemporary icon faded away but from these ashes, the legend of a princess shall always live.

●

09. MOTHER TERESA

would not be inappropriate to call Mother Teresa "The Saint of the Twentieth Century." Bent down in poised grace, with her white sari draping her head, she was the very image of God's love on this earth. During turbulent times like ours, which, the race for materialism has all but completely wiped out our consciousness, it was this apostle of love and mercy that was a beacon for millions all over the world. Her inspirational selfless work for the homeless, the poor, the aged, the handicapped and the unwanted was nothing short of the manifestation of the Divine self.

Mother Teresa was born as Agnes Gonxha Bojaxhiu on August 26, 1910, at Skopje. Her family belonged to the Albanian community. They were Catholics, though the majority of the Albanians were Muslims. Her father, Kole, was a widely travelled businessman. Her mother, Drana, was a housewife. They had three children of which, Agnes was the youngest. Unexpectedly, when Agnes was nine, her father died. Drana had to look after the family. She started earning her living by sewing wedding dresses and doing embroidery jobs. Inspite of these hardships, theirs was a religious family. They prayed every evening, went to the church everyday, prayed with the rosary and assisted in the service of the Holy Virgin. An annual pilgrimage to the place of Letnice, where Our Lady was venerated, was a custom of the family.

This scriptural upbringing had a deep impact on Agnes. As a little girl, she began to understand the quintessential meaning of the preachings of the Gospel and early in her life she tried to put to practice what was preached. Her mother' influence in moulding the little Agnes into a deeply caring human being cannot be undermined. Apart from taking care of her three children, Drana was much moved by the misery of an alcoholic woman in the neighbourhood and started to take care of her. She went to wash and feed her twice a day. She began to take care of a widow and her six children. When Drana could not go, Agnes went to do this work. After the death of the widow, the children were raised in the Bojaxhiu household as a part of it. So, it was this exemplary attitude of her mother that instilled in Agnes the love and concern for others. This was to become so much a part of her character that she left all other pleasures in her later life. She was to completely devote herself to the welfare of the poor and the needy.

It was at the age of twelve that for the first time, she felt a keen desire to spend her life doing God's work. But she was not sure. She prayed a lot and talked about it to her mother and sister. She even confided her earnest desire to a Father at the Legion of Mary whom she had helped with learning a language. "How can I be sure?" she asked. He answered, "... through your joy. If you feel really happy by the idea that God might call you to serve Him and your neighbour, then this is the evidence that you have a call. ... the deep inner joy that you feel is your compass that indicates your direction in life."

Agnes was eighteen when the decision was made. For two years, she had assisted several religious retreats in Lentice and it was clear to her that she would be a missionary in India. She then, decided to join the Sisters of Our Lady of Loreto who were very active in India. On September 25, 1928, she left for Dublin where the motherhouse of the Loreto Sisters is located. Here, Agnes learnt to speak English and was trained for a religious life. After receiving the Sister's Habit, she chose to call herself Sister Teresa in memory of the little Teresa of Lisieux. On December 1, 1928, Sister Teresa left for India to begin a new life.

After taking her vows at Darjeeling, Sister Teresa dedicated herself to the care of the sick and the needy in a small hospital. Later, she was trained as a teacher and became the headmistress of a secondary school in the center of Calcutta. Not only did Sister Teresa teach the students History and Geography, but also she took time to get to know the children's personalities and their families. She was loved by everyone who came in contact with her. So overwhelming was her concern for the children that they began calling her 'Ma.' Close to this institute, were the slums of Calcutta. The miserable appalling conditions in which, the poor lived, wrenched her heart. Sister Teresa could not turn herself away from such a misery. Along with some girls, she would visit the slums and would try to help out the poor in any manner that she could afford. But her contribution seemed to be insignificant to her in the face of such a misery. During these years, the Belgian Wallon Jesuit, Father Henry, was a great source of inspiration for her.

To clear her tormented soul and to look for direction, Sister Teresa went for a retreat to Darjeeling on the tenth of September, 1937. Many years later, Mother Teresa called it, "The most important journey of my life." It was during that journey that she really heard God's voice. His message was clear; she had to leave the convent to help the poorest of the poor and to live with them. "It was an order, a duty, an absolute certainly. I knew what to do but I did not know how." The tenth day of September is called "Inspiration Day."

To leave the convent was not an easy matter. It had to be considered carefully. The matter was taken up by the Archbishop of Calcutta, Mgr Perier. The decision had to taken carefully. The political situation at that time was precarious. India was about to gain independence. Questions arose — would a European be accepted after India became free? would Rome approve of this decision? Sister Teresa was asked to wait for at least one year before joining the Daughters of Saint Anna, sisters, who wore dark blue saris and worked to help the poor. Sister Teresa was disappointed. She did not simply want to work among the poor but wanted to live among the poor and the wait seemed endless. It was in August, 1948 that she received the permission from the Pope in Rome and the Mother General at Dublin to leave the Loretto community.

Mother Teresa was 38 when she took the vows of poverty, purity and obedience. Giving up the Habit of the Sisters of Loretto, she took to wearing a cheap white sari with a blue border. Sister Teresa then, went to Patna to train herself as a nurse. She realised the importance of such a training in her venture to help the poor who lived in dirt and unhealthy habitation. After completing her training, Sister Teresa came back to Calcutta and began her life's vocation — to live among the poor and to help them. Soon, she became a common figure in the slums and the streets of Calcutta. Her white sari, the fluent way in which, she spoke Bengali and her unrelenting effort to improve the hygiene and literacy in the slums, soon made her an endearing figure. Inspired by this lone European lady's dedication, one day, a young Bengali girl, who was former student of Sister Teresa, came to ask her permission to join her in this noble venture. The girl was from a well-off family and Sister Teresa, after explaining the hardships in this life of sacrifice, asked the girl to consider her decision for a year and then, to come back to her if she still wanted to be a part of her mission. On March 19, 1949, the girl came back in all simplicity and earnest faith. She was the first to join Sister Teresa in her mission to improve the lot of the unwanted and the poor. Rising early at dawn, the Sisters worked with dedication and inner spiritual strength that comes with sincere prayer. At this time, Sister Teresa, so sure of the virtue of her vocation, took Indian nationality.

Her will to help the needy became stronger with each passing day.

With continuous work, their community grew. Soon, Sister Teresa began thinking seriously about starting a congregation. This was approved on October 7, 1950. Thus the constitution of the "Society of the Missionaries of Charity," came into being. It was the day of the feast of the Holy Rosary. After five years, the congregation became papal as more and more Sisters joined the congregation and devoted their lives to the sick and the poorest of the poor.

At Calcutta, owing to this growing numbers, the Missionaries of Charity needed a residence. A Muslim leaving for Pakistan sold his house for a cheap price and this was to become the famous Mother's House at 54 A, Lower Circular Road, Calcutta. While the society grew, the Mother's work kept on increasing. Her work among the lepers of India got her international recognition. She received the Noble Prize for Peace in 1979. After receiving the honour, Mother Teresa said, "I choose the poverty of our poor people. But I am grateful to receive (the Nobel) in the name of the hungry, the naked, the homeless, the crippled, the blind, the lepers, all those people who feel unwanted, unloved, uncared for throughout society, people who have become a burden to society and are shunned by everyone."

On September 5, 1997, Mother Teresa died of a heart attack at 9.30 in the evening. It was an irreplaceable loss that was felt worldwide. Mother Teresa was buried on September 13, 1997, exactly 7 months after electing Sister Nirmala as her successor. The vacuum left by this Nirmal Hriday (Pure Heart) shall never be filled. Mother Teresa would live on in the memory of all those who were, during her lifetime, graced by her tender touch that made all the difference. ●

110. PANDIT JAWAHAR LAL NEHRU

Pandit Jawahar Lal Nehru was the first Prime Minister of India. He worked hard with Mahatma Gandhi during the freedom struggle. Invariably wearing a red rose, he was adored by the masses. He was a great leader and a master builder of modern India. That is why, he is known the architect of our nation. He had plans to build a great and strong India. He was a man with determination and strength of character. His love for people and affection for children made him very popular. He was a great writer and thinker. He wrote the famous book, *The Discovery of India.*

Jawahar Lal Nehru was born on November 14, 1889, at Allahabad. His father was Moti Lal Nehru who was a famous barrister. He took his primary education from English tutors at home. He was sent to England for high school studies. He took up education in law. After completing law, he returned to India. He had a burning passion for his country and independence.

He was deeply influenced by Mahatma Gandhi. His greatest desire was to set India free. Under the guidance of Mahatma Gandhi, Jawahar Lal Nehru took an active part in the freedom movement. He also followed the path of truth and non-violence. He was sent to jail may times. He was elected President of the Indian National Congress in 1929. The pledge of Independence was taken there. He said at the constituent Assembly, "whether we are men and women of history or not, India is a country of destiny."

When India attained freedom in August 1947, he became the Prime Minister of the country. His leadership and vision brought progress, prosperity and respect for the country. He laid the foundations of democracy. He believed in the principles of peaceful co-existence. In 1961, the Panchsheel Agreement was signed between India and China. He was a great supporter of disarmament. India got due respect from the world under his leadership. He worked hard to create an international order of peace and brotherhood. He followed the path defined by Buddha, Christ and Nanak.

After serving the nation and mankind for a long time, he died in May, 1964. He left behind the heritage of planning and development. He started the cycle of progress and social justice. He created a network of educational, technical and medical institutions. He built large industrial, agricultural, irrigation and power projects. His contributions are noteworthy in all the fields. He was one of the few men who could made an impact on the country and the world. His birthday on November fourteenth, is celebrated as the Children's Day. This reminds us of his great character, ideals and deeds. In the words of Winston Churchill, "he had conquered all things including fear."

Jawahar Lal Nehru had a profound vision. He was a great orator and an author of repute. He believed in the unity of the country and liberty of the mankind.

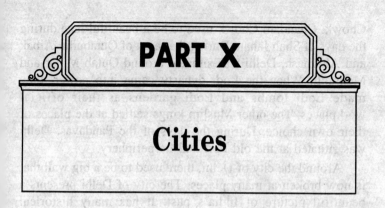

PART X

Cities

111. AN HISTORICAL CITY (DELHI)

Delhi is one of the most important historical cities. It has a rich historical background. One finds Delhi a land of ruined towers and turrets, tombs and temples, mausoleums and monuments and of forts and fortresses. Delhi has been the seat of power of many ancient empires kingdoms, marauders and invaders. Delhi was also the centre of great Indian movements. It was the capital of ancient Hindu kingdom as well as that of Mughal emperors. Factually speaking, Delhi is the star city of Indians and foreigners because of its great and rich historical background. It has been ruined seven times and rebuilt seven times.

Delhi was named as Indraprashtha by Pandavas and remained the capital of Hindu kingdoms for thousands of years. The Muslim kings also made it their capital, though every Muslim king rehabilitated it at a particular place around the walled city. For example, the present Delhi was found by Shah Jahan. Red Fort was a grand palace. Delhi of Shah Jahan's days was founded near Red Fort and Chandani

Chowk. Chandani Chowk used to be a beautiful lake during the days of Shah Jahan. During the reign of Qutabudin-Aibak and Altumash, Delhi was situated around Qutab Minar and Mehrauli. When the Lodi dynasty came into power, they made Lodi tombs and Lodi gardens as their official workplaces. The other Muslim kings settled at the places of their own choice. During the days of the Pandavas, Delhi was situated at the old Fort and its periphery.

Around the city of Delhi, there used to be a big wall that is now broken at many places. The city of Delhi presents a beautiful picture of India's past. It has many historical buildings and magnificent monuments. Humayun's tomb, a majestic piece of art and architecture, was built by the wife of Humayun. Qutab Minar is another tower of great importance that was built by Qutabuddin-Aibak and completed by Altumash, the Muslim king. There are also the tombs of Safdarjang and Nizamuddhin. These tombs are now ruined and broken while some have been preserved properly.

Delhi has been the capital during the period of British rule in India. Today, it is also the capital of the Government of free India and is a seat of the Central Government, embassies, high commissions, trading firms and many other organisations of India and the world. New Delhi is a lovely part of the city. It is well built and charming city. It has green gardens and beautiful parks. The Parliament House, *Rashtrapati Bhavan*, various offices of the central government, old houses and palaces of Indian kings and princes etc. are situated in New Delhi.

Among its trading centres, Cannaught Place is considered to be one of the most fashionable shopping arcades. This shopping centre hums with activity, especially during the evenings, amidst neon signs, glittering lights and coloured fountains.

Therefore, the city of Delhi is prominent because of its historical importance and is also the seat of central government but at the same time, it is a city that reflects the whole world. It has a strange blend of the ancient and the modern legacies, the ruined monuments and Mughal architecture. The city of Delhi is cynosure of all eyes. Everyone is interested and anxious to have a bird's eye view of this ancient historical city of India. Delhi, indeed, is a treasure-chest of antiquity.

112. THE CITY I LIVE IN

The Mughals shifted their capital from Agra to Delhi because they could not resist the charm of the Yamuna flowing on its outskirts. We are reminded of the scene when Noorjahan was drying her hair in the window at the Diwan-e-Khas in the Red Fort. A washerman looked at her with covetous (lustful) eyes and had to pay the price with his life. The arrow shot from the bow of Noorjahan pierced his heart and he fell down, dead.

His relatives pulled the golden chain of justice, which moved Jahangir. The emperor immediately ordered that Noorjahan should be beheaded. It was upon the intervention of the ministers that her life was saved. Such stories are written on each and every corner of the city. It is the city of Mirza Ghalib, the great Urdu poet. In the Red Fort, there is a museum that tells us about the lives of the people in the days of the Mughals and after the Mughal rule. The Jama Masjid calls the faithful to assemble for the prayer. This mosque is in old Delhi.

But there is another Delhi, which was built by the British as their capital. Lord Lyton had studied the designs of great historical buildings and had tried to blend them with Indian traditions. The Parliament House is a majestic building with beautiful pillars. The building is circular in shape and has gates on every side. *Rashtrapati Bhavan* is another wonder of the modern architecture. India Gate and the Secretariat lend grace to the whole view. People have come from every corner of India and have settled down here. They teach everyone a lesson in national integration. They have a cosmopolitan outlook.

During the last ten years, migration has started from every state. Those, who do not feel safe anywhere, shift to this city. The population is bursting to the seams and the amenities are not enough to support such a large population, which is 1 crore. There are traffic jams during the peak hours and the communers are packed in the DTC buses.

In spite of all these shortcomings, I love to live here and enjoy my life. ●

113. DOES OUR CITY NEED BEAUTIFICATION ?

I am live in Delhi. Delhi is the capital of India. It is the seat of the central government. Many government offices are located here. There are embassies, great and beautiful buildings, gardens, lawns, parks, statues and other places of interest. But still that there are some places in Delhi that are just slums and dirty spots and do not give a decent look to the city.

Therefore, there is need to beautify it. Without beautifying it, it cannot get a lovely look.

First of all, there is need for repairing the roads. The roads of this city are damaged. Whosoever from foreign countries visits this city, does not get a good impression of this city. To give a good impression, there is a great need for repairing and reconstructing the roads. Moreover, there are some old and ancient buildings, though ruined, in various parts of the city. Those broken and ruined buildings not only mar the beauty of the city, but also cause accidents. Therefore, these old buildings must be repaired.

There are many slums here and there. Dirty water and sewage get spread in the streets. This dirty water not only gives foul smell, but also breeds mosquitoes. The pools of stagnant water are very harmful for our health. They should be removed because in the capital of India, such places simply leave a bad impression on those who visit it.

Then, there are some unauthorised constructions in the city. The houses are not properly built. There are no proper drains and bylanes in many localities. The houses are not built after proper planning. This also mars the beauty and grandeur of the city. It is necessary to demolish all such structures. Instead, there should be built beautiful and grand houses. Modern designs in architecture should be used for their construction.

The number of public parks in their city is also small. Public parks and municipal gardens add to the beauty of the city. These parks and gardens act as the places of recreation and relaxation for the citizens of this city. Therefore, such places should be developed.

On the whole, the entire city needs to be renovated and overhauled. All such steps must be taken to beautify the city. The roads should be widened, the slums should be removed and the huts should also be removed from their present places. The slum dwellers should be allotted land somewhere else because the residents living in these huts cannot maintain their dwellings. ●

Life in a big city is a war in different battlefields. A neighbour's clarion call, "Sugar has arrived at the ration shop," is a signal to buckle up the straps for a fight. Foregoing his breakfast or dinner or tea, cutting short his meeting with a friend, the resident of the big city scampers to the ration shop in the pursuit of the sweet crystals. So, an array of men confronts him at the ration shop. Here, the resident of the big city fights heroically against fatigue, thirst, queue jumpers, dwindling stocks and the dishonest shopkeeper. After this heroic fight, he may get the booty; in case he does not get, he is scolded by his 'commander' at home.

The city-dweller's ordeal in a bus is another great epic. Every morning, he has to take part in one hundred metre sprint to the bus stop. He may have to elbow out pick-pockets, ignore frail kids, push ladies and argue with the conductor. The veritable hell moving on wheels may give him jerks and jolts, causing cramps in his limbs.

Train journey needs advanced planning. He must fight for getting his seat booked even two months before the actual battle. While waiting in a queue, he finds the privileged ones entering from the backdoor and getting their tickets. The booking clerk grins before he says that all the seats have been booked; money changes hands and there is smile on the face of the booking clerk. Sometimes, there is a gentle pat on the shoulder and as we look, we find a burly man offering us a ticket at a premium of fifty Rupees.

The city dweller's heroic deeds at the time of admission of his children in schools and colleges is another great saga. The queues for the registration forms, the interviews of the parents, the snobbish behaviour of the school teachers, clerks and peons, the demand for donations for the school auditorium and many more hurdles ought to be crossed. If the child is admitted, a heavy demand for money begins — money for the school uniform, money for the fete, money for the founder's day, money for decorating the classrooms and what not ? If the charges swell up a little more, it would become an effective step for restricting the expansion of families.

The campaigns at the milk booths, at dead public telephone booths and in the corridors of bureaucrats are not less significant. He has to defend himself against the speeding trucks that might knock him down, against the innocent looking rogues who might stab him for a five Rupee note and against the wily hawkers who might cheat him with their sweet talks. The traffic jams, the crowded shops, the money-spinning rich and the spectre of price-rise leave the residents in a state of awe and confusion. One murmurs, in a fit of desperation, "Devil made the city and God made the town!"

●

15. THE TOWN LIFE AND THE COUNTRY LIFE

Everything in this world has its own merits and demerits. Nothing is perfect in this world. Perfection is a privilege only of God. So, town life and country life have also their own advantages and disadvantages. Commodities, pleasures, scenes, entertainments and recreations that one finds in cities are not available in the country-side and *vice versa*.

There goes a saying that "God first made the country and then, the city." This sums up the belief that even God resides in villages or in the country side. Why ? Because villages and the country-side breathe due to fresh air of nature, the cool breeze. The villagers get fresh vegetables and diet that is nourishing. Moreover, a village is free from the din and dust, noise and clamour as well as smoke and heat of the cities. A village is near it is nature and so, nearer to God. The village people are innocent and lead simple lives. They are not aware of the practices, which are prevalent in towns and cities. A village is the very embodiment of simplicity and a symbol of God's bountifulness.

The countryside is superior to town in many other respects. The lush-green fields, the vast meadows, the groves of trees, the lovely landscapes and the farmers working in their fields, reaping the crops amidst chirping of birds, are the sights that are elevating and cheerful.

But there are certain other things that one does not get in the villages. These can only be found in towns. Cinema, telephone, television, refrigerator etc., are some of the facilities that are found only in towns and cities. The means of entertainment and recreation like clubs and coffee-houses, posh restaurants, theatres and other centres of art, culture and civilisation are found only in cities. The villagers are quite ignorant about these trends that are prevalent in the urban areas.

Moreover, the smoky atmosphere, the dirty and noisy roads, the poor sanitary conditions of cities because of factories and industries, the lack of good diet and fresh air are some of the deficiencies of town life.

So, the country life and the town life stand in a striking contrast. The facilities of one are the drawbacks of the other and *vice-versa*. City people are cultured, civilised and cleverer than their counterparts dwelling in villages. But still, the life in a small village is worth enjoying because it provides stability, calmness and peace of mind, which are conspicuously absent from the life in the towns.

PART XI

General Essays

116. READING HABIT

Knowledge knows no bounds. Even if we gain more and more of knowledge, we cannot be satiated as there is much more than we could absorb. Reading books contributes towards the enrichment of our knowledge in terms of human experiences and information. Unfortunately, we in India, do not have the reading habit. That is why, in India, 70 percent of the total number of books published are the text books whereas in the Western countries, this percentage is not more than 30 percent.

Once, the famous Indian writer, Mulk Raj Anand, was asked about reasons for low reading habit in our country. His reply was that India had a tradition of verbal communication of knowledge from one generation to another. The *pananiya shiksha* proclaims that those, who learnt from written records, were the lowest in the rank among the seekers of knowledge.

Even today, the formal teaching method of imparting knowledge to students is based on "note memory," lectures and reproduction. It hardly expects the students to delve into the vast mass of knowledge. This method touches students superficially and in effect, it has failed to arouse an inner urge among them for self-study.

The inculcation of the habit of reading depends upon three factors-pedagogical, bibliographical and bibliothecal. The first one is related to teaching and can play an important role. But the teaching profession unfortunately, lays more emphasis on achieving short term objectives rather than on the ultimate goal. In order to prepare for examinations, students prefer to consult more diluted and cheap text books rather than the standard texts. Teaching should lay stress on self improvement and self development of the students to prepare them for their lives. For self improvement, love for books and reading are the essential pre-requisites.

This should be supplemented with the right type of reading material and that is the bibliographical factor. Unfortunately, we do not have any reading material for children and adults. Language is another barrier. We are also divorced from the mainstream of literature because there is hardly any translation facility available in the country. So, we do not know anything about what has been written in the different parts of the country in various languages.

The third factor is the bibliothecal factor. It underlines the role of the library as an institution to coordinate the activities of described two factors earlier. There should be libraries that must be rich in terms of collections. The books should be easily available. ●

117. MY FAVOURITE BOOK

There are so many books that it is very difficult to read all of them. But of all the books, which I have read until now, I like *The Mahabharata* the most. *The Mahabharata* is an epic of profound interest and significance in the realm of Indian literature. This original book was composed as a Sanskrit verse and was written by Ved Vyas.

The Mahabharata, broadly speaking, is a great contribution towards the rich stream of Indian literature. It consists of famous principles and the doctrines. It has a very wide appeal. Its story is interesting and instructive. It reflects the picture of India during the turbulent days.

The story goes like this. Pandu and Dhritrashtra were two princes. Their capital was Hastinapur. Dhritrashtra was born blind and was also the elder one. Pandu became the monarch but he died due to the curse of a sage. After the death of Pandu, Dhritrashtra became the guardian of his sons. But Dushasan and Duryodhan were two notorious characters and were known as 'Kauravas.' Arjun, Nakul, Sahadev, Bhim and Yudhishthir were the five sons of Pandu and were called 'Pandavas' and used to be considered as superior, in every respect, to Kauravas. So, there grew a jealously between the Pandavas and the Kauravas. Kaurvas even tried their best to kill Pandavas but they escaped due to their prudence and valour.

Then, a plot was hatched by Duryodhan and his brothers who were aided and abetted by their uncle, Shakuni. Yudhishthir was invited to a game known as dice. A sinister trap was laid for the loser. According to this trap, the loser would go on exile for 12 years and also, would have to live in perfect secrecy and isolation for the thirteenth year. If he was detected, he would again have to live in exile for another twelve years. Yudhishtra agreed to this plan. But he lost the game due to the insidious role played by Shakuni and so, went into exile along with his wife and four brothers. On the expiry of the term of their exile, they demanded five plots of land but the stubborn Duryodhan did not sanction them even a bit of land. Pandavas were asked to get it after winning the war.

This lit the flame of war between Pandavas and Kauravas. Pandavas, no doubt, were very pious and holy while Arjun and Bhim were renowned for their acts of bravery, chivalry and heroism. Lord Krishna became the leader of Pandavas and so, a battle was fought between the two rival factions at Kurukshetra, which lasted for eighteen days. The Pandavas, who were guided by the then astute politician, a superb statesman and hero, Lord Krishna, emerged out victorious. Then, Yudhishthir became the king of Hastinapur. But his mind was moved by seeing the disastrous calamity brought about by war. Then, Yudhishtra along with his wife and brothers left for the Himalyas but all except Yudhishthir died on the way. Yudhishtra was carried to a heavenly abode.

The entire story is a study in human virtues and vies. The defeat of the vice and wicked plan is moral of the epic. Moreover, the worthy leadership of Lord Krishna and his famous and thought-provoking *updesha* to Arjuna have become a part of the culture and civilisation of India. *The Mahabharata* still continuous to be read and sung by Indians. This monumental epic is really a valuable addition in the literary treasure-chest of India. ●

118. INDIA'S NEIGHBOURS

India is a great country having extensive borders. Its total borderline is nearly 15,000 kms. Its Northern frontier stretches from Kashmir and goes up to Arunachal Pradesh and Assam, touching the borders of Burma and Bangladesh.

On the periphery of India, lie many countries. In the North, Kashmir is surrounded by Afghanistan, Pakistan, Tibet and China. Ladakh is the tri-junction where the frontiers of these three countries kiss one another. Afghanistan is not friendly towards India due to the rise of Talibaan power there whereas Pakistan and China also hostile towards India.

Along the entire Himalayan range lies, the Himalayan kingdom of Bhutan. The Himalayan kingdom has a benevolent king. The customs, costumes, religious and manners are quite akin to India. In fact, there are kingdom striking similarities between this tiny Himalayan kingdom and India. Then, there is the beautiful Himalayan kingdom of Nepal, which is also governed by a benevolent King Birendra Bir Vikram Shah. Nepal is a country situated in the heart of the mighty Himalayas. Its capital is Kathmandu. Kathmandu is a lovely valley. India and Nepal is based more upon close cultural and historical links with India than upon our social, political and economic links.

The borders of India also touch the plateau of Tibet. This heavenly kingdom is now under the direct control of communist China. As there are only lukewarm relationships between India and China and so, this heavenly abode does not have good relationships with India. Tibet is a Shangri-La, a land of tranquillity.

Pakistan is the closest neighbour of India. This country came into existence when the entire country of India was partitioned in 1947. India has always tried here best to be friendly and cordial with Pakistan but the latter has always been indulging in such activities as are injurious to India. Moreover, in September, 1965, in December, 1971 and in April-July, 1999, she launched attacks on India. The relationships with Pakistan have never been friendly.

Another neighbour of India is Bangla Desh and she is sandwiched between Assam and West Bengal. Bangla Desh was born after much blood-shed on December 16, 1971. She proclaimed her Independence on March 26, 1971 when General Yahya Khan let loose the military terror over the unarmed and innocent people of Bangla Desh. But the military might of the Pakistani rulers received a deadly blow in the war in December, 1971, against India. Again, military has taken over Pakistan and it is now, an unstable State. But Indians want to be friendly towards all of their neighbours.

Burma is another neighbour of India whose borders touch Assam. Sri Lanka is still another neighbour of India. It is an island that lies in the Indian Ocean, about 70 miles from Cape Comorin.

Therefore, India has many neighbours around her. Some of them are quite friendly while others carry on with a negative attitude towards India.

119. THE ROLE OF A SOLDIER IN THE DEFENCE OF INDIA

Every Indian contributes something as far as the defence of India is concerned. But the role, which a soldier plays in defending and protecting the borders of India, is really unparallelled. A soldier is the most disciplined lot of the nation. Upon him depends, to a great extent, the security and stability of the nation.

A soldier's life, no doubt, is very difficult and hard. It is he who obeys the orders of his commanders and does what is ordered by them. A soldier keeps nightlong vigils on the borders even in the face of great and grave dangers. He stands heroically before his enemies. For a soldier, in the words of Longfellow :

Their's not to make reply,
Their's not to reason why,
Their's but to do and die.

A soldier faces death bravely. He fights up to the last moment of his life in order to protect his motherland. He sacrifices everything for the sake of the nation. It is he who has to live miles away from his family. It is he who goes into the jaws of the death while defending his country.

His life is not a bed of roses; rather, it is a bed of thorns. With his meagre income, he feeds himself and his family. The life of a soldier is really very hard but he is not scared by it. For him, defence of the country is the foremost in his duties and responsibilities.

During the war, he fights bravely but at the same time, he helps the civilian population as well. The role, which Indian soldiers played during Indo-Pak war is exemplary. Our soldiers helped and assisted the civilian population of Pakistan. They offered them food and drinks and did not harm them. So, Indian soldiers acted in accordance with the noble military traditions.

A soldier is ready to face death. He never shirks responsibility. He fights in the most difficult terrains on the hills and mountains, plains and forests. The defence of the country is the only mission of his life.

A writer, a politician, a statesman, a businessman and a teacher play their own roles through their actions, abilities and aptitudes. But the role, which a soldier plays while safeguarding the frontiers of the motherland, is paramount and unique. He lives for the nation and dies for her dignity. He makes history and history immortalises him. ●

120. THE JOYS OF SUMMER

India is a land, which has been gifted with a variety of seasons. These seasons have their own importance and significance. Winter season provides the rich with an opportunity to show their wealth by wearing costly woollen clothes and to spend winter in the most comfortable manner. Then, we have the rainy season. Every season has its own pleasures and thrills. But the joys, which summer season brings, are really unparalleled.

It is the spring season that brings that the blooming and blossoming flowers. The gardens, the pastures, the meadows and the valleys are clothed in green velvet. Everything in nature seems to be at its full youth and maturity. The nature presents itself in the most delightful mood. Everything seems to be happy and cheerful. The birds chirp amidst green leaves and cool shade. On the whole, one finds a merry-spree in nature during the spring season.

The summer season is the time of tournaments and sports. Swimming contests are usually held in summer. The sports contests and other activities are also organised during the summer season.

It is also a time when blood circulates in our bodies at a normal pace. With the availability of fresh fruits and vegetables, there is a proper circulation of blood in our bodies. A new life dawns upon people.

The rich get the opportunity to go to the hill stations. The aristocratic families proceed to the health resorts and spend summer season there. The hill stations wear a majestic look during this period. They are packed with people. Recreational centres hum with activity, means of entertainments abound and other fairs and festivals, beauty contests, concerts and dancing programmes and dramas are planned and staged at the hill stations. People, in their lovely costumes and gay moods, enjoy the summer season. Dalhousie, Pahalgam, Simla, Mussoorie, Darjeeling and Nainital become the centres of great attraction for all the families.

It is also the time for the artists to show their artistic skills. They can paint the pictures of summer in its various moods. In one picture, they can express the very joy of summer. It is this season, which compelled Tagore to say :

"Spring scatters the petals of flowers that are not for the fruits of the future but for the moment's whim."   ●

121. COMPULSORY MILITARY TRAINING

Some of the recent events have given rise to the thinking that military training should be imparted as a compulsory training to every able-bodied citizen of India. The full-fledged aggressions of China and Pakistan have compelled the Indian leaders to give a second thought to this problem. Our leaders have realised that in order to meet this twin challenge, there must be a strong force that could prove to be morale-booster. So, the slogan "Militarise the Nation" has been given to the country.

Getting training in military science is important and useful in ways more than one. That it makes the people disciplined, is beyond doubt. It also inculcates the noble qualities of service, sacrifice, devotion and dedication. Military training serves as an insurance against foreign attack. Military training keeps the people physically fit and intellectually sharp.

It also increases our power to work. As a matter of fact, by imparting military training compulsorily to the youth of India, we shall not only be raising an army of millions to fight the enemies of India, but also we would be able to fight innumerable diseases and other wars at economic, social and health fronts. By raising our military strength, we would be boosting the morale of the nation.

Moreover, military training can be put to many civilian uses. It teaches one to obey and to command. Military training aims at preparing men to sacrifice themselves for the motherland whenever she is threatened by some hostile power. It teaches one to place service above self. For a soldier, duty is more important than food and rest. A soldier goes in the quest of opportunities to serve his people and country.

By getting military training, we shall inculcate those qualities towards which, we have a very casual attitude. We are lacking in many other virtues like team spirit, loyalty, sense of duty, value of time, dignity of labour, selflessness, nobility of character and a spirit of good fellowship. All qualities of head and heart can only be acquired through military training.

Military training helps at the time of an emergency or a foreign attack. The trained commandoes can be assigned some duties as they can handle fire-arms, revolvers and rifles and therefore, can safeguard the interests of the nation.

There is no doubt that the mass military training would take time to complete and it would cost a fortune but the nation would get great benefit from these new disciplined people. It would make people realise that the interest of the nation is first and their personal gains are secondary. This would also increase the output in our fields and factories. There would be no corruption and favouritism in our country. Efficiency and hard work would be the guiding tenets of our nation.

In order to understand the very significance of military training, the following instances are sufficient. It was this spirit that enabled Sir Winston Churchil, the worthy soldier-stateman of England, to come out victorious during World War II. Napoleon's daring feats could also be attributed to his military discipline. It was also this spirit, which moved Maharana Pratap and Shivaji to fight against the nefarious acts of their enemies. Indeed, military training is useful in many ways.

Therefore, if we really want to make India a great country that is free from all the evils of corruption, nepotism and selfish interests, it is high time that we imparted military training to our youth and made them the true soldiers and saviours of the motherland. This would also serve as the second line of defence during the wars.

122. DOMESTIC PETS

Domestic pets are very common in every country. In our country, many families are fond of keeping domestic pets. There are many kinds of domestic pets. Everyone selects pets according to his own taste. Domestic pets are not only a source of pleasure, but also are useful in some cases.

Domestic pets are countless. Birds, including parrots, pigeons, sparrows and peacocks, fall under the category of domestic pets. There are cats and dogs, horses, mules and mares. Then, there are cows and she-buffaloes, rabbits, deer, squirrels and mongoose and all these are domestic pets. But every family keeps a pet of its own liking.

Dogs are common pets in India as well as in the European countries. Europeans are really very fond of keeping dogs. Sometimes, they maintain and care for dogs even more than they care for human beings. Dogs are very faithful. That is why, many people prefer them as domestic pets. Dogs act as protectors of our property and scare away thieves during night. They play very good games as well. In sports, dogs are trained by their masters.

People also keep cats and mongoose at their homes. Cats not only kill rates, but also are a source of entertainment. But at the same time, they contaminate the eatables.

Peacocks are the national birds of India. In some regions of India, peacocks are quite common. In sandy areas, they are very happy. Peacock is a beautiful bird. In Rajasthan, peacocks are kept as domestic pets by most of the families.

Cows and she-buffaloes are very useful for the national economy. Even on religious grounds, cow is worshipped in India. Hindus call it mother cow. Cow's milk is very useful. Its dung is used as fuel and manure. Its urine is used in medicines. Some people eats its flesh. They are known as beaf-eaters. But majority of the people consider beaf-eating to be a great sin.

Horses are also very common in India. As they run very fast, they are used for riding and travelling purposes. In battles, horses were very common during the ancient times because in those days, there were no trains and planes. Racers also keep horses. In villages, the rich people keep horses for going from one place to another. Then, there are mules and assess as well. They are used for carrying loads. They are known as the beasts of burden.

Some people keep birds, rabbits, deer and doves in their houses. These pets really give enjoyment. The twitter of birds enchants the keepers. Parrot is one of the most important domestic pets. This bird can be trained to speak like men. Monkeys are also kept by some people. Their gestures and imitations thrill the people.

We can learn many things from the domestic pets. We can know about their typical sounds, food habits and likes and dislikes. Moreover, they give much pleasure and this is also a pastime for many people. Some people keep domestic pets as a hobby. Their upkeep and care are, no doubt, a costly affair. One will have to devote one's attention towards their rearing, otherwise they could fall sick or die due to malnutrition or disease.

123. A DUST STORM

Dust storms are very common in India. These are very common in the months of May and June. A dust storm has its own merits and demerits. While it is quite beneficial for people's health, its destructive power is really shocking.

Last year, I was living in Rajasthan. Rajasthan is a desert. Its sand dunes run into miles. One fine evening, I went out for a walk with my friends. We started our walk at 5 PM. As we were advancing, the sky became overcast with clouds. Then, it became red. We saw something floating in the sky. These were the gathering of dense dust particles. Soon, we were swept by the wind. The wind was becoming faster and faster every moment. We stood under a tree. Then, there came a very powerful puff of wind. This puff of wind was full of dust. We were unable to see anything. Then, there was a gale. In this gale, we heard horrible and deafening sounds. These sounds were because of the breaking of the branches of the trees. We were standing under the trees by catching its trunk tightly with our hands. A complete darkness fell over the entire area. Nothing was visible. Shrieks and cries of the people were also heard. The roofs of the huts and houses were blown away . One of the branches of the trees, under which, we were standing, also broke down. But thank God, it did not fall upon us. The gale was coming at a fast speed.

In the meantime, the thunder was heard. Soon, it started raining. It was a heavy downpour. After some time, the dust in the atmosphere settled down. The sky became clear. Now, we saw the ravages caused by the dust storm. Many trees had been uprooted. Tin sheets of the roofs of huts and houses had been blown away. Crops were damaged. Some of the people were seriously wounded. Many families had become homeless. Many cattle had lost their lives by falling into wells.

This was the worst ever dust storm witnessed by me. The very map of the earth changed around us. The sand dunes from one place had been shifted to another place due to the powerful winds. The destruction, which was inflicted upon the property and cattle, was incalculable.

We then, made a backward journey. On our way, there was the same painful scene. At some places, the road was blocked by the fallen trees. The aftermath of duststorm presented a scene of destruction. This would perhaps be one of the most unforgettable experiences of my life. ●

124. DISTINCTION BETWEEN PHYSICAL AND MORAL COURAGE

Physical courage and moral courage have their own significances. These two differ widely. To compare spiritualists like Swami Vivekananda and Mahatma Gandhi with wrestlers and racers is like comparing moral courage with physical courage. Gandhiji and Vivekananda were men of thin and lean figures, yet their deeds, utterances and speeches reflected the courage of a high order, which is quite different from physical courage.

Physical courage is the courage based on physical strength, which depends upon physical exercise and training while the courage of the heart and the mind is either a born one or a created one. Physical courage comes through the exercise of the body while mental courage can be cultivated through mental exercise or by remaining in touch with great spiritualists.

For the cultivation of moral courage, we shall have to shun the sensual desires of the materialistic world. By hating sensual desires, we shall rise in spirit. By foregoing the petty temptations of wealth, power and position, we shall have the strength of spiritualism and morality in ourselves. But this gigantic strength should not be used for selfish ends but should be used in the most civilised and humanitarian way.

Moral courage is more effective than physical courage. Mahatma Gandhi adopted the path of non-violence while dealing with the British government. He preached non-violence in our domestic and international relationships. Physical courage must be supported by moral courage otherwise the usage of physical courage is beastly and barbarous. It is most uncivilised and uncultured. All the great social reformers, religious divines, scientists, statesmen, saints and sages cultivated the spirit of moral and mental courage. Many people have been successful in impressing humanity and this is a rich tribute to the principle of moral courage.

Those people, who use physical courage, have been labelled as tyrants and despots, blood-suckers and marauders of humanity.

Persons must develop moral courage. It is more powerful than physical courage. Will-power is the key word for moral courage. It was the will of Kennedy, which made him President of America. It was the will of Napoleon Bonaparte, which made him an Emperor. And Gandhiji with his will-power, uprooted the mighty British empire from India.

Therefore, moral courage is more appealing and forceful than physical courage. Moral courage wins at the cost of physical courage.

125. A HOT SUMMER DAY

A hot summer is a punishment than a gift. It is unbearable and makes us uncomfortable and lazy.

The period between dawn and sunlight gives a lovely sight. The twilight scene is most appealing. The calm and serene atmosphere, the cool and bracing climate and the refreshing breeze soothe our spirits. The sweet chirping sound of birds appears to be most enchanting.

After some time, we can see the golden disc of the rising Sun in the East. It is slightly hot. But as the day advances, it becomes hotter and hotter. People, who are out, begin to come back in order to avoid the oppressive heat. At noon, the Sun is red hot. People are hardly seen outside. Farmers stop ploughing their fields during these hot hours. The doors and windows of the houses are closed. People sit in their rooms, which are kept cool by fans and air conditioners. Some have to go to the offices. Their clothes become wet with sweat. One feels very uneasy due to the sweat.

But the afternoon period is the hottest. The piercing rays of the Sun fall on the ground. The heat is unbearable and oppressive during the afternoon period.

But in the evening, when the Sun begins to set, people again come out. Gardens, public parks and fashionable centres again hum with activity. People take ice creams and cold drinks.

Modern science has made summer very comfortable. But it is for a rich man to enjoy. For a rich man, summer is not hot and winter is not cold. These people enjoy both the seasons alike. ●

126. PLEASURES OF GARDENING

Gardening gives me immense pleasure. Moreover, gardening is my hobby. During my leisure time, I take up gardening. The desire to grow fruits and flowers is but natural in me. I devote my extra time to gardening by growing flowers, fruits, vegetables and other plants.

In my garden, the plants of orange, lemon, mango, pomegranates and banana have been grown. Then, there are vegetables like spinach, carrot, radish, tomato, cauliflower, and brinjal.

The garden gives me a great pleasure. I keep myself physically fit with the help of this hobby. But the best benefit, which gardening gives me, is that I keep myself in the cradle of nature. Nature is such a supreme thing that even God resides in nature. Poets like Wordsworth, Shelly and Keats have written many poems on nature because nature appealed to them the most.

A poet has said, "One is nearer to God's heart in a garden." By staying and working in a garden, one feels quite close to nature. For a poet like Wordsworth, nature was everything. To him, nature was a teacher, a preacher, a mother, a healer, a consoler and a companion. So is the case with me.

I see the living God in plants and flowers. For me, these are the objects of delight and happiness. The cool and fresh air of the morning, the fragrance of the flowers, the humming of bees and the music produced by their sounds transport me into the kingdom of beauty and joy.

Moreover, gardening can give pleasures of all types. The poor can get monetary benefits by gardening while for the rich, it is a hobby and a source of joy and delight. Gardening inspires us to work during our leisure time and creates a taste for refinement and purity. It takes us away from the world of sorrow and sadness, rush and tension. *"A garden is a place lovesome thing,"* so says a great writer. It is a place of beauty and delight. It is one of the most enchanting spots because it gives us a pleasure that is quite natural and God-like and also, it keeps us away from the maddening crowd of cities. ●

127. ARE WE HAPPIER THAN OUR FOREFATHERS ?

The aforementioned remark is a puzzling one and so, cannot be answered categorically. Opinion remains divided on this subject because the world of today is quite different from and much improved than that of the world a century ago. If our ancestors were to wake up from the eternal sleep, they would be wonderstruck to see the marvellous changes brought about by science during the twentieth century and would really envy our lives.

Our ancestors had to experience a life full of inconveniences and troubles. There were no good schools and hence, they could not receive proper education. They remained illiterate. They were unaware of the civil and hygienic rules and the result was that they used to suffer from many diseases. There were no hospitals and people died premature deaths. They were a superstitious lot. They went even to the extent of sacrificing human beings in order to appease the deities. There were no means of communication and con-veyance. When people left for a place of pilgrimage, it took them months to reach there and they had to bid final goodbye to their near and dear ones as if they would never come back.

During the times of calamities, which could be floods or earthquakes, the people of one region could not help those of the other. There were so many difficulties of this type, which the people, a century back, had to face.

But now, things have changed. Electricity, the fairy child of science, has done much for the comfort of the modern man. There are motorcars, aeroplanes, trains and so many other means of conveyance. Wireless and radio have done a lot to keep the world well-informed through news. Distance means nothing these days. Schools and hospitals are functioning properly. More people are getting educated. Electricity is helping us all in our domestic chores. A housewife does not feel any difficulty in cooking and washing clothes. Life has become comfortable and worth living. With the invention of X-rays, many internal diseases can be detected without much pain. With the help of trains and aeroplanes, we can send help to the famine-stricken or to the flooded areas. After the day's hard life, when we listen to the sweet songs on our CD players, we feel much relaxed and soothed.

Modern scientific implements have increased agricultural output. The world no longer suffers from shortage of any type. Every possible effort is being made to increase literacy. People are not superstitious. They have developed scientific attitude towards every problem relating to their lives. The usage of telescope has also helped us explore distant planets, stars and even galaxies. People have learnt the laws of hygienic life and live for longer spans of life. In the world of literature also, the geographical boundaries have been crossed. Eminent writers, poets, novelists and essayists now do not belong to a particular race or country.

There creations are studied and enjoyed by all the lovers of literature who live in any corner of the world. Every possible effort is being made to bring peace and prosperity. Hence, the world now, is a better place to live in than it was a century ago because science has brought the kingdom of God on earth. This earth has become a paradise where every comfort and facility is being provided by the scientific inventions and discoveries. So, the man of today is certainly healthier, more cheerful and far happier than his ancestors.

●

128. AN IDEAL STUDENT

An ideal student is one, who is fully conscious of his duties and aware of his responsibilities. He paves the way for the younger generations to tread on. Every student should endeavour to be an ideal one. Students are the leaders of tomorrow. A nation can prosper and reach the zenith of glory if it has a disciplined army of students.

A student is well versed in his studies and is capable of passing examinations but he may not necessarily be an ideal student. Such students, though having brilliant records throughout their school and college lives prove to be utter failures when they enter the field of practical life.

An ideal student is intelligent and simple. According to Gandhiji, he should have the quality of "simple living and high thinking." A student should be fearless and bold enough to face the trials and tribulations of life.

An ideal student lives in accordance with the strict rules of conduct and discipline. This is the time of life when the foundation of character is laid. Without a sense of discipline, the student is like a ship without a rudder; it sails adrift and never comes safely to harbour. He must obey the rules of schools and colleges and the sermons of his teachers and professors.

He uses his discerning insight while selecting his companions. He is fully conscious of the moral code of conduct and no evil force could tempt him. He knows well that a single rotten apple spoils all the apples in the basket.

As we owe our duty towards the members of our families, an ideal student tries to understand how much he owes to his parents, brothers and sisters. It is his duty to realise that he is under heavy debt of his parents. The modern trend is that students, after completing their studies, forget their parents. As soon as they are married, they try to separate themselves from the parents and therefore, forget those days of hardship during which, the parents had suffered for the healthy growth of their children. An ideal student takes care of his parents when he grows to become an audlt.

An ideal student is a servant of the entire humanity. He should share the worries and other problems of life with the members of his family. He should also take keen interest in social work whenever this is possible. He should be active in finding out solutions for various complicated problems of the society.

According to Swami Vivekananda, *"What our country now wants, are men and women with muscles of iron; nerves of steel; gigantic wills, which nothing can resist and which can penetrate the inner-most secrets and mysteries of the universe and will accomplish their purpose in any fashion, though it means going down to the bottom of the ocean and meeting death face to face."*

An ideal student must possess the aforementioned qualities. This would also help the nation in the achievement of better prosperity levels for her masses. ●

129. A PICNIC PARTY

It was the month of July and some of my friends had arranged a picnic party. The venue chosen for the party was the Qutub Minar. This place was so chosen because it served two purposes — one, of seeing the historical monument and the second, of an excursion. The Qutub Minar is situated on the outskirts of Delhi.

We decided to have our breakfast, lunch and evening tea there. So, we packed our necessities and food-stuffs and went to the picnic spot. The day was very fine. Clouds were hovering in the sky. We reached the Qutub Minar at 9.00 AM. We prepared tea on the stove and took it with some snacks. We also carried with us some musical instruments like harmonium, *sitar* and transistor. After having our breakfast, a friend of mine, Sudhir, played on the harmonium. He played two songs, which were so thrilling, enchanting and pleasant that we enjoyed them to our heart's content. The lush-green lawns surrounding the Qutub and other shady trees make this place a natural spot full of beauty.

Then, my other friend Rakesh asked me to have a round of the area surrounding the Qutub. We decided to go, leaving two friends at the spot for cooking and preparing lunch. As we were roaming in the beautiful gardens bedecked with flowers and trees, we came across a foreign couple who were taking photographs of the ruined monuments and other important places of historical interest. They asked us a few questions and we answered them; we enjoyed the conversation very much.

We came back to our picnic spot. We found everything ready. We had lunch to our heart's content. In the meantime, there came a juggler who was having a monkey and a baboon with him. He showed such extraordinary feats and skills as left us wonder-struck. He made us laugh. The tricks played by the monkey and baboon were really marvellous. The juggler made the monkey dance to the tune of his *dumroo*, which enchanted the spectators. At the end of his performance, the spectators gave the juggler money according to their paying abilities.

After this, we enjoyed the songs, poems and other humorous couplets. Mr Sudhir's performance as a singer and reciter of poems and *ghazals* was really remarkable. His songs were so soothing and poems were so enchanting that he attracted the attention of everybody around us. As this programme was going on, some of my friends started feeling drowsy. In no time, they went to sleep.

Now, Sudhir and I started the preparations for the evening coffee. We prepared some snacks, *pokaras* and other fried things. In the meanwhile, I shook my sleeping friends and asked them to take coffee. They woke up and all of us enjoyed our coffee and snacks amid tit-bits, jokes and retorts, which were so interesting, amusing and humorous that we laughed to our heart's content. Now, it was about 5 PM. The other picnic parties were packing their paraphernalia and were preparing to go home. We also packed our utensils, crockery and other things and placed them on our bicycles. Then, we proceeded towards home, talking, gossiping, chatting and laughing all the way.

130. THE MODERN GIRL

The modern girl is no longer shy, meek, submissive and homely creature as she used to be. She is no longer confined to her hearth or home. She can fight for her rights. She can assert herself in the company and can also face the heavy odds. However, she is more a painted stick than a natural beauty.

Modern girl is imitating the male in fashion, behaviour, ambitions and professional endeavours. The colourful saree, which gives majesty to the personality, has been replaced by jeans, pants and hot pants. The curly long hair and the plaited hair are no longer the beauty of a girl. The boy-cut of her hair gives her a boyish look. She can play cricket, climb mountains and do every odd job that boys are supposed to do.

Modern girl is the charm of the parties, functions and meetings. Her lively conversation, her butterfly-like approach and her actress-like behaviour add more colour to every party. Men do not talk of money, business or other affairs but something that tickles their fancies. Nirad C Chaudhuri said that Indian women are more qualified for charming talks.

The modern girl does not want to stay at home. She does not want to miss concerts, fashion parades, cinema shows and other outdoor activities. She has no hesitation in talking to men as well as no desire to remain reserved and shy. If at all, there is shyness, it is a well-calculated shyness.

Modern girl is indifferent to her duties as a daughter, wife or mother. Her only interest is to derive maximum pleasure out of life. She wants her husband to take care of himself; she wants that the children should be looked after by the nurses. Latest fashions and cosmetics are very dear to her. ●

131. CRAZE FOR FOREIGN GOODS

We Indians are madly after the foreign clothes, foreign manners, foreign food, foreign education and what not ? The sweet Indian music is considered to be inferior to disco and jazz. The feminine shyness has been replaced by the blunt talks and vulgar looks of the ladies. Speaking a foreign language has become a fashion. The young would like to work as labourers in America instead of taking up a good job in their own country.

To entertain the guests, there are some cheap restaurants where young boys and girls in jeans sway and scream around a mike while the band blares rock music. The more discordant the music, the more happy the guests are. The guests jump about on the dance floor; their hearts throb wildly whereas their bodies jerk excitedly to the clang and bang of jet-set music.

People deliberately make foreign goods surround themselves. The imported crystal chandeliers and gilded furniture are some of the objects, which decorate their homes and restaurants. The restaurants must have a bewitching singer who may wear a skin-tight, a strapless flashy gown, a provocative waistcoat or even baggy trousers so that she could be looking like a Persian princess or a yankee American.

Some celebrate the Chinese New Year in Chinese style in a restaurant that has, for its name, the title of a song from an old Hollywood movie. The menus include Chinese, Japanese, American and Arabian delicacies. People want the hotels to organise Mexican, Swiss and French nights. The decorations, the music and even the chefs are imported.

Craze for foreign things is not in the larger interests of the country. In case we become the slaves of foreign cultures and foreign habits, we cannot be moulded according to our own culture. These developments in our society are dangerous and must be given a U-turn.

132. EVE TEASING

Sexual desire may be natural but it is wrong to resort to eve-teasing. Eve-teasing is the manifestation of sexual provocation of the person. An indecent remark or a vulgar comment is the mildest form of eve teasing. It goes to the extent of physical assault and harassment. It starts with winking eyes but making obscene gestures and singing irritating songs are the general methods employed by the teasers. These cause mental agony to the girls.

Eve teasing, it is said, is the offshoot of the segregation of sexes. Boys and girls were not allowed to mix up freely and so, their desires remained suppressed. Even now, free courtship and freedom in having friends of opposite sex are not socially acceptable activities. So, the suppressed feelings find expression in terms of eve teasing. Another cause is the influence of the Western culture. The grafting of Western culture through education, literature and cinema has tempted the younger generation to lead that type of life. As Indian culture does not give so much liberty, the suppressed feelings find expression in the form of eve teasing.

Eve-teasing, which is the manifestation of the suppressed sexual desire, is considered to be the cause and result of moral perversion of a society. Temptation to violate morality has been quite powerful.

Eve teasing makes the life of the young girls miserable. In a crowded bus, they are pinched, nudged, pushed and insulted. While walking on the road, they are chased and commented upon. The young lads whistle and name them after the heroes of heroines. They not only stare at them wistfully, but also pass obscene remarks on them. They have to tolerate all this patiently because their resentment may provoke physical assault. No person, however insensitive he or she may be, can tolerate all this. On the other hand, the passers-by derive vicious pleasure in seeing them embarrassed.

It is a crime, which is not taken so seriously by the police or the authorities. In a democratic State, if the weaker people are not protected, they cannot become fearless citizens. If the moral crimes are committed without having a conscience, the society would certainly degenerate.

Women are afraid to bring complaints to the notice of the police because the eve-teasers are not dealt with severely. But the action taken by the law or by the law-enforcing authorities alone cannot be enough. People's conscience must be aroused and they should be prepared to take up this problem at the grassroot level. Women should be respected; that is what Indian culture demands.

133. ADVERTISEMENTS

It is almost impossible to escape advertisements. Hoardings stare down at us from the sides of the roads, crude neon signs wink above the shops, jingles and slogans assault our ears and finally, pictures of washing machines and custard powders in magazines take up more room than the letter press.

Advertising attacks not only our eyes and ears, but also our pockets. Its critics point out that in this country, 1.6 percent of the national income is being spent on advertising and consequently, the costs of the products have risen. When a woman buys a few cosmetic products, she pays 20 percent to some advertiser or the other. In case she buys a product of a particular brand, she may pay more; for example, if she buys aspirin, thirty percent of what she pays may represent the cost of advertising.

These amounts seem a great deal to pay *viz-a-viz* the questionable benefits of advertising but there are also few things to be said in its favour. Although certain things cost more because of advertising, yet some other things cost less. Newspapers, magazines, commercial radio stations and television broadcasts carry advertisements, which help the producers lower the costs of production. In this way, we get information and entertainment at lower prices, which would otherwise, had to be paid for and so, what we lose on the swings, is gained by us on the round abouts. Apart from this consideration, advertising, to some extent, ensures that a product would maintain its quality. It also gives rise to competition among manufacturers and the customers get the benefit of choosing from a wide range of products. Competition may even succeed, in some cases, in reversing the influence of advertising and causing a reduction in price.

134. CINEMA : ITS USES AND ABUSES

Cinema has become one of the most popular sources of entertainment and engligtenment today. People often talk about film stars and their achievements. The young want to have the latest information about the film world. The strength of regular cinema-goers is increasing at a rapid pace. This has also increased the sale of film magazines and other related weeklies.

Cinema has a great educative value. A student can acquire permanent knowledge about a certain thing if he is able to read as well as see that thing. Knowledge thus acquired, would have an everlasting impression on his mind. We read so many things but when we are able to see those very things on the screen, they are imprinted on our minds.

In the Cinema hall, we get knowledge of foreign countries even if we do not have time or money to visit them. We come to know about their ways of life, cultures and traditions. Recently, a picture *Dilwale Dulhania Le Jayenge* was released. This picture presents very lovely and charming sights of Switzerland. After seeing the movie, we can understand how industrious the Swiss are. Although it is a small nation, yet it has been planned and designed skilfully and artistically. There is beautiful arrangement of homes, roads, hotels, railway stations and farms. There are many more movies that give us education, thrill and entertainment.

Cinema also helps the students in learning History, Geography and Science. It teaches these dry subjects in a fascinating manner; the TV and cinema professionals teach us about these subjects, by showing the movies with different examples and thus even the youngsters remember the same quite explicitly. For example, the serial "The Sword of Tipu Sultan" was a successful historical serial and was telecast on Doordarshan.

Cinema is our moral preacher and teacher. Every good film has a moral lesson to teach. The film *Savitri* shows us the devotion of a wife to her husband and how she is able to conquer death. *Krishna Sudama* teaches us how true devotion to God makes Sudama rise from extreme poverty to riches and power. Films like *Shaheed* infuse values of martyrdom in our souls.

This is only the bright side of the picture. Now, let us turn our eyes to its dark aspect as well. Every rose has a thorn as well. It is painful to note that now, film industry has become a money-making industry. Film producers worship money and pay scanty attention to the ethical side of cinema. Modern pictures have polluted the minds of young boys and girls. They easily fall a prey to modern fashions. They sing dirty and obscene songs. The vulgar scenes have completely changed the outlook and character of the youngsters.

It is high time when the film industry woke up from its deep slumber and tried to discourage such films as sow the seeds of immortality in the minds of the younger generation. The kids of today would be the administrators of tomorrow. So, care should be taken to infuse in them the spirit of sacrifice, hard work, honesty, selfless service and good conduct. More emphasis should be laid on these aspects.

Films should be classified into different categories — instructive, social, moral, amusing and literary — so that people from all the walks of life may have entertainment according to their tastes.

In sum, we can say that cinema has a great educative and recreative value. And it is a cheap source of entertainment, which even a poor man can afford. It can do a lot of good to the people at large if both the movie producers and government embark upon producing such movies as may promote moral and artistic ideals. ●

132. ADVANTAGES OF READING NEWSPAPERS

The newspapers have their own importance and advantages. In modern times, newspapers are considered to be the disseminating media of information, news and views. Newspapers have many advantages. They bring news from all the corners of the world to us. Someone has rightly remarked that modern world is a world of press and morning newspapers.

Newspapers, in the modern world, reflect public opinion. Newspapers are the true barometers of public opinion. They contain a great deal of useful information. The public remains in touch with the leading thoughts and trends of the country as well as those of the world. Through newspapers, we get news — National as well as International. Social, political, economic, scientific, literary and religious events are reported by all the newspapers.

They help in creating the spirit of goodwill and mutual understanding among all the nations of the world. Newspapers are a good mode of publicity and propaganda. In the columns of the newspapers, one can know about many things.

Some newspapers give news regarding murder, sex, crime, scandals, divorces, abduction and other such subjects. Such types of news can have bad effect upon the readers. But as compared with the merits of newspapers, these disadvantages could be safely ignored.

Now a days, every newspaper preaches a moral while the real aim of a newspaper should be to give impartial coverage of news. Some of the newspapers indulge in propagating their own ideological thoughts. These thoughts harm the real purpose of a newspaper.

Newspapers play a great role for mobilising public opinion on various national issues. These newspapers also help in educating the public. They make us realise our duties and also make us aware of our responsibilities. They give their own honest, just and right opinion on various grave problems that face the country. Therefore, they lead the masses in the right direction.

From the point of view of education, they have a great value. Newspapers can publish the latest reports regarding the researches made, discoveries done and inventions made in the various fields. The ideas and thoughts of world-renowned thinkers, writers, poets, scientists, reformers, philosophers and politicians are known to have emanated from newspapers. Thus newspapers are the important limbs of modern society. They encourage commerce and trade. They reflect the national will. They mirror the right sentiments. We can conclude that newspaper have many wonderful advantages in this world of commercialism and information. ●

Letters
&
Applications

PART I

Letters to Friends

1. *A letter to a friend, describing the Inspector's visit to your school.*

House No. B II-67
College Road
Quadian.

January 20, 19 —

My Dear Saurabh,

I hope that this letter of mine would find you in the best of your health and spirits. I am happy here. How are you ?

Once you asked me to write to you about the Inspector's visit to my school. Therefore, I append the following details.

The Inspector of Schools of our division — Mr BD George — paid a visit to our school on January 5, 19.... He was accompanied by his assistant. The Inspector's party reached our school at 11.00 AM. The Principal and other teachers of the school welcomed him at the gate. Then, he was led to the Principal's office where he was served tea.

The entire school wore an elegant look. The school was cleaned and decorated with flowers. The grounds were cleaned and watered. All the rooms were decorated with charts, placards and other gems of wisdom. Students came dressed in their nice uniforms. On the whole, our school was giving a charming look.

The Principal then, took him for rounds in the classrooms. He came to our class also. The moment he entered our class room, we all greeted him. Then, he gave us a small test in Mathematics. He asked some questions. Almost every student answered very well. He was very pleased at this remarkable performance of the students. Then, the Inspector went to inspect some other classes.

The Principal brought to his notice some outstanding activities of the school. The Inspector was very much pleased by our brilliant results and also, by medals, prizes and shields won by our school in various matches, tournaments and games. He gave very good remarks regarding our school. He was satisfied with its progress and performance in all the fields of activities.

At 4 PM, he was given a send-off by the Principal and the members of the staff. The Principal declared the next day as holiday. We all were very happy and came back in cheerful moods.

This was, in a nutshell, the Inspector's visit to our school. Hoping for an early reply,

Yours friend,

(Deepak)

2. A formal invitation to a friend to join a tea party.

Miss Nayan Tara requests the pleasure of
Miss Madhu Bala's company
at a Tea Party
on Sunday, December 26, 19... at 5 P M
at her residence, C-40, Hanuman Road, New Delhi.

R S V P
Ms Tarkeshwari

3. Reply accepting the invitation.

Miss Madhu Bala feels pleasure in accepting the kind invitation of Miss Nayan Tara to a Tea Party on Sunday, December 26, 19... at 5 PM, at the latter's residence. She extends her cordial thanks for the same.

1071-Sector VII
R K Puram
New Delhi.
December 24, 19...

4. Reply declining the invitation.

Miss Madhu Bala thanks Miss Nayan Tara for her very kind and cordial invitation to a Tea Party on Sunday. December 26, 19... at 5 PM at the latter's residence but regrets to express her inability to accept the same as she would be attending the marriage of her cousin on the same day and almost during the same time slot.

1071-Sector VII,
R K Puram
New Delhi.
December 24, 19...

5. *An informal invitation to a friend for a cinema show.*

18, Golf Links
New Delhi.

December 31, 19...

My Dear Gitanjali,

We are all keeping well here and pray that you may be happy there. As our final examination is over, we are quite free now to enjoy as we like. Now, nobody can check us if we wish go for some entertainment and enjoyment. The period after examination is a time for relief, rest and recreation. So, what about the idea of going to see a picture at Plaza on January 7, 19... A renowned English movie *Titanic* is being screened there now a days. It is attracting a record number of viewers and the house is always full. This picture is a vivid depiction of the sinking of a ship. It is a very adventurous picture. Don't you think that it would provide us with good recreation after these late-hour sittings and hard labour ? We can start at 2 PM and I shall give you a lift in my car. Please get ready by the time so that I may be able to pick you up from your house at 1.30 PM.

Your loving friend,
(Binny)

6. *Reply accepting the invitation*

C-60, Defence Colony
New Delhi.

January 2, 19...

My Dear Binny,

I extend my profound thanks to your kind invitation to a cinema show. I was just thinking about this issue when I received your note of December 31, 19…. This picture would provide us with immense entertainment after the period of late-night sittings and hard labour, which we had put in our studies. Going to cinema would be an escape from this world of boredom and monotony. Please get the seats reserved in advance to avoid the uncertainties of not getting tickets at the eleventh hour. I shall be ready by 1.30 PM on the 7th of January 19….

Rest is OK.

Your loving friend,

(Gitanjali)

7. Reply declining the invitation.

C-60, Defence Colony
New Delhi.

January 2, 19….

My Dear Binny,

It is really good to have proposed a visit to cinema show. I was really longing to see this adventurous and thrilling movie but due to unavoidable circumstances, it has become a little difficult. My elder brother is going abroad for higher studies on that very day. So, we all would go to the aerodrome to extend him a send-off. The plane would take off at 3 PM.

Anyhow, I wish you good time there. At least, do drop me a line, narrating your impressions of the movie.

Your loving friend,

(Gitanjali)

8. A letter to your friend, inviting him to visit the historical buildings of Delhi.

B-130, Malviya Nagar
New Delhi-17.

September 28, 19...

My Dear Ramesh,

I hope you are having Dussehra holidays, beginning from September 24, 19.... Since long, I have been requesting you to come over to Delhi for some days. But every time, due to some reason or the other, you have played tricks with me. I hope that you will not disappoint me this time. You must reserve these Dussehra holidays for us so that you could give us a nice company.

As you know, Delhi is an ancient city. It has seen the rise and fall of many kingdoms. Some historians contend that Delhi had seven lives. There are a number of historical buildings in Delhi. Students of history must see these buildings to have a first-hand knowledge of Delhi's history. The Red Fort, the Jama Masjid and the Qutab Minar are the famous historical buildings of the Mughal period. .The Secretariat, the Parliament House, the *Rashtrapati Bhavan* and India Gate are some of the famous buildings constructed during the British reign. Independent India has also seen the birth of many new buildings. The Ashoka Hotel, the *Krishi Bhavan*, the National Museum, the National Archives and the *Akash Vani Bhavan* are well known and newly erected buildings.

We have chalked out a nice programme to see there historical places. I am sure that you will love to see Lotus Temple and Chhattarpur Temple. You will never be able to forget the divine beauty of musical fountains at Kalindi Kunj.

We will also see the Dussehra celebrations at the Ramlila Grounds. I hope that you will comply with my request.

Please let me know the date and time of your arrival here. Please pay my regards to your respected parents.

Yours sincerely,

(Deepak)

9. *A letter to your friend, inviting him to your sister's wedding.*

C-169, Kidwai Nagar
New Delhi.

October 15, 19...

My Dear Deepak,

I am glad to inform you that my sister's marriage is being solemnised on 2nd November, 19.... It is a local marriage. The marriage party will come from Tilak Nagar by bus. The bridegroom is working as a Stenographer in the Ministry of Finance.

I request you to be present at the occasion. You should come at least two days earlier so that you may lend a helping hand while we would be busy making arrangements for the marriage. Please let me know the date and time when you would be reaching here.

Once again, I invite you and your parents on this auspicious occasion. I hope that you would not disappoint me.

Please pay me regards to your respected parents.

Yours sincerely,

(Vipin)

10. *A letter to your sick friend, who is an indoor patient in Dr Ram Manohar Lohia Hospital, encouraging him and praying for his early recovery.*

13/5, Shakti Nagar
Delhi.

December 2, 19…

My Dear Vanit,

I was really sad to learn that you had met with an accident yesterday. Your brother told me that you had received some injuries on your head and fractured your right arm. This sad news was a source of great anxiety for all of us.

Thank God, you are now in safe hands ! The doctors of the hospital are very well qualified. You will get the best treatment. I am sure your injuries will be healed very soon. Owing to fractured arm, you will have to take complete rest for some time.

You need not worry about your studies. No doubt, work in the school is in full swing but I am preparing notes of what is being taught in the school. After your recovery, I shall give you up-to-date notes on every subject.

I shall visit your home this Sunday. Please do not hesitate to write if there is anything that I could do for you.

Yours sincerely,

(Surendra)

11. *A few days ago, while one of your friends was reading, his oil lamp overturned and the furniture in the room caught fire. You were living next door and rushed to his help. A letter to your father, describing the part you played in putting out the flames.*

249, Kesar Ganj
Ludhiana.

December 4, 19…

My Dear Father,

Since long, I have not heard from you. I am very much worried. I hope that you and others at home are enjoying sound health.

A few days ago, a very sad event occurred here. You know that my friend, Varinder, lives next door. At about 10.30 PM, when I was about to retire to my bed, I heard him calling me for help. I was wearing sleeping gown at that time. Without wasting even a single second, I rushed to him bareheaded and barefooted and found that all things in the room were aflame. I raised an alarm and soon, a number of persons arrived there for help. We all brought buckets of water and tried to bring the fire under control. All the furniture and the books were reduced to ashes. Fortunately, the walls were cemented. So, fire could not spread to other parts of the building. It took us roughly half an hour to put out the fire. During the course of the fight with the fire, I got some injuries on my shoulder. But those were of minor nature.

Upon enquiry, I was told that when my friend was about to put out the lamp, it overturned. Immediately, the oil fell on the table and the books caught fire. In this manner, the fire kept on spreading. Some of the students have decided to help him financially.

Please convey my respects to dear mother. Love to Sharda, Ravinder and Titu.

Your loving son,
(Surendra Pal)

12. A letter to your friend, describing your visit to a famous temple or a shrine.

45, Iqbal Ganj
Ludhiana.

October, 12, 19...

My Dear Ashvini,

I have not heard from you for a pretty long time. I hope that you would be in good health.

Last week, I had to go to Amritsar with a marriage party. It was the marriage of my colleague. Among other places, we visited the Golden Temple, also known as *Darbar Sahib*. It is a temple that is most sacred for the Sikhs and was built under the divine guidance of Guru Amar Dass. It is situated in the middle of a deep tank, full of clear water. It is a two-storey building. The walls have been painted with beautiful pictures, depicting the events of the Sikh History. The building is connected with a bank of the tank through a narrow bridge. The temple is visited by hundreds of men, women and children daily who pay their respects and reverence before *Shri Guru Granth Sahib*. A *Granthi* is in-charge of the temple and is appointed by the *Shiromani Gurudwara Prabandhak Committee* for its management.

You should make it a point to see the Golden Temple whenever you find an opportunity to go to Amritsar. It is really a divine place and is worth seeing.

With best wishes,

Yours sincerely,
(Satinder)

13. *You were to attend a friend's marriage but on account of an accident, you could not do so. A letter of apology to him, describing the accident that did not allow you to attend the function.*

14, Prem Niwas
Karnal.

November, 9 19...

My Dear Naresh,

I am extremely sorry for my inability to attend your marriage yesterday. As I informed you in my last letter, I would have come to you a day before marriage. But when I was going to the railway station the other day, I met with a serious accident. My tonga was running at full speed. Suddenly, a taxi, coming at full speed from the opposite side, collided with the tonga. I was thrown off with a great force. I got serious injuries in my head and fracture in my right leg. Soon, I was removed to hospital nearby. Now, I am improving and therefore, you need not worry.

Please accept my apologies for my absence and my hearty congratulations on your happy marriage. I am sanguine that the function must have been a great success.

I am sending you the present and the greeting card through registered parcel.

Yours sincerely,

(Harinder)

14. *Suppose that you have a friend who is a bookworm. A letter to him, persuading him to take part in the games.*

G8/12, Malviya Nagar
New Delhi.

January 25, 19...

My Dear Parveen,

Recently, I received a letter from Ranjit who informed me that you have become a bookworm. You do not take part in physical exercise; so much so, that you don't even go for a morning walk. I am really very much pained to learn all this. You know that all work and no play makes Jack a dull boy. You are trying to secure good marks and a scholarship. It will really be creditable on your part. But at the same time you should not underestimate the importance of physical fitness. Health, is the most valuable gift offered to man by God. Its maintenance is very necessary.

I would sincerely advise you to devote some time to games. Actually, this will not be a wastage of time. Rather this would nourish your brain and you will feel afresh for hard work.

I do hope that you will pay heed to my advice and start participating in games.

With best wishes,

Yours sincerely,

(Narinder)

15. *A letter to a friend, inviting him to visit a hill station.*

Primrose, Cart Road
Darjeeling.

August 1, 19...

Dear Chand,

I hope this letter will find you in the best of your health and spirits. It has been long since you have dropped any line to me. I do not know what is the reason of this long silence.

You know that it is the summer season and the hill station, Darjeeling, is wearing a new look. Streams of visitors from foreign countries as well as from the various parts of India are pouring into Darjeeling daily. Everything here seems to be in a fine trim.

Darjeeling, you know, is situated in the heart of the Himalayas. This place is really an ideal place to visit, especially in summer. In summer, Darjeeling becomes the venue of many conferences and exhibitions. Its natural surroundings make this place a queen of all the hill stations. The tall pine trees, the green vegetation on the surrounding hills, the beautiful lake, the lush-green parks, meadows and gardens, the crystal clear cataracts and lively springs make this place a fairy land.

Now a days, there is hectic activity in Darjeeling. In the evening , crowds of people, who are in their multi-coloured dresses, adore the Mall.

Now a days, it is the seat of many social gatherings, ballet troupes and music festivals. Moreover, on August 20, 19..., dance performance is going to be staged by the renowned dancer of India, Meenakshi Seshadri. There are many more means of entertainment and recreation.

I would, therefore, invite you to visit this place this month. A trip to Darjeeling would also remove boredom and monotony of your daily routine. Please write to me about your entire programme. I shall be waiting for you very anxiously.

With kind regards to your father and mother.

Yours sincerely,

(Kanwal Kishore)

16. A letter to a friend, congratulating him on his success in the examination.

15, Hornby Road
Mumbai
April 3, 19...

My Dear Anil,

It is a matter of great pleasure and joy that you have been successful in this year's Senior Secondary Examination. You have also secured first division. I would, therefore, congratulate you on your brilliant success. All the members of my family are very much pleased to know this.

Please pay my best regards to our respected Uncle and Auntie. Love to Meena. A prompt reply is solicited.

Yours lovingly,

(Ramesh)

17. A letter to a friend, showing sympathy on his failure in the examination.

40, The Mall
Mussoorie.
April 5, 19...

Dear Tapan,

I was shocked to know about your failure in this year's Higher Secondary Examination. My heart plunged in grief when I could not find your Roll No in *The Indian Express* dated 3rd April, 19....

I know very well that you burnt mid-night oil while studying. You made all efforts for passing this examination. Even your past record speaks of your intelligence. All along, you have been an extraordinarily diligent student but this result has proved to be different. For the moment, the result appears to be unbelievable.

But what cannot be cured must be endured. I request you to keep on working hard on the academic front. You should again put your heart and soul into the studies. Success will certainly kiss your feet.

Please do not take this failure to your heart. Failures are the stepping stones to success. Take this result in a sportsman spirit. You would do better in your forthcoming examination. I hope that you would study earnestly and diligently and would come out as successful.

Please convey my respects to your parents and love to kiddies.

With best wishes for you,

Yours sincerely,

(Rajesh)

18. *A letter to your friend, condoling the death of his mother.*

91, Rouse Avenue
New Delhi.

September 29, 19...

Dear Pal,

I have received your letter. My eyes became dim and heart began to palpitate when I read about the untimely and sudden demise of your mother. This news was so shocking that I lost my wits for some time.

The news about the dramatic and sudden death of your mother came like a bombshell to me. This is an irrepairable loss. Her death has left a vacuum in the family. When I visited you last year, I saw her quite hale and hearty. She used to tell us so many things, incidents and ancedotes. I really used to enjoy her company. She used to love me like a son. I cannot compensate for this great loss.

The service, which a mother renders to her sons and daughters, cannot be repaid. How she brought you up and made you a man, is better known to you. She fulfilled all your requirements. This moment of grief is really unbearable. Your family has been made poorer due to the sad demise of one of the most precious jewels.

But I do opine that you should not take this death to your heart. There is a stage in the life of man, in which, everyone is helpless. So, you should try to console your younger sisters and brothers in this sad time of bereavement.

I send my heart-felt sympathies to the entire family in this hour of sorrow. I pray to the Almighty to grant eternal peace to the departed soul !

With deep sympathies.

Yours sincerely,

(Ajay Kumar)

● ● ●

PART II

Personal Letters

19. *A letter to your father, describing your first day experience in the school.*

Ramjas School
Darya Ganj
Delhi.

August 16, 19....

My Dear Father,

After the long summer vacation, we have taken up our studies with great zeal and enthusiasm.

We got our new time-table on the very first day. Except English, all other subjects have been allotted equal number of periods. Our class teacher, Mr Sinha has been retained. Mr Sinha teaches us English. Mr Akhil, who used to teach Hindi, has been selected as a lecturer in a college. We really miss him badly. Mr Akhil had endeared himself to all the students during his short stay in the school.

We have started our studies systematically. All the teachers give us home task. They check it regularly. Proper emphasis is also laid on English Grammer. Now, I do not make any mistake in the usage of tenses. My progress in other subjects is also satisfactory.

Our school is really an ideal one. Here, everything is neat and tidy. There is no noise anywhere. There are big play- grounds. Flowers add to the beauty of the school lawns. The News Board and the Wall Map keep our knowledge about the world quite up-to-date. Please come some time and see all these things yourself.

Please convey my regards to dear mother and love for Neetu.

Your loving son,
(Gulshan)

20. *A letter to your father, asking for money.*

124 D, Kamla Nagar
Delhi-7.
August 17, 19...

My Dear Father,

I hope this letter would find you in the best of your health and spirits.

I am giving my entire attention to studies. The academic session in our school is in full swing. All the teachers give us a lot of home task and check it regularly.

Our teachers have suggested a number of books. Our English teacher has asked us to buy *Oxford English Dictionary* and a book for composition. I am thinking of purchasing *Current College Essays*. Our History and Geography teacher wants every student to have an Atlas and a Wall Map of India. Moreover I want to purchase exercise books, pencils and a good pen.

Kindly send me Rs 1,000 by money order. Father, please take it for granted that I shall make the best usage of every single paisa sent by you.

Please convey my respect to dear mother and love to dear Bobby.

Your loving son,

(Lucky)

21. *You have recovered from a long illness; at one time, even your life was in danger. Write a letter to your cousin, describing the nature of your illness, the medical treatment and the care you received.*

C-272, Kidwai Nagar
New Delhi.
November 18, 19...

My Dear Paras,

I hope that you would be hale and hearty as you always have been.

I could not invite you for a pretty long time. This was due to my confinement to bed. I have just got rid of illness. I did not inform you intentionally. Perhaps, it would have disturbed your studies.

On the fifth of the last month. I had a sudden attack of typhoid. I felt very thirsty and had many sleepless nights. Doctor Bawa treated me for ten days. But there was no improvement. So, we had to call Dr Banerjee. He started giving me two injections daily. I was allowed nothing but liquid food. Mother and Lalita attended to me during the days and nights. They also had sleepless nights along with me. Now, I am feeling better. The temperature of the body has come to normal but I do feel physically weak. I am taking a nourishing diet.

How is Auntie ? Please pay my respects to her. Please also let me know how are you pulling on with your studies?

Yours affectionately,

(Surender)

22. A letter to your younger brother who has asked for your advice on the choice of a profession.

18/3, Shakti Nagar
Delhi-110007.
June 17, 19...

Dear Ravinder,

I hope that you are having a nice time after the examinations. How is everybody at home ? I am fine here and in a good mood.

I was really delighted to know from your letter that you have passed the Matriculation Examination, securing first class. I congratulate you on your splendid success. You have sought my advice regarding choosing a suitable profession. It is my sincere advice that you should continue your studies. Try to seek admission in a good college. As you are very hard working, it would not be very difficult for you to secure a first class or a high second class in the examination. You are very good at Drawing and Mathematics. Later on, you should try to get admission in Engineering College, Roorkee. Now a days, as an engineer, you would be able to have a decent living and would help your parents as well as your country.

Please convey my respects to respected mother and father. Love to Titu.

Your affectionately,

(Sukhwant)

23. A letter to your father telling him about your new friend. Describe what you have liked about him.

Room No. 11, Students' Hostel
Modern School
Barakhamba Road
New Delhi-110001.
September 13, 19...

Dear Father,

How are you. I am fine here and hope that everybody is fine at home.

You will be glad to know that I have included one new friend in my company. He is my classfellow. His name is Rajesh Bhakri. I have developed intimacy with him. Perhaps, you may wonder why I am developing friendship with new friends, though I already have a wide circle of friends.

But father, my new friend is very intelligent. He is very good at English. The English teacher has a very high opinion about him. In Mathematics, Physics and Chemistry, he is equally competent. He is also an excellent player of cricket. I have decided to develop friendship with him. We study together for hours daily.

He is very active and energetic. He takes part in school debates and dramas as well. He has secured many prizes.

He comes of a respectable family. He is the son of a Principal. His mother is a religious type of lady. She gives me due affection whenever I visit their home.

I only need your good wishes for fostering friendship with him.

Please convey my regards to dear mother and love to Bimla and Gulshan.

Your loving son,
(Lokesh)

---

24. *A letter to your father who is away from home, telling him how the family has been doing.*

B/130, Malviya Nagar
New Delhi-110017.
December 20, 19...

My Dear Father,

I received your letter yesterday only. I was very much pleased to know that you would be returning home during the next few days.

Dear mother remained confined to bed for a fortnight due to cough and cold. Cough and cold, as you know, are the gifts of winter season. Sharda was also not well due to her tonsilitis. Gulshan is making good progress at school. He is burning midnight oil. I always find him engrossed in studies. I am also busy in my studies.

Yours loving son,

(Anil)

25. *Letter to your elder brother, congratulating him on his recovery from illness.*

A-225, Moti Bagh
New Delhi.
September 8, 19...

My Dear Brother,

How are you ? I am fine here.

Yesterday, I received a word from father. He has written to me that you have now recovered almost fully from your illness. It has really given me great joy and a sense of relief. I wanted to see you but due to heavy burden of work, it is not possible for me to take leave.

Please accept my hearty congratulations on your successful recovery. I also thank the Almighty for having released you from the confinement to bed! I pray to Him for your long life !

Kindly convey my regards to dear parents. Love to Gulshan, Ravinder and Nitu.

Yours affectionately,

(Dharam)

26. *A letter to your younger brother who is in the habit of keeping away from the school. Give him a suitable advice for giving up this habit.*

B-30, Malviya Nagar
New Delhi-110017.
18th December, 19...

My Dear Ravinder,

How are you ? I hope that you are keeping good health and pysche.

I am very much pained to learn that you are not regular in attending the school. You never return to school after recess. Further, you are also not keen about your studies.

Perhaps, you do not realise the financial crisis through which, the family has been undergoing for the past few days. We want to give you better education so that you may become an earning member of our family and may be able to help in reducing the financial burden of the family.

Further, this is the golden period of one's life when one can build strong foundation for a bright career. The time once gone can be never recalled.

So, it is my sincere advice to you to take keen interest in your studies. Try to be regular and punctual and be in the good books of your teachers.

I hope that my advice would imbibed by you in the right perspective.

With best wishes,

Yours affectionately,

(Surendra Bhandari)

27. *A letter to your brother, admonishing him for having neglected his studies and exhorting him to be diligent at his work.*

1/11, Railway Quarters
Lodi Colony, New Delhi-110003.
September 5, 19...
Dear Sudershan,

I hope that this letter of mine would find you in the best of your health and spirit.

I have just received a letter from your Principal that you are not paying any attention to your studies. In order to prove this, he has also sent me the marks sheet of your Half Yearly Examination. I am sorry to note that you showed such a poor and discreditable result. You have scored very low marks in every subject.

You know that you have been studying in DAV College for the past three years but uptil now, you have not been able to get through the examination. Let it be known to you that this period is the most precious period in the life of a man This is the formative period of your life. If one misses this opportunity, one is bound to repent throughout his whole life.

I shall, therefore, exhort you to focus your attention on studies. Do not wander here and there. Do not waste time over trifles. Give up all such company of friends as it is harmful to your character and your studies.

Moreover, for securing admission in a good college, you will have to secure good marks. You can decidedly secure the same if you work hard. So, invest your hard and earnest labour in your studies. It will pay you later in life.

I hope that you will give some thought to these warnings and views. Hoping for a better results from you next time.

Yours affectionately, •

(S S Bhakri)

PART III

Letters Concerning Schools

28. *Letter on behalf of the students of your school to the Mayor of Delhi, inviting him to be the Chief Guest at the Annual Day of the School.*

Dolphin School
Green Park
August 17, 19...

The Mayor
Delhi Municipal Corporation
Delhi.

Sir,

I am the President of our School Students' Union. I have been directed by the Principal of the School to approach you for the occasion of the annual day of our school, which falls on 25th August 19.... You are requested to be the Chief Guest.

At the function, games of various types would be played. Dramas will also be presented by the students of the school.

Further, as desired by the Principal of the school, the prizes are also to be distributed by you. The prizes shall be given to those students who have topped the lists of candidates in various examinations, extra curricular activities, competitions and sports activities.

I do hope that you will oblige us with your benign presence.

Yours faithfully,

(Parveen)
X-C
President, Students' Union

29. An application to the principal for fee concession.

The Principal
Khalsa Senior Secondary School
Qadian.

Sir,

Most respectfully, I wish to submit that I am a student of class X of your esteemed school. I belong to a family, which is very poor. My father is a clerk in a Government office. He gets a very meagre salary. He has a large family to support. It is very difficult for us to make both ends meet in these days of rising prices and inflationary trends.

I have a great interest in studies. But under the present circumstances, it is very difficult for me to pursue my studies. In every examination, I do very well. I am in the good books of all the teachers and they have a very good opinion about me. I have also won the trophy of "Best Player" in hockey. I am a good player of hockey as well as an athlete of repute.

Therefore, keeping in view my merits and financial shortages, I am compelled to request you, sir, to grant me full fee concession. I promise that I shall do my best to enhance the prestige of my school.

I shall be extremely grateful to you for this act of kindness on your part.

Yours obediently,

(Surinder Pal)
Class X B.
Oct 3, 19....

30. *A letter to the Principal applying for the Testimonial (Character Certificate).*

The Principal
DAV Higher Secondary School
Qadian
Sir,

With due respects, I wish to submit that I have been a student of your institution for the last five years, *ie,* from 19... to 19....

I passed my Senior Secondary Examination in the year 19.... As is known to the school authorities, I stood first in the whole school and got high first class. My teachers used to hold me in high esteem. I was considered to be the best student of my school.

Apart from studies, I used to take an extra part in the extra-curricular activities (debates, dramas, athletics and other related activities.) During my years as a student of the school, I bagged many prizes, trophies and awards. I was also the captain of the school Hockey Eleven.

As I intend to join a good college for higher studies, kindly give me a character certificate at an early date.

I shall be really grateful to you for this kind favour.

Yours obediently,
(Saurabh)
September 27, 19....

The Principal
Government Girls Senior Secondary School
Jang Pura
New Delhi.

Sir,

With due respects, I wish to state that I am a student of class XI of your school. I have been fined by Mr Yash Pal, my Economics teacher, for not appearing in the test of Economics.

Truly speaking, I was fully prepared for the test but unfortunately, my father suffered a heart attack on that very day. I had to go to the hospital and stay there for the whole day. My elder brother had gone on an official tour and there was no one else to attend to him. Some students have misled the teacher. He has imposed a fine of ten Rupees upon me. I am prepared to appear in the test even any time.

I shall, therefore, request you to remit my fine. I shall be very careful in future regarding appearance in the tests.

I shall be highly thankful to you for this favour.

Yours obediently,

(Priyanka)
Class XI A
October 31, 19....

32. A letter to the Principal of the college, asking for necessary information about admission to the first year and for a copy of the college prospectus.

D-17, Model Town
Delhi
16th June, 19...

The Principal
Deshbandhu Gupta College
Kalkaji
New Delhi.

Sir,

I have passed my Senior Secondary Examination this year, securing first division. Now, I intend to join B Sc class (non-medical group) in your college.

I shall be grateful to you if you could arrange to send me a copy of the prospectus of your college with necessary information about the dates of interview and submission of forms, together with a blank application form.

I am sending Rs 50/- only by money order as the sum for covering the cost of the prospectus as well as the postage charges.

Thanking you in anticipation,

Yours sincerely,

(Rama)

33. *A farewell letter with thanks to the Principal of your school after leaving the school and joining college.*

C/274, Laxmi Bai Nagar
New Delhi
August 28, 19...
The Principal
DAV Senior Secondary School
Kalkaji, New Delhi.

Sir

I wish to express my sincere thanks to you for the kindness and generousity extended to me when I was a student of your school. Throughout our stay in the school, we were taught by the teachers with untold sincerity and dedication. They paid whole-hearted attention to our studies. We do not remember even a single instance when any teacher gave us a harsh treatment. All the teachers sincerely wanted to pave the way for the bright careers of the students.

When I recall my school days, I feel delighted to remember the sense of discipline in the school. There were sufficient library facilities. In the sports ground also, we were at liberty to play any game.

I have stood first in the school and this is due to your earnest efforts. I really appreciate your sincerity in teaching. I am very much grateful to you. I cannot express my sense of gratitude in words.

Now, I am planning to join Deshbandhu college. I, need your blessings.

Thanking you,
Yours faithfully,
(Anil)

34. A letter to your mother complaining about the poor quality of food served in your hostel.

Student's Hostel No. 4
Modern School
Barakhamba Road
New Delhi.
September 5, 19...

Dear mother,

I hope that this letter of mine would find you in the best of your health and spirits.

I am aware that you would be very much angry and annoyed with me as I could not write even a single letter to you for more than a month. But I shall tell you the truth. I have suffered three times due to stomach problem. My other colleagues are also not well.

Now, we have been able to analyse the cause of our illnesses. We have come to the conclusion that it is due to the dirty foodstuff, which is being served in the hostel. The contractor of our mess is very careless and cunning. He is playing with the health of the students. The *chapatis*, which are served to us, are not properly baked. The pulses contain small stones.

In spite of the repeated requests to the contractor for regulating the supply of healthy food-stuff, he is turning a deaf ear. But we have brought this matter to the notice of the Principal and the Superintendent of the Hostel. They have promised to look into our grievances regarding the mess.

I shall inform you about the action and steps taken by him in this regard in my next letter.

Your loving son,
(Varinder)

35. *An application for leave.*

25th Oct., 19...

The Principal
Delhi Public School
New Delhi-110003.

Sir,

You would be proud to know that the undersigned, a student of class X-G, has won second prize in the Asian Art Competition organised by the Government of Japan. The prize distribution ceremony would be held in Tokyo on 6th, December, 19.... My air ticket for Japan has been arranged by the Japanese Embassy in New Delhi. I shall request to you to grant me leave for five days, *ie*, from December 5th to December 10th, 19..., so that I may be able to attend the prize distribution ceremony. I am sure that my attendance at the ceremony shall bring laurels to our school.

Thanking you,

Yours obediently,

(Ankur Jain)

36. *An application for a scholarship.*

4th January, 19...

The Principal
Model School
Daya Basti
New Delhi.

Respected Sir,

With due respects, I wish to submit that I am a student of Class XI-C of your school. I belong to a poor family. My father, who was head clerk in the railways, retired last month.

This has brought financial scarcity for our family. With his meagre pension of Rs 2000/- per month, he has to feed the entire family, besides making adequate provisions for housing, clothing and education. It is becoming very difficult for me to continue my education, which is beyond our means. However, I am very keen to continue my studies in your school.

I am not only a good student, but also the captain of the Junior Football Team. I have brought laurels to the school in Inter-School Debate Competition. My keen ambition is to pursue higher studies for serving the nation in the capacity of a doctor.

I would be grateful if you could kindly waive the fees and grant me a Merit-cum-means Scholarship. I am sure that you would find me most deserving for this favour. Your kindness would permit me to continue my studies and to fulfill my dream of becoming a doctor. I shall always remember your kindness. I am confident that you will certainly grant me a scholarship.

Thanking you,

Yours obediently,

(Gautam Pal)

Class XI-C

37. An application for remission of fine.

December 23, 19....

The Principal
Central School
Arya Samaj Road
New Delhi.

Respected Sir,

I wish to state that a fine of Rs 100/- has been imposed upon me for reaching the school late yesterday. I agree that this act of mine was against the discipline but the circumstances, under which I was forced to reach late, were beyond my control.

I started on my bicycle from my house at the usual time. Near the railway crossing, I saw an old woman bleeding prously. It seemed as if some vehicle had hit her and had been driven away from the scene. I took the woman to Ganga Ram Hospital and got her admitted in the casualty ward. I thought that the victim deserved priority over my routine as it was a question of her life. After one hour, I was assured by the hospital by the hospital staff that she was out of danger. After some time, her relatives arrived and then, I left the hospital. As such, I was late for the school by three hours. However, when I reached the school, the gatekeeper did not allow me to enter unless the permission was obtained from the Bursar. The Bursar did not listen to me and imposed a fine of Rs. 100/- upon me.

Most humbly, I would request you to kindly order the withdrawal of the fine in view of the facts appended above.

I assure you of my strict adherence to the discipline of the school at all times.

Thanking you,

Yours obediently,

(Suresh Manchanda)
Class X-B

PART IV

Letters to Editors

38. *A letter to the Editor of a newspaper about frequent breakdowns in water supply.*

1071, Sector VII
Ramakrishna Puram
New Delhi.
August 5, 19....

The Editor
The Times of India
New Delhi.

Sir,

Kindly permit me to draw the attention of the Municipal Corporation of Delhi, through the columns of your esteemed daily, towards the inefficient and inadequate water supply in our colony.

The citizens pay a good amount of taxes and in return, expect the corporation to provide them with proper civic amenities. It is really very unfortunate that the corporation has not been able to provide the basic needs of the citizens.

It does not bother to make proper arrangements even for water and power supplies.

Every now and then, we find people arguing and fighting over water because water is supplied only for three hours during the evening. A long queue is formed at the water taps. The pressure of water is also very low.

The office-goers are delayed and become the victims of the anger of the officers. After all, the officers cannot tolerate late arrivals if the same become a matter of routine.

The authorities must take some steps. They must make an earnest effort to ensure regular water supply and help us in the performance of our respective duties. Besides, this would earn a good name for the corporation.

Thanking you,

Yours faithfully,

(Jagdish Rampal)

39. *A letter to the Editor of a newspaper about the rising prices.*

C-6/8, Rana Pratap Bagh
Subzi Mandi
Delhi-110006.
September 22, 19...

The Editor
The Times of India
New Delhi.

Sir,

I shall feel highly obliged if you publish the following text in the *Letters to the Editor* column of your esteemed daily. The text deals with the skyrocketing prices.

During the last few months, the prices of essential commodities have been rising. Due to their meagre salaries, it has become difficult for the majority of the people to make both ends meet. A man with a fixed income finds it all the more difficult to pull on.

No one knows where this vicious circle of rising prices is likely to end. The common man has been crushed by these prices. He cannot fulfill even his daily requirements. The essential commodities and things of daily usage become dearer almost every other month.

In order to put a check on these ever-soaring prices, it is imperative for the government to plug all the loopholes and check black-marketers, hoarders and profiteers. These elements are the enemies of the society. Such unworthy elements should be eliminated. Then alone, can the common man heave a sign of relief otherwise, he will be terribly crushed.

Yours truly,

(Indu Bhatia)

40. *Letter to the Editor of a Newspaper about the need of parks and gardens in different localities of the city.*

S-430, Greater Kailash
New Delhi-110048.
December, 1, 19....

The Editor
The Statesman
New Delhi.

Sir,

Let me draw the attention of the public and the Municipal Corporation of Delhi towards the ever-growing need for public parks in all the localities of the city through the columns of your esteemed daily.

It is well known to the authorities that Delhi has become a crowded city. The population is increasing day-by-day. The people are living in very congested localities. They are unable to get fresh water and air for their survival. Parks and gardens are the lungs of a city. The provide a method for purifying the air. Animals and birds are also able to find solace in them. The citizens of the city would also be able to have some mental peace in the parks. They give us pure and fresh air and thus keep our bodies healthy. The young and the old men as well as women and children can take up exercises, relax and entertain themselves in these parks and gardens. The city dwellers would really have a sense of relief as they would be relieved from their congested houses for some time.

It is, therefore, requested that the authorities should seriously consider this aspect and should provide public parks in those parts of the city in which, there is a dire need for the same.

Thanking you,

Yours faithfully,

(Sangeeta)

●●●

PART V

Letters of Complaints

41. *A letter to the Superintendent of Police for reporting a case of theft.*

B-99, Malviya Nagar
New Delhi-110017.
August 19, 19....

The Station House Officer
Police Station
Parliament Street
New Delhi-110001.

I wish to report a case of theft, which took place three days ago. It was Sunday and we were invited by our nearest relative in Moti Bagh to attend the *mundan* ceremony of his son. For the whole day, we had to remain there.

It was late evening when we came back. To our utter dismay, we found that all the locks of our home had been broken. After examining, it was found that Rs 1,500, which had been kept in the Almirah the other day, were missing. Further, two new terylene shirts, one new woolen pant, a stereo and a watch were also taken away by the thief.

It really surprised me very much to visualise how the thieves dared to strike whereas the police post is hardly at a distance of 10 yards from our house. I immediately got the case registered at the police station.

Unfortunately, no action seems to have been taken by the police so far. I have a doubt about the integrity of one of the policemen.

I hope that you would not disappoint me and would look into the matter and institute an enquiry into the matter.

Thanking you,

Yours faithfully,

(N L Malik)

42. A letter to the Postmaster, complaing against the irregular delivery of your letters.

C-279
Kidwai Nagar
New Delhi-110003.
December, 2, 19...

The Postmaster
G P O
New Delhi.

Sir,

It is really a matter of regret to bring to your kind notice that my letters are not being delivered properly at my residence. The postman throws the letters carelessly near the door, though the letterbox has been fitted on the wall. My name is inscribed in bold letters but still, he does not take the trouble of inserting the letters in the letter box.

The postman turns a deaf ear to our genuine requests. After all, he is a public servant. Such type of irresponsible behaviour is certainly undesirable on his part.

Recently, I have not received some urgent letters from my friend. I had to cut a sorry figure when one of my friends reminded me. I am sure that you would personally enquire from the postman and would suitably instruct him for mending of his misconduct.

I hope that you will take an early action.

Thanking you,

Yours faithfully,

(D P Kochhar)

43. *A letter to the Health Officer, complaining against the poor sanitary conditions of the street you live in.*

U-35
Lajpat Nagar
New Delhi.
July 4, 19....

The Health Officer
Municipal Corporation of Delhi
Delhi.

Sir,

Please allow me to draw your attention towards the poor sanitary conditions prevailing in the street I live in.

The moment one enters the street, one gets such a stinking and foul smell that even the nose feels irritated. All along the street, there lie heaps of excreta and dirt that breed mosquitoes. The drains are in a deplorable state. The dirty water containing filth and waste material flows over the drains and the spreads in the whole of the street. This results in diseases like malaria and cholera.

For the last two years, the street has not been repaired. It is broken here and there. The sweepers also do not work properly. They are most irregular and work according to their own convenience. Moreover, some people have kept some domestic animals. They also throw animal dung and human excreta in the street. This makes the street a living hell.

I have already brought the deplorable condition of my street to the notice of the Sanitary Inspector of this locality. But he is the most irresponsible and negligent official and pays least attention to our requests.

I shall, therefore, request you to make **on-the-sp**ot study of this street at your earliest convenience **so that, this** locality may not fall prey to the grip of an epidemic.

Thanking you,

Yours faithfully,

(Indu)

PART VI

Miscellaneous Letters

44. *A letter to the Post Master General for providing a post office in your village.*

Village and PO Rampur
Tehsil Sirsa
District Hissar.
March 6, 19....

The Post Master General
Hissar Division
Hissar.

Sir,

I, on behalf of the resident of village Rampur, like to bring the fact to your kind notice that till date, there is no post office in our village.

The villagers have to face many difficulties and hardships because there is no other post office within a radius of five miles. Villagers have to go a long way for sending their telegrams, parcels, despatches and money orders. Over and above, sometimes, the most important messages and telegrams do not reach our village at an appropriate time. The result is that villagers sometimes suffer a great deal.

Under such circumstances, it is a necessity to open a post office in our village. I shall, therefore, request you earnestly to provide a post office in our village. We are ready to donate land for the post office building.

I hope that our genuine request would be considered favourably.

Thanking you,

(Darshan Dayal)
Pradhan Village Panchayat
Village and PO Rampur
District Hissar.

45. An application to the Secretary of CSIR for the post of a lower division clerk.

A-76
Lajpat Nagar
New Delhi.
December 5, 19...

The Secretary
Council of Scientific and Industrial Research
Rafi Marg
New Delhi-110001.

Sir,

With reference to your advertisement in *Indian Express*, dated December 1, 19... for the posts of Lower Division Clerks. I am an efficient and experienced LDC and offer my service for one of the posts.

I have passed the Senior Secondary Examination of the Central Board of Secondary Education, Delhi held in 19... in high second division. I have learnt typing at a good institute. At present, my typing speed is 60 WPM.

I have sufficient experience of office work, accounts and business tools.

I am a young girl of 20, enjoying sound health. I am capable of putting in hard work. I come of a respectable family.

I am submitting my testimonials for your perusal.

Awaiting your esteemed favourable reply.

Thanking you,

Yours faithfully,
(Usha Tahiliani)

46. *An application for a job.*

Anuj Kishore
Junior Programmer (Computers)
C/o Delhi Public School
Mathura Road
New Delhi-110003.
June 7, 19....

Mr Anil Kumar
Vice President
ITC Ltd
New Delhi.

Sir,

I am interested in working as a Senior Programmer for your organisation. I am an expert programmer with more than 10 years of experience. I am enclosing my *Curriculum Vitaé* as first step towards exploring the possibility of employment your company.

My most recent experience was gained in the design of an automated billing system for a trade magazine publisher. I was responsible for the overall product design, including the user interface. In addition. I developed the first draft of the operator's guide.

As a Senior Programmer in your organisation, I would bring a focus on quality and ease of usage. Furthermore, I work well along with others and I am experienced in project management.

I would appreciate if you keep this application as confidential. I shall call you in a few days to arrange an interview at a convenient time. I shall be grateful to you for your consideration.

Thanking you,

Yours sincerely,

(Anuj Kishore)

● ● ●

Paragraphs

1. MY FIRST DAY IN MIDDLE SCHOOL

It was a Monday, the fifteenth day of April. This was my first day in VIth class of middle school. Like a mountaineer, who has to climb and win over Himalayas, I was having a thrill in my heart. I was looking forward to a year in which, every-day would be full of adventure and a new chapter of knowledge would be opened. It was a day of mixed feelings. I was happy to see most of my friends but also missed some of them who were allotted other sections. I could see some new faces with whom, I became friendly. On the face of everyone, I could see a feeling of confidence. The boys and girls were feeling more independent as they had joined the middle school. I myself felt grown up and responsible. Perhaps, the best part of the day was to find a very fine and friendly teacher, a teacher who makes everyday a beautiful day. She introduced herself and asked the names of all the students. Her name was Rachna Goyal and she had done MA (English) from Saint Stephens College. She was smiling and cheerful. She made our day. At the same time, I found that most of my classmates had a sad feeling as they missed their last year's class teacher.

2. THE SCHOOL ASSEMBLY

Most of the schools follow certain traditions. The school assembly is one of such conventions. The assembly implies — to get together. The students generally assemble in the forecourts of their schools on certain days, every week. They have to wear proper uniforms. Like a military regiment, they have to form queues and stand straight. The ritual invariably includes singing of the national anthem and address by the principal to the students. There is also presentation of a wards and some announcements, sermons and warnings. It is often argued that an assembly is a wonderful occasion to know each other and exchange information. Frankly, I hardly find it a place of communication and interaction. On the contrary, it makes one feel like a petty worker among thousands in the assembly line of a factory. I am puzzled about the purpose of having regular assemblies. In fact, most of the students find it boring, except on some special occasions, like some entertainment shows and magic shows. I would suggest the school authorities to think whether frequent assemblies serve any goal or it just wears out the tender students in the morning for no purpose. Perhaps, some alternative and innovative method of assembly could be evolved that might be less cumbersome, more relevant and interesting. ●

3. A CROWDED MARKET STREET

It was the time around Deepawali. We wanted to buy clothes, Deepawali lights and many other items. Chandani Chowk is famous for such items. My mother asked me to join her and also, visit this famous market along with her. My mother and I went to Chandani Chowk. It is near the Red Fort in Old Delhi. There was a lot of crowd. Everyone was pushing each other. There were traffic jams and the vehicles were blowing their horns. Street vendors were selling various items, which were very cheap. They were shouting on the pitch of their voices to incite the customers for buying their wares. Many customers were bargaining with the shopkeepers. Some poor beggars were asking for food and money. We went inside a saree shop where my mother bought a saree. She bought some artificial jewellery for me. We also bought some sweets from the famous shop of Ghantewala. From the Electrical Market, we bought Deepawali lights and a mixer-juicer. I also bought some CDs of classical music and some toys. We were very tired after the shopping spree. We took a cold drink to refresh ourselves. Thereafter, we returned home. I enjoyed the shopping very much, though the market was very crowded. ●

4. HOW I INTEND TO SPEND MY HOLIDAYS ?

During the holidays, one can do what he likes. One has enough time for entertainment or for learning something new. The holidays give us an opportunity to develop a new skill. There is complete freedom. But this does not mean that we should waste our time. We should make the best usage of time by developing new skills, learning many things, playing and enjoying holidays. I do not want to spend all my time in gossiping and reading the comics. During the holidays, I wish to spend at least one hour everyday for writing articles for newspapers and magazines. In order to improve my health, I would like to spend two hours daily for sports and physical exercise. I am planning to go to Panchmarhi for a week. There, I would do some trekking and would also carry out an ecological study. Now a days, computers are becoming very popular and indispensable. I shall try to learn some basics of computers. During the holidays, one has a lot of time for entertainment, games and also, for his hobbies. I would like to do a lot of swimming to beat the heat and to keep myself cool. I am also planning to commence the practice of guitar, take up gardening as well as expand my coin and stamp collection during the holidays. I also intend to study several encyclopaedias and improve my general knowledge. Holidays provide an opportunity to learn many new things. Beside this, holiday can be an experiment for learning the time management and becoming self-reliant. ●

5. MY PET ANIMAL

A pet is a domesticated animal or bird. People keep pets for their pleasure. Pets are a good company for the lonely persons. There are many types of pets like dog, cat, rabbit, snake, tiger, crocodile and birds. My pet animal is dog. She is as white as snow and we call her Snowy. She is very beautiful and smart. She possesses a small body with agile eyes. She is a member of our family. She loves all of us and shares our moments of joy and sorrow. She responds well to my call. She waits for me to return from the school. She is not afraid. She enjoys playing with the ball but dislikes taking bath. In the event of an occasional tragedy or grief, she becomes very sad and refuses to eat. Sometimes, she acts mischievously and teases us. Snowy has certain natural instincts. She performs various jobs like picking up the newspaper, calling father for dinner and guiding my grandfather to the market. She has an extremely sensitive nose for food, animal and people. She can recognise the strangers and unwelcome visitors. She has a good hearing power. She wags her tail when she is happy or when I return from my school. Though small in terms of physique, Snowy is strong, agile and intelligent. Snowy has clean habits. She does not make the house dirty. She eats in her plate. I feed her bread, milk and *chapatis*. She is very fond of mangoes and sweets. She often goes with me for an evening walk and we play together, hop, run and jump. She makes friends with children. She is not only a member of our family, but also she is like a doll. She taught us to love animals as they also have sentiments and feelings like us. ●

6. A RAINY DAY

The earth was hot and the Sun was burning. The tress were dying and the birds appeared to be lifeless. Everyone was eagerly looking forward to the monsoon. It was a surprise that suddenly, the sky was overcast by dark clouds. Soon, with a thunder, the rain started. The earth started smelling in a nice manner. Lifeless trees came back to life. The rain washed the buildings and roads. People, cars, buildings and trees looked attractive with their reflections in water. People, with bright umbrellas and raincoats of various colours, created an interesting scene. Birds had started singing and the peacocks were dancing with joy. Everyone was happy to see the rain. When the rain stopped, a beautiful rainbow appeared in the sky. The rainy day was like a dream. ●

7. AN ACCIDENT

It was a pleasant sunny day during the winter. We had come to Chennai and I was keen to see the sea. So, we went to the beach. We took a boat and went out at the sea. There, many people were enjoying boating and fishing. There were some motorboats also. Suddenly, a motorboat come very close to our boats with a very high speed. It created strong waves. This turned one of the boats upside down. The boat started drowning in the sea. However, out of six fishermen, four were saved by another boat but two fishermen were not found. Perhaps, they were drowned in the sea. I was frightened to see this accident. I felt very much afraid of water and we returned to the shore. Since that day, I am frightened by the sea and motor boats. The memory of this accident flashes before my eyes whenever I see the sea or the motorboats. ●

8. A FRIGHTENING DREAM

It was a windfall. I was very much thrilled to bag the first prize in a lucky draw. It included a free holiday and travel to the Disneyland in the USA. I boarded a jumbo jet. Immediately, it became airborne in the high sky. But my joy was short-lived. It kept on going higher and higher. I was terribly frightened. While the plane was wandering, it struck against a satellite and broke into pieces. I started falling down. Suddenly, I saw a huge bird, which was as big as a helicopter. I managed to catch its wings. The bird, after some time, landed on a ship. I landed on the deck. I was thinking that my life, had been saved. But this was not so. Suddenly, there was a big blast and the ship broke into pieces. I tried to save my life, holding on to a plank and swimming. It was a deep sea and was full of sharks and whales. I was so terrified that I shouted "Mummy-Mummy." As soon as I shouted, mother heard my call. She woke me up and asked me what had happened. I was so happy to realise that my experience was only a frightening dream. ●

9. IF I WIN A LOTTERY !

The other day, I read in the newspaper that an Indian boy in the USA had won US Dollars 50,000 in a lottery. I thought that it was wonderful! What a lucky boy! If I had won the lottery, I would have been perhaps the richest girl of India. First, I would have given a treat to my entire school. Then, I would have donated Rupees ten lakh to my school. For myself, I would have bought a lot of books, clothes and shoes. Further, I would have bought a Mercedes car and a farm house. In order to earn more money, I would have run a large departmental store, something like the "Kids' Camp" at Bangalore. I would also have used this money for the poor and orphans. You might be thinking how can I do all this with such a small sum ? Yes, If I win a lottery, it should be at least enough to meet my basic needs as well as those of my countrymen.

●

Stories

1. LITTLE RED RIDING HOOD

Once upon a time there was a little rabbit who always wore a bright red cloak with a hood. Her name was Little Red Riding Hood.

One day, Little Red Riding Hood and her mother packed a basket full of good things to eat. They filled it with her grandmother's favourite foods like fresh-picked carrots, orange blossom honey and home-made breads and tarts.

"Please take this basket straight to your grandmother's house," her mother told her.

Little Red Riding Hood nodded her head as her mother helped her put on the red cloak. Her mother tied a beautiful bow under her chin as only she could have done that. Then, with a kiss on the forehead, her mother sent Little Red Riding Hood off through the woods to Grandmother's house.

Little Red Riding Hood hadn't gone far when a wolf leaped out from the trees. "Where are you going?" he asked.

"I'm not supposed to talk to strangers," said Little Red Riding Hood.

The wolf looked her basket. "A picnic?" he asked.

"It's not a picnic," said Little Red Riding Hood as she held the basket close to her. "It's a basket for my grandmother. Now please excuse me so that I could take it to her."

The wolf sniffed the basket. "No flowers? I would never visit my grandmother without a beautiful bunch of flowers.

Perhaps you should stop and pick some. You wouldn't like her to be disappointed."

Little Red Riding Hood thought that it was a good idea. She picked buttercups and daisies while the wolf ran down the path toward her grandmother's house.

Grandmother was rocking in her favourite rocker, mending her favourite apron. She hummed a little tune as she worked and so, she didn't hear the door being creak opened. Grandmother also paid careful attention to her needlework so and she didn't see a big and hairy wolf sneak into the house and into the closet.

"Grrr," snarled the wolf as he sprang from the closet.

"Oh, my!" cried Grandmother.

"You seem to be tasty," said the wolf.

Grandmother jumped up from her chair and knocked over the table. She ran out of that house as fast as she could.

The wolf looked through Grandmother's closet and found her nightcap, gown and some glasses. He put them on, leaped into the bed and pulled the covers up over his nose.

Little Red Riding Hood arrived a few minutes later.

"Grandmother, are you home?" she called from the open door.

"In here, my little darling!" said the wolf softly.

Little Red Ridding Hood hurried inside. "Grandmother What big ears you have?" she said.

"All the better to hear you with," said the wolf.

Little Red Riding Hood thought that her grandmother sounded funny. She leaned in a little closer to hear her better

276

when she saw the eyes. "Grandmother, what big eyes you have?" asked Little Red Riding Hood.

"All the better to see you with," said the wolf. Then, the wolf slowly pulled down the covers from his face.

"But Grandmother," said Little Red Riding Hood, "What big teeth you have?"

"All the better to eat you with," growled the wolf as he jumped off the bed.

"You're not my grandmother!" said Little Red Riding Hood.

"Why, you're the big, bad wolf from the forest! What have you done to my grandmother?"

The wolf chuckled. "you'll never find out," he said.

"That's what you think," said someone behind them.

Little Red Riding Hood and the wolf looked up. There was Grandmother and there she was standing in the doorway with a big, strong lumberjack!

The wolf chuckled again, "One old lumberjack can't catch a quick and smart wolf like me."

The wolf leaped toward the bedroom window. But he could not get very far.

Little Red Riding Hood grabbed the wolf's tail while Grandmother snatched up her nightcap and pulled it down over the wolf's eyes.

The lumberjack picked up the wolf and carried him off to the bank of the river. Little Red Ridding Hood and her grandmother followed closely behind.

The lumberjack set the wolf on a big log. He pushed the log into the water and the wolf quickly sailed down the river.

"He doesn't look so big in the middle of that wide river," said grandmother.

"He doesn't look so bad when he's so far away," said Little Red Riding Hood.

"And he doesn't look like he'll be coming back any time soon," said the lumberjack as the wolf floated out of sight.

With the wolf safely gone, everyone went back to the house and enjoyed the food in the basket. As grandmother sipped some tea, she smiled at Little Red Riding Hood, "You are very brave. And I'm glad I'm your grandmother." ●

2. THUMBELINA

There was once, a woman who lived in a cottage with a beautiful garden. One day, she found a golden ring among the flowers.

"What a beautiful ring!" exclaimed the woman. She didn't know that it was really a magical crown, lost by a fairy who had once visited her garden.

The woman put the ring on her finger. Suddenly, a new tulip bloomed in the flower patch. Its pretty petals opened and there sat a tiny girl, hardly as big as a thumb. She wore a buttercup for a dress and had long and golden hair.

"You are the most beautiful child I've ever seen! Would you like to live with me in my cottage?" asked the woman.

"Oh, yes!" replied the tiny girl. "Then, I will call you Thumbelina," said the woman.

They lived together very happily.

One evening, a frog hopped through the garden. He heard Thumbelina singing by the pond. When the frog saw the tiny girl, he said, "I have never seen or heard such a beautiful creature! I must take her away to be my wife."

The frog waited until Thumbelina's mother went inside. Then, he jumped out from behind the reeds and captured Thumbelina. The frog carried her away to his lily pad on the river.

"Rest here while I go and make plans for our wedding," said the frog. After saying that, he hopped away.

"I don't want to be the wife of a frog," said Thumbelina. Thumbelina became so sad that she began to cry.

A fish in the river heard her crying. "I'll help you," said the kind fish.

"But how ?" Thumbelina asked.

The fish nibbled through the stem of her lily pad until it broke free. The lily pad floated down the river.

"Thank you," said Thumbelina as she sailed far away.

Soon, the lily pad came to rest on a grassy bank of the river. Thumbelina climbed up the bank and found herself on the edge of a meadow.

"This would be a fine place for me to live," said Thumbelina.

Soon, the days began to grow cold. The meadow was covered in snow.

"How would I keep myself warm in the winter?" cried Thumbelina. A field mouse, who lived nearby, heard Thumbelina. The field mouse was always happy to have visitors.

"Come into my burrow!" said the field mouse. Come and sit by the fire and have a warm cup of tea."

Thumbelina and the field mouse soon became close friends.

Would you like to stay with me for the winter?" The field mouse asked.

"I would like that very much," said Thumbelina. They filled their winter days with storytelling. Thumbelina loved his stories of fairy princes and princesses.

One day, Thumbelina peeked out of the burrow. She found a young swallow, with a broken wing, lying on the ground nearby. Thumbelina helped the swallow down into the cozy warm burrow.

"I surely would have frozen to death if you hadn't found me," chirped the swallow.

All winter long, Thumbelina took care of the swallow. She fed him warm soup and helped him heal his wings.

One morning, Thumbelina poked her head outside the burrow again. The snow had nearly melted and tiny green shoots had appeared all over the meadow.

"Spring is coming!" she shouted to her friends.

The swallow decided that it was time to leave. "You saved my life, Thumbelina," he said. "Now, I would like to help you."

Thumbelina said goodbye to the field mouse then and climbed onto the swallow's back. She held onto his feathers as they flew off into the sky.

Thumbelina held on tightly as the swallow flew deep into the forest and landed gently in a thicket. Sunlight streamed down from between the trees. All around her, beautiful flowers of every colour blossomed.

"This must be a magical place," said Thumbelina, "like the places in the field mouse's stories."

Suddenly, a beautiful lily opened before her. Inside the lily, sat a tiny boy, no bigger than a thumb. He had a beautiful pair of silvery wings.

"Who are you?" asked Thumbelina.

"I am the Prince of the Flowers," said the boy. "You are so sweet. Come and live with us here and be the Princess of the Flowers."

"Thank you," said Thumbelina.

"I would be happy to live here," she added.

With that, the meadow became alive. Tiny fairies stepped out of the flowers.

"These are fit for a princess," said the fairies as they gave Thumbelina a pair of beautiful silvery wings.

All the animals of the forest also came to see the beautiful new princess. Thumbelina stayed with them in the magic thicket where it was summer all the time and where it never grew cold.

3. GOLDILOCKS AND THE THREE BEARS

Once upon a time, there was a family of three bears. There was a great big Pappa Bear, a middle-sized Mamma Bear and a little Baby Bear. The three bears lived in a cozy little house right in the middle of the forest.

The three bears always started each day in the very same manner. Firstly, they washed their faces and paws with sparking fresh water and sweet-smelling soap. Then, they made their beds and fluffed their feather pillows. After they were dressed for the day, they went downstairs for a nice breakfast of delicious porridge.

One bright morning, Mamma bear cooked the porridge and called her family for breakfast, just as she did everyday, be it rain or sunshine. She spooned the porridge into their three bowls and they all sat down to eat.

"It's too hot!" exclaimed Baby Bear, tasting the porridge in his little bowl.

"We must let the porridge cool for a little while," agreed Pappa Bear and Mamma Bear after they tasted the porridge in their bowls.

The three bears decided to go for a walk while their hot breakfast got cooled. Mamma bear took her basket in a case and they happened to find ripe blackberries to put on the top of their porridge.

Now, it just so happened that a little girl — named Goldilocks — was out walking through the woods that morning, all by herself.

She had been walking since the early hours and was feeling rather tired. She was hungry as well because she had left her house without eating breakfast. When Goldilocks saw the bears' little house she thought it was the perfect place to have some rest.

Goldilocks marched up to the front door and knocked but there was no answer. The bears were still out, taking their walk. So, goldilocks just let herself in !

Goldilocks saw three bowls of porridge. Her mouth started to water and her stomach started to rumble at once. She decided that she simply must taste the porridge.

First of all, she dipped the spoon into the great big bowl that belonged to Pappa Bear. She cried "Oh! this porridge is too hot !"

Next, she tired the middle-sized bowl that belonged to Mamma Bear. "This porridge is too cold !" she said.

Finally, she had a taste from the little bowl that belonged to Baby Bear. "This porridge is just right !" she said and she gobbled it up.

After she had eaten the porridge, Goldilocks wanted to rest. She went into the bears' sitting room where she saw three chairs.

First of all she sat down in the great big chair. "This chair is too hard !" she said.

Next, she tried the middle-sized chair. "This chair is too soft !" she said, struggling to get out.

Finally, she tried the little chair that was just the right size for her to sit in. "This chair is just right !" she smiled. But Goldilocks sat down so hard that the wee little chair broke to pieces !

By this time, Goldilocks was sleepy. She tiptoed up the stairs and found three beds.

First of all, she lay down on the great big bed. "This bed is too high at the head ! she said.

Next, she tried the middle-sized bed. "This bed is too high at foot !" she frowned.

Finally, Goldilocks lay down on Baby Bear's little bed.

And she said, "This bed is just right !" Soon Goldilocks fell asleep.

A short while later, the three bears returned home from their walk. They noticed right away that things were not quite right.

Pappa Bear looked at his great big voice, "Someone has been eating my porridge !"

Baby bear looked at his wee little bowl and said in his wee little voice, "Someone has been eating my porridge and has finished it to the last drop !"

The three bears then, went into their sitting room. When he saw his great big chair, Pappa Bear said in his great big voice, "Someone has been sitting in my chair !"

Mamma Bear looked at her middle-sized chair and said in her middle-sized voice, "Someone has been sitting in my chair !"

Baby Bear looked at his little chair and cried in his little voice, "Someone has been sitting in my chair and has broken it into pieces !"

The three bears went up the stairs to their bedroom.

Pappa Bear looked at his great big bed and said in his great big voice, "Someone has been sleeping in my bed !"

When Mamma bear looked at her middle-sized bed, she said in her middle-sized voice, "Someone has been sleeping in my bed !"

Baby Bear looked at his wee little bed and cried in his wee little voice, "Someone has been sleeping in my bed and there she is !"

Baby Bear's wee little voice woke Goldilocks. She sat up to find three bears staring at her. They did not look pleased to see her !

Quick as a wink, she rolled out of bed and ran straight to the window. She jumped right out and ran off as fast as her legs would carry her.

The bears never saw Goldilocks again.   ●

4. HANSEL AND GRETEL

Long ago, a woodcutter lived on the edge of a large forest with his two children and his wife who was the children's stepmother. The woodcutter's son was called Hansel and his daughter, Gretel. Although the woodcutter worked hard, yet he was very poor. Once, there was a terrible famine throughout the land. The woodcutter did not have enough food for his family.

The woodcutter's wife complained that the whole family would soon die of hunger. So, one night, she told her husband that he must take the children deep into the woods and leave them there.

Hansel heard them talking and told Gretel about their stepmother's idea. The children were very frightened. Then, Hansel made a plan.

Later that night, when his parents were sleeping and the moon was high, the boy sneaked outside and gathered as many white pebbles as his pockets could hold.

The next morning, the stepmother told Hansel and Gretel that they were all going to gather firewood. As they walked deeper and deeper into the woods, Hansel would stop now and then, to look towards his house. Hansel was scolded by his stepmother for being slow but he was really dropping the white pebbles to mark the way home.

When they finally stopped, the woodcutter built a fire and left the children with some crusts of bread for their supper. He said that he and his wife would return after they had completed cutting wood. Hansel and Gretel knew that they would not be back. They slept for a while by the fire, waiting for nightfall. Then, with the moonlight shining on the white pebbles, Hansel and Gretel followed the pebbles straight back to their home.

"You bad children!" cried the stepmother when she saw Hansel and Gretel. "Why did you sleep so long?" But she was secretly angry because they had returned.

The next day, the woman made her husband lead Hansel and Gretel back into the woods.

This time, the woodcutter led Hansel and Gretel for deeper into the forest. Hansel had not had time to gather pebbles and so, he crumbled his bread and left a trail of crumbs instead. Hansel and Gretel slept until the moon rose and then, they searched for the path of bread crumbs. But the bread had been eaten by the birds in the forest and so, they could not find their way home.

They searched until they were so tired that they had to stop and sleep. The next morning, they searched again. Then, Hansel and Gretel saw a beautiful white bird who sang so sweetly that they followed him as he flew from branch to branch.

Soon, they found themselves in a small field where they saw the most amazing house. It was made up of gingerbread with a roof of icing and windows made of sugar !

The children were so hungry that they didn't stop to think. They each broke off a piece of the house and started eating it. No sooner had they stuffed their mouths than they heard a gentle voice calling :

Nibble, nibble like a mouse
Who's that nibbling at my house ?

The door of the house opened and there stood an old woman, leaning on a heavy cane. Hansel and Gretel were so frightened that they dropped what they were eating.

The woman smiled and invited Hansel and Gretel into her house. Seeing how hungry and tired they were, she gave them a wonderful dinner of pancakes and apples. Then, she made up beds for them and put them to sleep as kindly as any grandmother.

Hansel and Gretel did not know that the woman, who seemed so nice, was really a wicked witch ! Before Hansel and Gretel wake up in the next morning, the witch carried Hansel to a little cage that she had built and locked him inside.

"Now," she laughed and said, "I'll fatten him up. He'll make a tasty treat for me to eat !"

Then, she woke poor Gretel and ordered her to fetch water and cook food for Hansel because she wanted him to grow plump. Hansel and Gretel cried and begged to be set free but the witch just laughed.

Everyday, the witch, who could not see very well, wanted to feel Hansel's finger through the bars of his cage. She wanted to know whether he was getting plump enough to eat. But he cleverly gave her only an old bone to feel. She thought that he was still much too thin for her to eat!

Four weeks went by and Hansel didn't seem to grow any fatter. Gretel could see that the witch was becoming very impatient.

One morning, the witch ordered Gretel to make a fire. After a while, she told Gretel to climb up into the oven to see if the fire was ready. But Gretel said, "How can I get into the oven to see ?"

The witch became angry at that and climbed up into the oven to show Gretel how to look at the fire. Quick as a wink, Gretel gave the witch a hard shove that sent her tumbling all the way in. Then, she banged the door shut.

Gretel ran to free Hansel. Now that they had nothing to fear, they explored the witch's house. They found boxes of jewels and gold coins in every corner.

The children filled their pockets with riches and set out to find their way home. They had not gone very far when they came to the edge of a big lake.

"How will we ever cross without a bridge or a boat ?" asked Hansel.

"Here comes a swan," answered Gretel, "I will ask her whether she would be able to help us."

The good bird agreed to carry them across the lake one at a time. Once on the other side, Hansel and Gretel found themselves in a familiar little wood. Soon, they were running down the path for home.

The woodcutter cried with tears of joy to see his children once again. He had not had one moment of peace since he had left them in the forest. And his wife had died while they were gone.

Gretel emptied the jewels from her apron into her father's lap. Pearls and rubies scattered on to the floor. Hansel added handfuls of gold from his pockets.

Hansel and Gretel and their father lived happily for the rest of their days with the help of the witch's gold !   ●

5. PUSS IN BOOTS

Once upon a time, there was a poor countryman who had raised three sons. When the man died, they agreed to divide up the few things he had owned. The oldest took his house, the middle son got his donkey and the youngest son was left with only his father's cat, Puss.

"What on earth would I do with a cat ?" moaned the young man. He could barely keep himself fed and had nothing to offer to the pet.

Puss overheard the third son and answered, "Don't worry, master. If you give me a sack and a pair of boots, you'll find that you have the most valuable things your father ever owned."

The youngest son, feeling that he had nothing to lose, gave the cat what he asked for.

The cat put on the old boots and took the sack to a place where he knew many fat rabbits came to find dinner. He put some tender young grass in the sack and lay down beside it as if he was dead. Soon enough, Puss caught a plump, brown rabbit in his sack.

He carried his catch straight to the castle and asked to see the king himself ! When Puss was brought before the king, he bowed low and offered the king the nice fat rabbit, saying, "please accept this gift from my master, the Duke of Carabas." (For that is the name he had chosen for his master.)

"Thank your master for this," answered the king.

A few days later, the cat returned and gave the king a pair of fat, white doves and a few days after that, he brought a dozen quail eggs.

For several weeks, Puss brought many gifts to the king, explaining that the presents were from the Duke of Carabas. The king was charmed by such a well-mannered cat and enjoyed the presents very much.

But he was beginning to wonder about his master. Who was the mysterious Duke of Carabas and why had the king never heard of him ? The king finally decided that, whoever he was, the Duke was certainly a friendly and a generous person.

One day, the cat learned that the king and his daughter would be riding near the river. Puss went to his master and told him to take off his shirt and stand in the river near the bridge at noon the next day.

Trusting Puss, his master did everything he was told to do. The next day, at noon, as the king's carriage was crossing the bridge, the cat cried out, "Help! Help! My master, the Duke of Carabas, is drowning!"

The king knew the cat and the name of the Duke well enough and he ordered his guards to save the man.

Puss told the king that his master's clothes had been stolen from him. The king insisted on dressing the Duke of Carabas in an extra suit of his own clothes. The Duke was grateful and thanked the king for his kindness. He looked quite handsome in fine clothes. The king's daughter, who was very beautiful, told him so.

The king invited the Duke to ride with his daughter and him. As they rode happily in the carriage, the cat ran ahead of the royal coach, quite pleased with himself.

As he ran ahead of the coach, Puss ordered every farmer and worker that he met on the road, "You must tell the king the land you work on belongs to the Duke of Carabas. If you do not say that, the ogre, who lives in that far-off castle, would chop you into tiny pieces for stew !"

All the farmers and workers were very afraid of the ogre in the castle and so, they all did what the cat asked.

When the king stopped to ask whose land he was crossing, he heard, "the land of the Duke of Carabas !" no matter how far he went.

"You certainly do have a lot of land," the king said to the Duke.

The princess smiled at him and the Duke smiled back. He had no idea what was happening. He was just thinking how beautiful the princess was.

At last, Puss came to the great castle, which really did belong to the ogre and so did all the land they had passed through. Puss knew all about the ogre. He went right into the castle and asked to see him.

Soon enough, the cat was brought before the ogre.

"It is said that you can take the shape of any animal you choose," said Puss to the ogre, "that you can't if you wish, turn yourself into a lion."

"True enough," said the ogre proudly and he turned himself into a lion.

The cat, seeing a fierce lion suddenly appear, was so frightened that he jumped onto a tall cupboard. But his boots slipped out from under him and he slid back down. The ogre had turned back into an ogre again.

Puss admitted that he had been quite frightened and complimented the ogre on his skill.

"People also say that you can change yourself into the tiniest of creatures," said Puss, "A mouse, for example. But that is impossible !"

"Impossible ?" cried the ogre, "Watch this !" And he changed himself into a mouse right then and there.

Well of course, Puss, being a cat, gobbled him up in one quick bite !

Just then, the king's carriage arrived at the castle gate. Puss ran to meet it, saying, "Welcome, sirs, to the castle of the Duke of Carabas.

"Why, is this your castle, my friend?" the king asked the Duke. "May we come in?"

The Duke only smiled and turned to help the princess out of the carriage. At the cat's orders, the ogre's servants prepared a wonderful meal for the guests.

While they ate, it was decided that the princess should marry the Duke of Carabas right away because it was evident that they were in love.

As for Puss in Boots, he became a great lord and never had to hunt for mice again - except sometimes, for the sake of fun. ●

6. JACK AND THE BEANSTALK

Long ago, there lived a poor woman and her son, named Jack. They had no money and no food and so, the woman decided that they must sell their milking cow.

The woman asked Jack to take the cow into the town and offer it for sale. On the road into town, Jack met a strange man who asked to buy the cow.

"I will give you five magic beans for your cow," he said to Jack, "Do you know how many that is?"

"Two for each of my hands and one in my mouth!" answered Jack.

"Right!" said the strange man, "here are the beans."

So, Jack traded the cow for the five magic beans.

When Jack returned home, he proudly told his mother of the good trade he had made.

"You foolish boy!" she said," now we will go hungry!" And she threw the beans out of the window because she did not believe that they had any magic. She sent Jack to bed without any supper and there was nothing to eat anyway.

The next morning, Jack awoke to find a large beanstalk growing from the spot where the beans had fallen. It was so tall that it grew all the way to the sky !

Jack climbed the beanstalk until he was high in the sky, even higher than the clouds. And there, before him he saw a great castle.

Jack walked up to the castle. There, in the doorway, stood the biggest woman he had ever seen !

"Please, Ma'am, I am very hungry. Could I come in and have something to eat ?" asked Jack.

The woman said that her husband, who was a giant, was coming home soon and would eat Jack for supper. But Jack asked again so nicely that the woman brought him inside and gave him some breakfast.

No sooner had Jack finished eating than he heard the tramp, tramp, tramp of the giant's boots.

Quickly, the woman hid Jack in the unlit oven.

The giant filled the kitchen door and roared.

Fe-fi-fo-fum
I smell the blood of an Englishman !
be he live or be he dead,
I'll grind his bones to make my bread !

"You only smell the stew I have cooked," said his wife, setting a huge bowl in front of him.

After the giant had eaten his fill, he called for his gold. His wife brought bags of gold coins. The giant counted them until he grew sleepy. Soon, he began to snore.

Jack slipped out of the dark oven and grabbed one of the bags of gold. Then, he ran as fast as he could to the beanstalk and climbed down.

Jack's mother was happy to have him home and the gold bought them food for many months. But as soon as the coins were spent, Jack disguised himself and climbed the beanstalk past the clouds. Once again, he asked the giant's wife to let him into the castle.

The woman did not recognise Jack in his disguise. But she did not want to let him in. She told Jack that the last boy she had let in for food had stolen a bag of her husband's gold.

But Jack asked so nicely for a drink that she brought him to the kitchen and gave him a thimble of water.

No sooner had jack finished the water than he heard the tramping of giant boots and ran to hide in the oven.

The giant roared,
Fe-fi-fo-fum
I smell the blood of an Englishman !
be he live or be he dead,
I'll grind his bones to make my bread !

His wife said "You only smell the delicious soup I have cooked for you." Then, she fed the giant his supper.

After the giant had eaten, he told his wife to bring hi magic hen.

"Lay an egg!" commanded the giant. The hen laid perfect golden egg. Soon, the giant fell asleep and Jack crep out from his hiding place. He grabbed the hen and did no stop running until he was safely home.

Each day, the hen laid another golden egg. Jack and hi mother were able to sell the eggs to buy plenty of foo Jack's mother was very happy.

But Jack still longed for adventure. So, he climbed up the beanstalk once more and tiptoed into the giant's castle. He ran into the kitchen and hid behind a giant broom.

Soon the giant and his wife came in. The giant looked around the kitchen and cried,

Fe-fi-fo-fum
I smell the blood of an Englishman !......

His wife quickly ran to look in the oven but no one was there.

The giant sat down in his chair with a thump that rattled the kitchen floor and told his wife to bring him his magic harp. Jack watched as a lovely golden harp was set before the giant.

When the giant roared, "Sing!" the harp came to life and played a beautiful song all by itself. It even sang along with its music in a soft and sweet voice. The giant ate his super while the harp played and sang. When the giant was full and was snoring loudly and so, was certainly asleep, Jack crept from his hiding place behind the broom. He picked up the golden harp and ran away with it.

The magic harp called out, "Help, master !"

This woke up the sleeping giant. When he realised that his prized harp was being stolen, the giant leaped up with a mighty roar and grabbed Jack with one of his huge hands.

Jack jumped off the table and ran just as fast as his legs could carry him. He could hear the tramp, tramp, tramp of the giant's boots behind him and that made him run faster than he had ever run before !

When Jack reached the beanstalk, he climbed all the way down to the ground with the magic harp clutched tightly in his arm.

As soon as Jack reached the ground, he grabbed an axe and with one sharp blow, he chopped down the huge beanstalk. Down it crashed and with it the giant was also crushed.

That was the end of the magic beanstalk and the end of the giant !

As for Jack and his mother, they lived happily ever after with the wonderful hen and the magical golden harp.

7. THE LITTLE RED HEN

Once upon a time, in a small but cozy little house, a little red hen lived with her chicks. The little red hen worked very hard, taking care of her house and her family. She was a happy little hen and she sang cheerful songs while she did her chores.

The little red hen had three friends _ a cat, a dot and a pig — who lived very near her. Everyday, she watched her three friends playing but the little red hen didn't have time to play. She was too busy with her chicks and her house.

The little red hen started each day, early in the morning. First, she cooked breakfast for all her chicks. Then, she made the beds and tended her garden. She cooked the meals, washed the clothes and scrubbed the floors. She worked hard from morning till night.

But her three lazy friends — the cat, the dog and the pig — never seemed to work at all. They went for long walks in the sunshine, lay about in the soft grass and spent their time reading stories and playing games.

One sunny day, the little red hen was outside, working hard in her garden. She looked down at the ground where she was pulling some weeds and she noticed some grains of wheat.

Who will plant this wheat ?" the little red hen asked her three friends.

"I shall not," said the cat.
"I shall not," said the dog.
"I shall not," said the pig.

"Then I shall do it myself," said the little red hen.

The little red hen planted the grains of wheat. Soon, the wheat grew. The little red hen looked at the growing wheat and asked, "Who will help me tend this wheat ?"

"I shall not," said the cat.
"I shall not," said the dog.
"I shall not," said the pig.

"Then, I shall do it myself," said the little red hen to her three friends.

The days went by and the little red her worked very hard, farming the wheat. She watered the field and hoed the ground and pulled the weeds. Finally, the wheat was ripe and was ready to be harvested.

The little red hen asked, "Who will help me cut all of this wheat ?"

"I shall not," said the cat.
"I shall not," said the dog.
"I shall not," said the pig.

Then, I shall do it myself," said the little red hen.

The little red hen worked from morning till night, cutting the golden wheat. When she finished harvesting all of the wheat, she loaded it in her wagon.

The little red hen looked at the wagon filled with wheat and asked, "Who will help me take the wheat to the mill to be ground into flour?

"I shall not," said the cat.

"I shall not," said the dog.

"I shall not," said the pig.

"Then, I shall do it myself," said the little red hen to her three friends.

The little red hen walked a long way into the village. She pulled her wagon of wheat behind her.

When she got to the village, she went to see the miller. "Will you grind this wheat into flour for me ?" asked the little red hen.

"Oh yes," said the miller. "This wheat would make enough good flour for bread for all your chicks."

The miller ground the wheat into flour and the little red hen set out for home. This time, in her wagon, she had a large sack of flour for making bread.

When the little red hen came back to her house, her three lazy friends were waiting for her. She showed them the flour.

"Now, I shall bake some bread with the flour", said the little red hen. "Who will help me make the bread ?"

"I shall not," said the cat.

"I shall not," said the dog.

"I shall not," said the pig.

Then, I will do it myself," said the little red hen and she began to wonder if the three were really friends.

When the bread was baked, the little red hen asked,

"Who will help me to eat the bread ?"

"I shall !" said the cat.

"I shall !" said the dog.

"I shall !" said the pig.

But the little red hen stamped her foot and said angrily to the cat, the dog and the pig, "Oh no. I found the wheat. I planted the wheat. I tended the wheat. I harvested the wheat. I took the wheat to be ground into flour. And I made the bread."

The little red hen said, "All these things I did by myself. Now my chicks and I shall eat this bread all by ourselves !" And they did.   ●

8. SNOW WHITE

Long ago, in a far-off land, a princess was born with hair as black as night, skin as white as snow and lips of the colour of rubies. She was called Snow White.

As the baby grew into a little girl, she became more beautiful every year. Her stepmother, the queen, was also very beautiful. The queen was so vain of her beauty that she had a magical mirror made. Everyday, she looked in the mirror and asked,

Mirror, mirror on the wall,
Who fairest of us all ?

The mirror would answer,

You my queen, are fairest in the land.

And the queen was very pleased because she knew that it was true.

But one day, when Snow White had grown to be a young maiden the vain queen asked,

Mirror, mirror on the wall,
Who fairest of us all ?

The mirror would answer,

You, my queen may lovely be,
But Snow White is fairer still than thee.

The queen was very angry because she could not stand to have anyone who would be prettier than her. From that time on, the queen hated Snow White. When she could no longer bear to look at beautiful princess, she called a woodsman and ordered him to take Snow White away and kill her.

The man, fearing for his own life, took the girl deep into the forest but could not bring himself to kill her. Instead, he left Snow White there alone.

Snow White found herself all alone in the dark woods. Around her, were mysterious noises and frightening shadows. She was so sacred that she began to run. Tree branches caught at her black hair as she ran through the forest. Wild beasts watched her but they did not harm the beautiful girl.

She ran as fast and as far as she could, until she saw a little cottage with a red roof. When no one answered her knocks, Snow White went inside.

There, she found a little table set with seven plates and seven little beds were all lined up against the wall. The hungry princess nibbled a bit of food from each plate and then, threw herself down on the seventh bed and fell asleep.

Seven dwarfs shared this little cottage. Soon, they came back from the gold and copper mines where they worked. How surprised they were to find Snow White sleeping in their home !

They let the lovely girl sleep until morning and then, asked her how she had found her way to their cottage that was so deep in the woods. When they heard Snow White's story, they felt sorry for her and asked her to stay. She took care of the cottage and dwarfs gave her food, friendship and shelter in return.

Snow White was happy living with the dwarfs. But one day back at the castle, the evil queen again asked,

Mirror, mirror on the wall,
Who fairest of us all ?

The mirror answer,

You, my queen, may lovely be,
But Snow White is fairest still than thee.

Then, the queen knew that Snow White was still alive. She decided to kill the girl herself. The queen disguised herself as an ugly old woman and then appeared at the dwarfs' cottage. She called out, "Belts for sale! Buy my pretty belts!"

Snow White saw no danger in opening the door to let in the disguised queen. Snow White tried on one of the lovely silk belts. The queen pulled the belt so tight around the girl's waist that she fell down as if she were dead.

When the dwarfs returned, they found Snow White lying on the floor. Right away, they saw that the girl's belt was too tight and cut it off with knife. She began to breathe again and told them what had happened.

The dwarfs realised that the old woman must have been the evil queen and they warned Snow White to be very careful. Above all, she must not open the door to let anyone in.

Meanwhile, at the castle, the queen asked once more,

Mirror, mirror on the wall,
Who fairest of us all ?

The mirror would answer,

When the mirror answered that Snow White was still the fairest, the queen shook with rage and vowed that Snow White must die.

The evil queen again set out for the cottage in a new disguise.

This time, she offered to sell Snow White a lovely comb-through the window this time-and put it in her hair. She fell right where she stood because the comb was poisoned.

The dwarfs soon came home. They realised at once that the comb was poisoned and quickly removed it from Snow White's hair before it could kill her. Back at the castle, the queen asked yet again.

Mirror, mirror on the wall,
Who fairest of us all ?

When she learned that the princess was still alive, the queen used all her magic to make a single perfect and poisoned apple.

Then, the queen dressed herself as a poor woman and went once more to see Snow White. She offered the girl the apple and Snow White could not resist it. A part of the apple's magic was that everyone who saw it must taste it. Snow White bit into the fruit and she instantly fell down as if she were dead.

When the queen returned to the castle, her mirror told her at last, "Queen, thou art fairest of us all !"

The dwarfs could not wake Snow White but she looked as healthy and as pretty as if she were comfortably sleeping. They laid her in a glass case so that they could have a watch over her.

One day, a prince was hunting in the woods. He came to Snow White who was lying in the glass case and thought that she was most beautiful princess he had ever seen. He fell in love with her right away. He believed that the glass box must be a part of some evil enchantment and so, he opened the case and lifted Snow White in his arms.

As the prince picked up Snow White, the piece of poisoned apple fell from her mouth and she woke from her sleep. Snow White slowly opened her eyes to find herself in the arms of the prince !

When the dwarfs learned that Snow White was alive, they danced with joy and agreed happily that she should marry the prince.

As for the queen, her hatred made her so ugly that she could no longer bear to have a look in her mirror. She finally smashed it in a fit of rage and so, she never found out about Snow White's happiness.   ●

9. THE THREE LITTLE PIGS

Once, there was a mother pig who told her three little pigs that it was now time for them to seek their fortunes. She warned them that each one must build a house to keep himself safe.

The first little pig met a man with a bundle of straw. He asked the man for some straw and built himself a little straw house. Soon enough, a wolf came along and knocked on the door, saying, "Little pig, little pig, let me come in."

"Not by the hair of my chinny chin chin," answered the first little pig.

"Then I'll huff and I'll puff and I'll blow your house in !" said the wolf. And he huffed and he puffed and he blew the straw house down.

The first little pig was not safe in that house !

The second little pig met a man with a load of sticks. He decided to make his house out of sticks.

Along came the wolf, who knocked on his door and said, "Little pig, little pig, let me come in."

"Not by the hair of my chinny chin chin," answered the second little pig.

"Then I'll huff and I'll puff and I'll blow your house in !"

And the wolf huffed and he puffed and he puffed again and he blew the stick house down !

The second little pig did not have his house either !

The third pig met a man with a load of bricks. He asked or some bricks and built a sturdy little house. Soon the big, bad wolf came knocking at his door, saying, "Little pig, little pig, let me come in."

"Not by the hair of my chinny chin chin," answered the third little pig.

"Then I'll huff and I'll puff and I'll blow your house in !" said the wolf. So, he huffed and he puffed and he puffed and he huffed and he huffed and he puffed ! But he could not blow down the brick house.

When he saw that house was still standing, the wolf gave up all his huffing and puffing. He sat down for a while and wondered how he could get his paws on that little pig, because he dearly wanted a plump pig for his dinner. Then, he had an idea.

"Dear pig", he called, "come with me to farmer Smith's turnip field. I happen to know that it is full of nice turnips. I will come for you at six o'clock tomorrow.

"All right," agreed the little pig. But the clever pig got up at five o'clock, went to Farmer Smith's and gathered all the turnips he could carry. He was back home by six when the wolf arrived.

The wolf was very angry when he discovered that he had been tricked but he did not show it. Instead he said politely, "Friend pig, I know of a lovely apple tree just up the hill. Its branches are heavy with ripe and delicious apples. I will come for you at five o'clock tomorrow. You must wait for me."

Of course, the little pig had a better idea. He woke up at four o'clock and hurried off to pick his apples, hoping to return before the wolf came. But this time, he had to climb a tree and it was not so easy to climb back down !

When the wolf arrived at the little pig's house, he was very angry to discover that he had been tricked once again ! He decided to go to the apple tree anyway. The wolf was delighted to find that the little pig was still there, struggling to get down.

"Good morning, pig", said the wolf, licking his chops. "I am pleased to find you here. Tell me, are these apples as delicious as I said ?"

"Let me throw one for you," answered the pig and he threw it as far down the hill as he could. When the wolf ran to get it, the pig managed to climb down and trotted home as fast as his little legs would carry him. There, he baked himself a plumb apple pie and had quite a feast.

The next day, the wolf was back. He had thought of another way to get the pig to leave his house.

"Charming pig," he called, "won't you come with me to the fair this afternoon ?"

"Oh, I love fairs !" said the pig, "What time would you stop by ?"

"Three o'clock sharp," said the wolf.

The little pig slipped out early and went to the fair by himself. He had a wonderful time there. He admired the flowers, ate some candy and bought a nice barrel for rainwater.

On the way home, with his new barrel, the pig saw the wolf, coming along the road to meet him.

The pig climbed inside the barrel to hide and it began to roll. It rolled right down the hill. The sight of the rolling barrel frightened the wolf so much that he turned and ran straight home !

The wolf came to the little pig's house later that day and told him how frightened he had been by the strange thing that he had seen. The little pig laughed and said that it had only been a barrel and that the pig himself had been inside it !

The big, bad wolf did not like being laughed at and he was getting very hungry. The little pig had cheated him and he was without his dinner !

"Pig", he said, "I am tired of your tricks. The time has come to eat you up."

Because he could not huff and puff and blow that sturdy house down, the wicked wolf climbed onto the roof of the little pig's brick house. He shouted down the chimney, "Little pig, little pig, I'm coming in !"

When he heard this, the little pig put a big pot of water over the fire.

The big, bad wolf came down the chimney and fell into the boiling water. That was the end of the big, bad wolf !

10. THE TORTOISE AND THE HARE

Once upon a time, in a great forest, there lived a hare and a tortoise. Tortoise was slow with everything he did. He, sometimes, ate his breakfast so slowly that it was almost time for lunch before he had finished. He kept his house clean and neat but he did it at his own pace, very slowly.

Hare, on the other hand, was quick as a wink in all that he did. He would be up in the morning, finished his breakfast and go for an early walk in the forest before Tortoise had come out of bed. Hare could not imagine how Tortoise could stand to be so slow all the time.

Tortoise lived next door to his good friend, Squirrel. Squirrel had a cozy little home high up in an old oak tree. She loved to spend her time scurrying around. She thought it was fun to jump from branch to branch. Squirrel, like Hare, wondered how Tortoise could always be so slow.

Hare lived near his old friend, Owl, who was not nearly as quick as Hare was. In fact, he spent a lot of his time sleeping. Sometimes, he thought to himself, "Hare always seems to be rushing somewhere in a hurry. I wonder if he ever slows down ?"

Every afternoon, when the weather was nice, Tortoise would gather up his paints and brushes and would go out into the woods. Tortoise loved to paint pictures of the flowers and trees and the stream near his house. He worked slowly but his pictures were beautiful.

Hare thought painting a picture was not at all exciting. "What a dull fellow Tortoise is !" he said. Hare had the most fun leaping about the forest. He liked to visit his friends, rushing from house to house. Wherever he went, he always ran very fast. -

There was just one problem. Hare was sure that he was the smartest, fastest and the most handsome animal in the whole forest. And he never failed to tell his friends how splendid he was. "I think I look especially fine today," he would say to himself as he stood in front of his mirror.

Tortoise never bragged about himself. He knew that he was not particularly handsome and that he was very slow but he did not mind. He was happy to spend his time, working hard and painting his beautiful pictures at his very slow pace.

One day, Tortoise was sitting beside the stream, painting a picture of the pretty wildflowers on its bank. Hare came up and said, "You are such a slowpoke, Tortoise. You've been working on the same picture all week !"

"I'm not so very slow," protested Tortoise.

"Silly fellow," said Hare. "You're so slow that I could beat you at anything you can name. Just name something, and I'll win."

"All right," said Tortoise. "How about a race ?"

"What an idea !" Hare laughed and laughed at the thought of running a race with Tortoise ! Hare laughed so hard that he thought he would explode.

Word of the race spread quickly through the forest. All the animals were talking about how Tortoise had boldly challenged Hare. "What was Tortoise thinking ? Why did he do such a thing ?" they wondered. Even squirrel had to laugh at the idea of Tortoise racing against Hare.

Squirrel hurried down her tree and went over to tell Owl the exciting news. When Owl heard about the big race, he blinked his eyes slowly and said in his deep, wise voice, "I am not so sure that Hare would win. You can never tell what is going to happen."

On the day of the big race, all the animals in the forest gathered at the starting line. Skunk and Chipmunk had been busy laying out the course for the race. Bear had made a banner to mark the finish line. Squirrel had a bunch of balloons, which she was giving to the animals in the crowd.

Fox was to be the judge. "If the race is finished, I will tell who is the winner," he declared.

"Don't worry," said Hare. "You won't have a problem. I will be so far ahead and there will be no doubt about who is the winner of the race ?"

Tortoise and Hare stepped upto the starting line. Tortoise looked nervous when he saw all the animals. Hare smiled and waved to the crowd. He could hardly wait to show Tortoise a thing or two about running a race.

Fox looked at both runners. He shouted, "Get ready. Get set. Go !"

The race was on ! Hare dashed across the starting line. In the blink of an eye, he disappeared over the first hill.

"Oh dear," said Squirrel to herself. "There goes Hare. Sure enough, Tortoise was just beginning to climb the steep path very slowly."

Hare ran and ran until he was sure he would win.

"This isn't even a race," he said to himself, "I think I'll lie down and rest a bit. Then I'll finish and still have plenty of time to spare. There's no way that slowpoke will ever catch up with me !" So Hare lay down under a shady tree and soon fell asleep.

Suddenly, Hare awoke with a start. He could hear cheering. He leaped to his feet and began running as his long legs would carry him. But when he saw the finish line of the race, he could not believe his eyes.

Tortoise was about to win the race. Hare could not believe it. Tortoise was crossing the finish line !

The crowd cheered and cheered. They ran to the finish line to congratulate Tortoise. The wise Owl blinked his eyes and said what all the other animals were thinking, "Slow and steady wins the race !"

11. THE UGLY DUCKLING

Once, there was a little farm, with a pond full of geese and ducks. One fine morning in May, a duck sitting on her nest full of eggs, felt something moving underneath her-crack, crack, crack.

Peep, peep ! Her eggs were started to hatch. She was very glad because it seemed as though she had been sitting on the nest for a long, long time.

One by one, her little ducklings broke through their eggshells, each fluffier and softer than the previous one. Finally, the last egg started to crack open. It was a very big egg and the duckling that came out was large and clumsy and dirty gray one. He did not look at all like any of the other duckling !

The mother duck thought, "How big and ugly this duckling is !" But she loved him just the same. When the mother duck led her babies to the pond, the ugly duckling swam just as well as the rest and she so didn't worry about him any longer.

The next day, the mother duck took her babies to the farmyard for the first time. The proud duck lined up her ducklings in a neat row, with the ugly duckling at the very end and told them to quack properly and bow their heads to everyone whom they met.

When the duck family entered the farmyard where the plump chickens, ducks and geese were gathered, the other ducks were quite rude.

"Look at that ugly little fellow ! He's not one of us !" said one snowy white duck. A mean old goose even reached out and bit the ugly duckling on the neck.

"Leave him alone !" cried the mother duck but the other birds continued to tease the poor duckling. Soon, even his own brothers and sisters were calling him "ugly duckling" and wouldn't play with him.

Days passed and the duckling grew bigger and uglier. The teasing and bullying got worse and worse. Finally, the duckling decided to run far away. He wandered through overgrown fields, often frightening the little birds who lived there.

"They think I'm ugly, too," he sighed.

On he went, until he came to a swamp where wild geese lived. As he was too tired to go any farther, he stayed there for the night. The wild geese found him in the morning.

"What kind of bird are you ?" they asked. Before he could answer, some men came with their dogs and scared the geese away. The ugly duckling hid in the grass because he was too frightened to leave.

As soon as he was sure that the dogs were gone, the lonely little duckling set off again, looking for somewhere to live. At last, he came to a crooked little hut where an old woman lived with her cat and her prized hen. She took the duckling in, hoping that she would be able to sell him in the market.

The cat and the hen thought that they were wonderful creatures and were very rude to the duckling. Besides, he was used to being outdoors and although the hut was warm and dry, yet he longed to be swimming on the water and diving down among the weeds.

So, one fine day, he ran away to find a lake.

He was happy on the lake, though none of the wild ducks there spoke to him. They thought that he was too ugly to talk to.

One day, at sunset, he saw a flock of beautiful birds flying overhead. Their feathers were so white that they glowed and their necks were long and graceful. The sight of them made the ugly duckling cry, though he did not know why.

Soon afterwards, the wild ducks flew off. They knew that winter was coming. The duckling stayed on the lake as the weather got colder and colder. It grew so cold one night that the duckling wake up to find his feet frozen in a sheet of ice!

Luckily, a farmer found the duckling held there and broke the ice to free him. The kind farmer took the duckling home with him, thinking that the odd bird would make a fine pet for his children.

When the farmer set the duckling down in his kitchen, the noisy children frightened the bird and the duckling flew right into a pail of milk and spilled it. From there, he ran across a plate of butter and knocked over a bowl of flour. What a mess he made !

The farmer' wife was angry with the ugly duckling and chased him right out of the kitchen door.

The frightened duckling did not run very far because it was dark and cold outside. He knew that the icy pond was not a safe place to spend the winter and so, he found a safe hiding place in an empty barnyard and made a nest for himself.

The ugly duckling spent the whole winter, nestled snugly in his hiding place. He came out only to search for food. It was the longest winter he could imagine.

Spring came at last ! The ugly duckling stretched his neck and tried to fly. His wings were now very strong and he landed easily on the little lake !

Just as the ugly duckling was enjoying his first swim of the spring, three snowy swans appeared from the grass along the shore. The duckling felt the same excitement he had felt when he had first seen them flying overhead.

He wanted to be near them so much that even though he was sure they would treat him cruelly, he swam towards them anyway. As he drew near, he bowed his head.

When he lowered his head, what do you think he saw ? A fourth swan, the most beautiful of all, was looking back at him from water. It was his own reflection !

You see, over that long winter the ugly duckling had grown up. He was not a duckling at all. He was a swan !

As the other swans joined him, the happy bird promised himself that he would never forget the things he had learned as the ugly duckling, even though he would spend the rest of his life as a handsome swan. ●

NOTES